GOING THE DISTANCE

BY KEN NORTON
WITH MARSHALL TERRILL
AND MIKE FITZGERALD

FOREWORD BY JOE FRAZIER

SPORTS PUBLISHING INC.
WWW.SPORTSPUBLISHINGINC.COM

Director of Production: Susan M. McKinney
Dustjacket and photo insert design: Terry Neutz Hayden
Proofreader: David Hamburg

ISBN: 1-58261-225-0

SPORTS PUBLISHING INC.
804 N. Neil
Champaign, IL 61820
www.sportspublishinginc.com

Printed in the United States.

To my father, John Norton, who passed away during the writing of this book. Thanks, Pop, you and Mom gave me a wonderful childhood.

—Ken Norton, Sr.

We dedicate this book to Jerry Haack for his infinite patience in keeping this project together—and we also thank Judy Haack for keeping Jerry together.

—Marshall Terrill & Mike Fitzgerald

CONTENTS

ACKNOWLEDGMENTS

A heartfelt thanks goes to Suki Meredith Coonley, who edited our manuscript as if it were her own. To Greg Korn, my childhood friend and boxing historian, who made sure there were no errors of fact.

Special thanks also go to those who contributed in other areas of the book: Muhammad Ali, Duane Bobick, Ed Brophy, Jeff Brophy, Gerry Cooney, Angelo Dundee, Pete Ehrmann, Buford Green, Sean Foley, Eddie Futch, "Smokin'" Joe Frazier, Marvis Frazier, Mike Fitzgerald, Sr., Harold Lederman, Scott LeDoux, Bob Lynch, Larry Holmes, William Martin, Arthur Mercante, Bobby Moore, Trina Moore, Keith Norton, Ken Norton, Jr., Kenisha Norton, Ruth Norton, John Norton, Kenejon Norton, Gary "Chub" Pliner, Patty Pliner, Sandi Spaude, Richard Steele, Bill Slayton, and Al Rosenberger.

We would also like to thank our wives, Zoe Terrill and Debbie Fitzgerald, for their patience in putting up with two immature adults who have a passion and a dream to write.

FOREWORD

by
"Smokin'" Joe Frazier

Bad things happen to good people.

Ken Norton is a true friend, and the determination he showed in recovering from his automobile accident in 1986 is amazing. To know Ken as I do, you wouldn't be so amazed. Although Ken has always been a hard worker and is a great guy, he hasn't always been nice to me. I employed him as a sparring partner for two years in the early '70s. He was anything but friendly to me in the ring. I knew right away he had the potential to one day become heavyweight champion of the world.

One of the first times we sparred, there was a crowd on hand. We went at it toe-to-toe. Instead of a workout, it was more like a major battle in a war.

That's how it usually was with Ken, and I can't say that I enjoyed it. Sometimes I even contemplated calling in sick to avoid sparring with him. Two rounds with Norton was more than enough any time. I had trouble connecting on him with that unique style of his.

Another time, when I was managing Duane Bobick, Ken again presented me with trouble.

The other two people financially backing Bobick thought Norton was over the hill. Ken had the name recognition to launch an opponent's career, and Bobick hoped it would propel him to the top. I warned them about Ken, but I was outvoted 2-1. Ken laid out Bobick in the first round.

I should have let them spar with Ken first; maybe then they would have believed me.

I also think Ken whipped Ali three times. For the last fight at Yankee Stadium, I had the best seat in the house. There was no way "The Butterfly" deserved the nod. I had no salt in my eyes, but the judges must have had fog in theirs. Ken clearly won their last bout by a large margin. Ken is a tough former Marine who I'm glad is my close friend. I'm just happy we never had to fight. Who knows who would have won, but it would have been one of the toughest fights of my career. I'm glad it never happened, because it would have been a war!

Prologue

LOS ANGELES, CA—*Ken Norton, former boxing heavyweight champion of the world, is in critical condition at Cedars Sinai Hospital today. Norton was involved in a mysterious car accident when his car veered off the Santa Monica Freeway off-ramp late last night. Medical experts are stating that his chances for survival are slim.*

—Associated Press
February 23, 1986

It was the deepest sleep I'd experienced. I felt as if I was stepping lightly through the cosmos, walking on air. I was a spirit soaring above the clouds. I wasn't imprisoned by my body. My mind was clear and free of any negative thoughts. Everything was easy and simple, peaceful and pure. If this was heaven, I was home free.

This wonderful walk in the clouds slowly was being interrupted by a noise. At first, the noise was merely in the background of my subconscious, not even an annoyance.

Blip...............Blip...............Blip . . .

My dream became less and less defined. The vivid colors that had once dominated the canvas like the windows of my mind were now blurring together as one, turning and spinning slowly.

The noise emerged from the background into the forefront of my subconscious, becoming a little louder and pounding a little faster.

Blip… Blip…Blip…

No rest for the weary on this day.

Blip…Blip…Blip…

The noise became an uncomfortable fixture in my head, pounding louder, faster. It raided my precious sleep, awakening me from a state of death.

Death? How had that word entered my thoughts?

Was I dead? Was I alive? Was I in limbo? Heaven? Iowa?

Only moments before, there were no questions, only answers. There was no darkness, only light.

The colors swirled furiously, mixing together into one color: black. Someone had turned out the lights, but I hadn't left the party.

Blip..Blip..Blip..Blip

There was that annoying noise again. Anger entered my subconscious as the dream came to an abrupt end.

I opened my eyes slowly, blinking a hundred miles a minute, but the picture was way out of focus. I squinted and tried to focus my gaze. It took about a minute before I realized I was flat on my back, staring at white ceiling tiles.

What?

Blip.Blip.Blip.

There was that noise again. I turned my head to where the noise was coming from; it took a moment for me to realize it was a heart monitor. This heart monitor was hooked up to me. Clear tubes filled with various fluids ran to and from my body.

I couldn't move an inch from the neck down. Three body straps had been placed over my chest, stomach, and legs. Obviously, somebody didn't want me to get out of bed.

I brought my head down, my chin touching my chest, and looked at my hands, my arms, my feet, my entire body. To my sheer horror, I discovered I was a bloody mess.

What happened? What the hell happened?

I breathed faster. My eyes darted around the room, looking for some kind of answer.

Where was I? How did I get here? Why am I here?

Anxiety now entered the picture, and my curiosity turned into rage. I felt like a caged tiger, mentally pacing back and forth in a confined space, desperately seeking freedom.

I sprang from the bed like a bolt of lightning. My blind rage fueled the raw strength it took to get on my feet while the hospital bed was still strapped to my back, and that included the frame.

I tore the tubes from my arms and headed for the door. A nurse tried to stop what must have looked like the African American version of "The Incredible Hulk."

"Mr. Norton, you must not leave this place. You have been in a very serious car accident. If you leave, you'll die."

I looked at her with fire in my eyes, causing her to take a step back. She wasn't looking at a sane man. Like me, she was horrified.

I tried to walk out the door with a bed strapped to my body, but the metal frame of the bed was taller than the door. I smashed into the wall with such force, my right knee snapped in two. I crashed to the floor, the bed and frame following shortly thereafter.

I was definitely going to feel that in the morning.

When I came to, the doctors gave me a hospital menu, specially prepared for Ken Norton. They predicted that if I lived, my head injuries were so severe that I was going to be a vegetable, and here was the dessert: Now that I had broken my right leg by my fine display of lunacy, they also predicted that I would never walk again.

I had lived a relatively charmed life for 42 years. I had an idyllic childhood, worldwide fame through my boxing—and millions of dollars—parents who loved me unconditionally, a wife and children whom I loved and adored. And now this.

I had been a physical man my whole life. My existence centered on my body and my God-given talent to accomplish what few men could. My body was my paycheck. My mind played a healthy role as well, but that, too, was affected by the accident.

The doctors served me a healthy portion of humble pie that day in my hospital bed at Cedars. Served it to me on a huge platter with a sterling silver fork, and I was forced to take a big bite.

Chapter One

Never a Dull Moment

Mischievous.

That's the word that best describes me as a child. I wasn't mean-spirited, I wasn't hateful, and I wasn't spiteful. Just plain ol' mischievous. Let's just say for the record that I've always liked to have fun.

Like the time when I was eight and raced my bike against a train—and lost. I thought it would be crazy and exciting to have the train whiz by me within a whisker as I passed the tracks. Well, it didn't quite work out as I had planned. The bike's front tire crashed into the side of the speeding train, throwing me backward and demolishing my two-wheeled ride. But that was OK. I just asked my parents for a new one, and I got it!

You see, not only was I mischievous, I was spoiled. Spoiled rotten.

I don't know how or why I was born with that disposition, but I was. I just about drove my parents crazy with my rambunctious behavior, always finding trouble right around the corner. My father, John Edward Norton, and I were complete opposites. He was very strict. He meant what he said and he said what he meant.

When I messed up, which was often, he didn't mind putting the belt to my behind. And there definitely was punishment if I stepped out of line. He was the type of individual who had to work hard for everything in life. My father only stood 5 foot 7 inches and had a slender build, but he had the strength and energy of several men. I've never known anyone with a more intense work ethic.

My father had to quit school when he was 10 to help his parents make ends meet during the Great Depression. There were 10 mouths to feed in his immediate family. Poverty is serious business, and John was a serious man.

Throughout most of his life, my father held three jobs at a time to put food on the table and clothes on his son's back. I can remember him hauling coal into basements in the morning, cleaning the local barber shop in the afternoon, and driving a fire truck in the evening for the Jacksonville, Illinois, Fire Department because he didn't want his wife or son to yearn for anything. After working for the fire department for 11 years, he had to have his right leg amputated. The loss of his leg only fueled his fire to work. He left the fire department and went right to work at the police department as a dispatcher. No handicap was going to hold my father back from making a decent living.

John Norton, however, is not my biological father. I consider him my father because he raised me since I was three, as if I were his own. However, my biological father was George Florence. My mother, Ruth, gave birth to me out of wedlock when she was 16.

George and my mother went their separate ways after I was born, but it wasn't as if the town didn't know whose kid I was. Jacksonville has had a population of approximately 20,000 people for the last five decades, and like most small towns, everyone knows everyone else's business.

Having a child out of wedlock today is not even given a second thought, but back in the '40s, it was shameful for both parties concerned, and my mother was no exception. I never brought up George Florence or even asked about him once. It was a situation that bothered my mother; therefore, it bothered me.

Ruth Norton (Ken's mother): *At that time in our society, if you had a child by someone who wasn't married to you, you didn't have any association with that person. I was 15 when I became pregnant by George, and he was not much older than me, so marriage was out of the question. In our generation, if you didn't marry a person, you didn't have any contact with them. They didn't come back to your family's home to visit with the child. Nothing.*

George and I went our separate ways, as much as you can in a small town. George later married and had a couple of kids, and I married John three years after Ken was born. When Kenny was growing up, George lived right down the street. George and Kenny saw each other, but it was nothing more than mutual acknowledgment when they passed. Ken knew George was his biological father, but they were just like two ships passing in the night.

The one thing I possess that I will always give credit to George Florence for is genetics. George Florence stood 6-foot-1 and possessed a muscular build and athletic body. I heard that he boxed as a hobby when he was in the Army during World War II. From George Florence I inherited my physique; from John Norton I learned integrity, honesty, and decency. In my head and in my heart, John Norton has always been my father.

As I grew older, I didn't grow more curious about George Florence, nor did I try to get to know him as an adult. I wasn't mad or angry at him, I just didn't really care. We never kept in touch, but town gossip was that he moved to Iowa, and then later to Northern California when I was a teenager. He was killed a few years back in California when his car got caught between a set of railroad tracks and he was crushed by the train.

When I was born on August 9, 1943, I was named Kenneth Howard Florence. My last name was officially changed to Norton when my mother married John Norton on June 21, 1947.

My parents grew up in Jacksonville and knew each other their whole lives. My father was born there, and my mother moved there from Missouri when she was one. They would see each other in town at various functions and church-sponsored events. My mother was only 18 when my father asked for her hand in marriage. They remained married for the next 53 years.

Unlike many professional boxers, I grew up in a normal, well-adjusted, hardworking, middle-class family with Midwestern values. I definitely can hold claim to a wonderfully happy childhood, having never felt deprived in any way, shape, or form. Because I was an only child, my parents went out of their way to give me almost anything I desired. My own room, new clothes, a bike, toys—anything was mine for the asking.

It's only in retrospect that I can appreciate how hard my mom and dad worked to give me the things that gave me pleasure. I certainly didn't or couldn't appreciate that at the time, because when you're a kid, you don't know any different. Years later when I became a father, I definitely understood the concept of sacrificing for your children.

My parents worked their behinds off so that I could be given a higher quality of life than anything they ever knew growing up. In fact, I was downright spoiled. I was spoiled by my mother, I was indirectly spoiled by my father by his working so hard, and I was definitely spoiled by my Aunt Mary.

In my formative years, my mother worked full time at the hospital as an activities director. During the day, while she worked, I stayed with my Aunt Mary. She was more of a mother to me in those early years than my actual mother. Aunt Mary was the family matriarch, the glue that held the whole family together, and she watched over her nieces, nephews, and grandchildren while their parents went to work.

I don't ever remember Aunt Mary having a career, but taking care of children, feeding them, loving them, was a full-time job and she loved it. Aunt Mary also was the best cook in the world and relished feeding anyone who entered her house.

Aunt Mary was a special lady who possessed a wonderfully up-beat personality and was quick to laugh aloud. There was an inner beauty and shining spirit within her that I can only attribute to her total devotion to God. Aunt Mary was a very religious lady who attended church every Sunday. She loved everyone and everyone loved her in return. To me, she was a world-class lady in a league all by herself.

Ruth Norton: *Mary lived only two houses away and was my aunt, and was really Ken's great-aunt. Mary raised me because my mother died when I was young. After my mom got sick and passed away, my brother, sister, and I moved in with Mary. She had three children who all died young, and I'm sure she ached to be a mother. Mary's husband was a World War I veteran who died in combat, and she never remarried, so she chose to dedicate her life to taking care of our family's kids.*

She loved to cook and she loved children. Anything those kids did was fine with her. She didn't discipline them much, and so they loved her for spoiling them. But it was a special relationship she had with those kids, kind of like a grandmother always spoiling her grandchildren.

Between my side of the family and John's, Ken had plenty of cousins and relatives to play with. We all lived on the same street, and Mary either took care of them in their infant years or watched them when they got out of school, making sure they had something to eat and loving care. Kenny was special to Mary because he was such a sweet, rascally, happy-go-lucky child. Mary and Kenny had a special bond, and she always had a special place in his heart.

I was always bigger and had more energy than other children my age. I was ready to play at the drop of a hat and could go all day and night. I was a handful. An endless supply of restless energy, combined with my playful personality, got me in trouble most of my childhood.

I loved to tease and antagonize my cousins and friends, but I never harmed anyone. If there was snow on the ground, it would be reasonable to assume I was going to make a snowball and aim at one of my relatives or friends as a target. If there was no snow, then a mud ball would do just fine. Just dumb, stupid things—pulling on pigtails, untying shoelaces, firing spitballs, getting dragged through the mud by a hog, riding on the back of the city garbage truck at 60 miles an hour—anything for a laugh or thrill.

Occasionally, I would cross the line and would have to pay the price for my mischievous deeds.

Like the time my family visited my uncle's house and he fell asleep. I was a snoopy little kid and somehow I found a pistol that he kept hidden in a bedroom drawer. The following day was a Sunday, and I was sitting with all of my friends at church, having brought along my new prized possession. I secretly brandished the gun and passed it around to my friends, basically showing off. One of the kids told their parents, and in one phone call, my father, John "Mr. No Nonsense" Norton, was informed that his innocent little boy was "packing heat" in the house of the Lord. That little prank cost me half of my precious behind when I got home from school the next day.

Spankings were a way of life for me. I got spanked more in one week than most kids did in a year. The main reason I got whipped so much was not only that I committed the dirty deed as accused, but I made the mistake of lying about it. The truth never set me free because I never told it!

Whenever something was amiss in Jacksonville, my parents instinctively knew that somehow or some way I was involved, if not the ring- leader. The local police could never solve the crime I committed, but Ruth and John Norton knew the culprit. It was as if they had a special radar that tipped them off every time I pulled a fast one.

John Norton (Ken's father): *I knew just by instinct. Ken's not a person who's good at hiding things, and he was an awful liar. The local police couldn't figure it out, and I'd just look at him and ask, "Did you do this?" and he'd try to talk his way out of it and couldn't. Rather than just say, "I didn't do it," he'd go into these long, elaborate responses, and give himself away. I nailed him every time. For the most part, Ken wasn't much trouble. He was a good kid. Never a dull moment, that's for sure.*

I think when I discovered sports, my parents' prayers were answered. I finally found a release for all of my pent-up energy and focused my attention on being the best athlete in school.

The year was 1952. I was nine and in the third grade when I was introduced to the Jaycee Junior Olympics competition at school. I entered many events that day: the 100-yard dash, the standing broad jump, the long jump, and the 440-yard relay with my friends John Mann, Joe Clem, and Bobby McCaan.

My chest was decorated with blue ribbons by the end of the day. Those ribbons represented first place, the best of the best. I was without a doubt the best athlete in all of Jefferson Elementary, and those blue ribbons brought me special attention, adulation, and a newfound respect. I developed a hunger for winning because winning meant attention. I was an only child and so used to the attention I was getting at home that I wanted it from my peers at school as well. I wanted to feel unique and special 24 hours a day. No exceptions.

That one blue-ribbon day turned my life around in an instant. It was probably the driving force behind what I eventually did with my life, my career as a professional athlete, and who I am today. From that moment on, I strived to be the best possible all-around athlete that I could be. That included track and field, football, basketball, and baseball.

I was a naturally gifted athlete. I was the only kid in my school who could walk on his hands. I could easily walk on my hands 100 yards. When I played in the park, I used to swing so high, I tried to wrap the swing around the bar and got darn near close to doing it. I had no fear as a kid. I prided myself as a youngster who accomplished physical feats other kids only dreamed about.

Jacksonville in the 1950s wasn't liberal by any means, but it wasn't the Deep South either. However, it had its fair share of discrimination. Blacks and whites didn't openly intermingle in public, nor did they live in the same neighborhoods. Jacksonville had hotels and restaurants that blacks couldn't patronize. I remember that the one movie theater in town had a balcony that was reserved only for blacks. Because I excelled in sports, I was protected from some of the racial prejudice that surrounded Jacksonville. Many white adults treated me as special or acknowledged me when I walked by. They would cheer for me if I was on their son's Little League team, as well as pat me on the back to congratulate me after the game. I brought attention to the town and to the school, so again, I was protected from the ugliness that others experienced.

While I was protected from a lot of racism as a child, my eyes were opened as an adult. Recently the Jacksonville City Council wanted to name a street in my honor, but the street was located in the projects: A 40-yard street in the ghetto where people live in substandard conditions, drink beer out of paper sacks, play dominoes, smoke crack, and shoot each other in gang vendettas.

I don't have anything against the people who live in the projects. I'm sure they all want to get out, but why rename a street after me there of all places? Is that what they think Ken Norton's name stands for? Why not rename one of the streets where I was raised, like Hackett or Clay Street or a main thoroughfare that runs through the middle of town? That's an honor? I considered it a total slap in the face. Is it any wonder I backed away from the idea?

I give credit to my parents for raising me to have respect for human beings of every color. I was raised by old-fashioned people with old-time values. I was taught to say "Yes ma'am" or "No ma'am" and respect my elders. Women always were addressed as "ladies." I didn't know anything about being cool. There was nothing cool or hip about being disrespectful. It was a genuine, old-fashioned belief system that I was firmly rooted in, which included respecting everyone in your community. Sadly, that type of hospitality is sorely lacking in our society today, and that includes children and the parents who have raised them.

Over the years, I've been able to enjoy many close relationships with people of different colors, nationalities and members of the opposite sex. It makes no difference to me what the color of a person's skin is; it's what's inside their hearts that matters to me.

During my youth I also discovered I was gifted in academics, although I must admit I wasn't willing to work as hard scholastically as I did athletically. I got along well with my teachers and classmates, had a lot of fun in class, and did the work required of me. I did just enough to get by, a constant theme that would haunt me most of my life. It was my one trait I wished that I could have changed; a glaring weakness that I despised.

Ruth Norton: *Ken was a very bright child, but he could have been a straight-A student had he applied himself. Everything came too easy to him, and he didn't have to work hard to make good grades, so he did a minimal amount of work to get passing grades. As a kid and growing up, Ken always took the path of least resistance, and that caught up with him as an adult.*

Chapter Two

The Norton Rule

People have always asked me how I got my sculpted physique. I can only attribute it to good genes. Honestly, I never worked out with weights, and that includes when I was boxing professionally. Everything, the physique, the talent, and the finesse, are gifts from the man upstairs. However, as my story will tell you, natural talent alone is not enough to make it to the top.

By the time I reached the ninth grade, I stood 5-foot-11 and weighed 160 pounds. I thought I was a man because of my physique. In my spunkiness, I decided to put my father to the test. One night at the dinner table I was smarting off to my father and he threw a glass of water in my face. "You need to cool off, boy," he said I challenged him to escort me outside to a fistfight. My father was a good three inches shorter and 30 pounds lighter than me at the time, but don't forget, I was a "man."

I was no such thing.

When we reached the front yard, I started getting a little nervous and it showed, but my father had to make a stand with me if he wanted to keep my respect. I wasn't making any kind of first move, so my father asked, "Are you sure you want to do this?"

"Yes, sir," I replied, taking a big gulp and regretting the action I had set in motion.

"Then put up your hands," he said politely.

As soon as I raised my hands, my scrappy little father popped me in the chin and instantly I fell back on my beloved behind. The little guy packed a mean wallop! Right square, smack in the jaw, and man, I was seeing stars. I stayed there on the front lawn, sitting on the ground, thinking about what I had done. I was hanging my head in shame, realizing that I had disrespected my father by talking back to him. Sensing my guilt, my father came over and offered his hand out to me.

"C'mon son," he said quietly, "let's go back inside."

I grabbed his hand and he pulled me up. We were face-to-face when he embraced me in a hug. It was important for him to let me know that he still loved me. That was the last time I ever disrespected my father.

Lesson learned.

I was not the biggest guy on the football team, but I was one of the top three. As a freshman, I played freshman football and basketball, but I competed on the varsity level in track, my first love.

That first year of high school I was introduced to one of the most influential men in my life: Coach Al Rosenberger. Al was not only a wonderful coach, he eventually became my close friend and mentor. Today, after 30 years of friendship, we maintain the same relationship we had when I was in high school.

Al Rosenberger (Ken's high school coach): *I knew about Ken when he was an eighth grader. He was a good-sized freshman, but I knew he was going to grow, and there was no way to predict how good an all-around athlete he was going to be. Let's put it this way: He surpassed everyone's expectations and yet he still wasn't giving it his all. He lettered three years in football and basketball and four years in track and field. Many people don't know this, but he played summer league baseball and threw a 90-mile-an-hour fastball. He had a professional-league fastball at 16! I'd never seen a kid with his potential—and you know it when you see it.*

Ken was the best all-around athlete I had ever seen in my 30 years of coaching. I was the varsity defensive line coach at Jacksonville High and I worked with Ken a lot. He was the defensive end but he also played running back. He had long arms and big hands— strong, quick, and agile. He also had a good attitude when he came in as a freshman. I told those kids they were going to be good when they were juniors and seniors. In 1956, 1957, and 1958, we went undefeated and we competed against the biggest schools in Illinois.

In 1959, we had a so-so year, but the year Ken was a senior, 1960, we went undefeated. He was a co-captain that year and one game in particular stands out. There's a town west of us called Beardstown and it was in our conference. One night we just beat the tar out of them, 74-0. In football, he played on offense and defense, played all the special teams, kicked off, kicked field goals, and kicked extra points. He was a one-man wrecking crew. Ken was running the ball superbly that night and the only thing he didn't do properly was run down low like a fullback should. He ran with his upper body straight up.

His style of running reminded me of the great Jim Brown. I asked him why and he said, "Coach, I wanna see where I'm going." Well, it sort of made sense to me. Hell, what am I gonna do? If the kid's running 60 yards for a touchdown, am I gonna change his style of running? No way, man!

As I said before, football was fun, but I loved track and field. The one-on-one competition is what I enjoyed the most. Just me and my competition. No team out there to make up for the weak link in the chain. In all, I competed in eight events in track: 100-yard dash, 220, 400, 120-yard hurdles, 440 relay, 880 relay, high jump, discus throw, and shotput.

I took to track because it was a case where it was a very natural transition that utilized all of my athletic skills, but again, I did just enough to stay in shape. I was the type of individual who didn't go for the best time or distance, I did just enough to beat the competition. I didn't push myself, and looking back, I regret being so lazy and relying solely on my talent. Al Rosenberger also was the track coach, and I gave him fits with my lackadaisical attitude in preparing for a meet.

Al Rosenberger: *I knew Ken was a great athlete, far superior to the rest of the athletes, but I knew he was shortchanging himself. Ken's best event was the 180-yard hurdles, and anytime you run that in under 20 seconds, you're really scorchin'. Ken would regularly run it in 19.8 seconds. In the discus throw, he had one of the longest attempts in school history, 174 feet. He already held the school record at 165 feet, but he'd regularly throw around 170 feet.*

I used to ride him all the time and make him do extra laps, and he'd do it, but it wasn't his best. In fact, I'd go over to John and Ruth Norton's all the time and get together to see what we could do. Ken just wanted to have fun, and I can understand that at that age, but I would have loved to seen his personal best-effort then. His only competition was himself.

I did please Al at one track meet my senior year in the spring of 1961 when a big school out of Decatur, Illinois, called Eisenhower came to Jacksonville with a loaded track team. They were the city champs and because we were the best two teams in the state it was decided that the two schools would compete in a rare dual meet. Track meets back then consisted of four to five different schools competing in one meet, but this was a special occasion. However, Eisenhower didn't like the way it turned out.

Coach Rosenberger decided to put me in my customary eight events, and on this particular day, I cleaned up. In the last event of the day, the high jump, I entered the event late. I didn't start jumping until the bar hovered around 6 feet. I guess my casual attitude didn't help; I cleared the bar wearing my sweat pants and not only won the event, my score was the deciding factor in the meet. In all, I placed first in six events and second in the other two.

Decatur Eisenhower was disgusted with Al for entering me in eight events and had a rule imposed into the Illinois High School Association, which is the overall governing body that consists of principals, athletic directors, and the state board. The association voted that one athlete could not compete in more than any combination of four track events. They called it "The Norton Rule," and the ruling still stands today in Illinois.

Al Rosenberger: *Boy, do I remember that day! Eisenhower's coaching staff blew its top when Ken pulled it out for us. The word got around that some of the athletes thought that Ken was monopolizing all of the events. In other words, if he was entered in eight events, what are the other athletes going to be in? Hell, that's the name of the game—competition! You can't go through life expecting people to back off. Somehow, a few people got together and implemented the Norton Rule. My argument against the rule was, "How in the world are we going to promote and train for the decathlon?" I fought against the ruling: so did several other coaches, but somehow the rule was passed. If you got a big stud horse, turn him loose! Any other coach with a kid of this potential would have done the same thing.*

Sports were my first love, but there was a new challenge on the horizon when I entered my teens: chasing the ladies!

Athletics drew the attention of female admirers in Jacksonville and I have to admit, I not only loved the attention, I craved it. I have a deep appreciation for physical beauty. I honestly can say that I am a man who is very comfortable around women because I not only love their beauty, I just plain love everything about them. The way they carry themselves, the way they think differently than men, the way they converse, the way they dress, and the way they compete. It wasn't just the women in school—I enjoyed being around my Aunt Mary, my mother, and other female relatives and friends.

I can be myself around women; which means mainly having a good time, joking around, putting them at ease, and making them feel good about themselves. I'm very flirtatious, but I'm also respectful. I learned at a very early age that if you can make a woman laugh, you've won half the battle. But don't think that I talk only to beautiful women; I talk to almost anyone who wants to engage with me in a conversation. Young, elderly, pretty, white, black, orange—it doesn't really matter. I'm a people person at heart and I enjoy people as people; however, if that person is a nice-looking female, well, it just makes the conversation a whole lot easier!

I was in the ninth grade when I met my first girlfriend, Gloria Trumbo. Gloria lived in Jacksonville, and to me, she was the prettiest girl in the world. We went steady all through high school, and when I was about to graduate I really wanted to marry her, although we had a few obstacles to overcome. You see, Gloria was also very flirtatious and that just drove me up the wall. I'm not a jealous person by nature, but Gloria had a way about her that made me get a little crazy whenever she flirted in front of me. She knew she had me, and there was nothing I could do about it.

Our relationship came to an end the summer after high school graduation. Gloria was a year behind me in school, so she was staying in Jacksonville. We knew our time was ticking away, but Gloria wanted to make a nice, smooth transition of boyfriends without any withdrawal symptoms and began seeing someone else before I went away.

One summer night, I was in my bedroom gazing out the window when I spotted Gloria and her new boyfriend driving in his car. I had no clue that I was being replaced. She was sitting so close to him while he was driving, it looked as if two people were steering. Gloria was laughing her fool head off, not noticing that I saw her out the window. She had eyes only for her new beau.

With cat-like reflexes, I jumped into my parents' car and sped down the road after the two lovebirds. I took a turn too fast and put a nice dent in the side of the automobile when I slammed into a parked vehicle. The car could still function, and I caught up to the lovebirds and cornered them in a cul-de-sac. I got out of the car and slammed the door shut with authority, my teeth and fists clenched, steam coming out of my nose and ears, ready to kick some "You've-been-replaced" boyfriend butt.

This dude was smart. Too smart. He waited for me to get out of the car so he could run me over. He did a nice job, running me over like a speed bump. Once I was five feet in front of his car, he accelerated, lifted

my natural black ass over the hood and hoisted me up on the front wind-
shield. The concrete broke my fall and I fractured my left collarbone in
the process.

Man, I was an A-1 chump for getting out of my car in the first
place. This guy might not have had a lot of brawn, but he sure had a
whole lot more brains than Ken Norton did!

I got hurt physically as well as emotionally. Either way, I came
out worse for the wear. That injury would affect the way I played football
in college; thus, it affected my future in more ways than I could possibly
imagine.

Despite the appearance that I had everything—the good looks,
the God-given physique, the natural athletic ability, the happy-go-lucky
demeanor—inside I was a very insecure. I couldn't really pinpoint why I
felt that way at the time, but I think perspective has allowed me to examine and explain those pangs of insecurity.

All my life I was involved in sports and chasing the ladies. I never
had to study hard to make good grades. Everything I did was easy. The
result was that I was a spoiled brat, only 17, and an only child who had
always been protected, always got what he wanted. As a result of not facing hardships, I suffered from a lack of confidence. I was terrified of high
school ending. No one in my family had ever been offered a full athletic
scholarship before and that doubled the pressure I was feeling.

In 1960, during my senior year in high school, our football team
went undefeated and easily won the state championship. I had been a
defensive standout and was selected to the state's All-Defensive team.

By the end of my senior year, I had grown into a man's frame,
standing 6-foot-3 and tipping the scales at 195 pounds. I was offered
more than 90 different athletic scholarships from some of the finest insti-
tutions in the country. Those colleges included nationally ranked power-
houses such as Nebraska, Ohio State, Oklahoma, Michigan, Miami, Wis-
consin, Illinois, San Jose State, and Iowa. I had my pick and I chose a
college close to home, Northeast Missouri State. The college was nowhere
near the competitive level of the other schools, but frankly, I didn't want
to venture too far from home because I was still a small-town guy. That
would soon change.

Al Rosenberger: *I would have liked to have seen Ken go to
a warm-weather school on the west coast, preferably San Jose State,
because it was a powerhouse in track. Bud Winter was the track
coach there and he had some tremendous athletes under him. He
knew about Ken and wanted him, but that's a long way for a guy to*

go from the Midwest. Had Ken attended San Jose State, I believe he would have been great in the decathlon, possibly competing in the Olympics and winning a gold medal. He worked much harder in track and field than in football or basketball.

Do I feel he shortchanged himself when he could have gone to a bigger school and competed on a higher level? Sure I do, but Northeast Missouri State wasn't a bad little football team. The bottom line was this was what Ken wanted to do, so this was the right move for him at the time.

At college, I was alone for the first time in my life and I was terrified of not knowing a soul. I had always been surrounded by family and relatives; safe in my little protected plastic bubble called Jacksonville. It was especially tough saying goodbye to my mother and Aunt Mary. I would miss my father, too, but the women in my life have always had a special place in my heart.

My fears were soon allayed when I got my first taste of college life and college ladies. I got poor grades, not from being depressed and away from home, but because I was having too much fun. I was like the fox let loose in the hen house. I had no supervision or parental guidance, and I went wild. No, I wasn't John Belushi dressed up in a sheet belting down frosty beers at a toga party, but I gave the lamp-shade man a pretty good run for his money.

I partied hard that first semester, and my grades mirrored my efforts. Al got wind of my exploits, and when I got back to Jacksonville, he gave me a much-needed lecture. "Ken, right now you are having the time of your life, and I'm happy for you," said Al. "You're playing ball, seeing a lot of different girls, and you fit right in. However, that ain't going to last too long if you keep up your current behavior. You're going to end up right back here in Jacksonville if you don't switch directions."

That got me thinking. Al always had my best interests at heart and I continued to listen to him. He ended the lecture with some simple advice. "Ken, when you can get to class, get there on time, sit there, and do your work," said Al. "Make an honest attempt, keep your mouth shut, and you're gonna make it." It was easy to apply his advice, and from that point on, I made good grades. I wasn't on the dean's list, but I made grades that I could live with. Had I applied myself like I should have, I would have been a straight-A student.

Looking back, academics should have been the No. 1 priority in my life, not sports. When I talk to youngsters today, especially those involved in athletics, I tell them to get their education first. It is so important to get that diploma because if you can earn a degree, anything in life is obtainable. Knowledge is the key to happiness, not financial security.

My freshman year in football at Northeast Missouri was much harder than I had anticipated. I started on the freshman squad but I also played on the varsity team. The broken collarbone I had suffered in the scuffle with Gloria's boyfriend had not healed properly, and I played my first year with intense pain. I didn't let any of the coaches know about the shoulder because I feared my scholarship might be revoked. I hid the pain by favoring my other shoulder. Whenever I made a tackle, it was always with the right shoulder. Actually, I did pretty well, and the coaches never found out.

If my first year at Northeast Missouri had been unremarkable, my sophomore year was an outright fiasco. My left collarbone was still hampering my play, and the coaches were expecting more from me. They ran me ragged and dogged my every move. It got to where I couldn't take the pressure, and I exploded at the head coach and had a few choice words regarding his comments about my play. I spoke my piece and then walked off the field, abandoning my scholarship and my education. College, I felt, just was not for me. I took a shower, got dressed, and took the next bus back home. My dream of a life outside of Jacksonville, Illinois, just crash-landed me back into reality.

It was childish to just up and leave school without telling anyone. I behaved like a spoiled brat. All of my life I had gotten my way, and now life was throwing me a little hardship, and I just walked away from the situation. Real mature.

I wasn't welcomed into John Norton's home with open arms. Of course, my mother and Aunt Mary were glad to see me, but my father looked at me with a real hard look, his arms crossed. His posture was stern and his eyes hurled daggers in my direction. He didn't say a word, but I knew he was disappointed that I had walked away from a free education. My behavior after that drew his attention and he presented me with three choices that I didn't want to make at that time. I wanted some time to chill out, think things over during the summer, maybe even have a few laughs. But John Norton wasn't laughing.

John Norton: *A few weeks passed by before a pattern started to emerge: Ken would sleep until noon, walk around the house in his underwear, sweet-talk the girls on the phone, and run the air-conditioner full blast. At the time I was working three jobs, Ruth was working full time at the hospital, and Ken was not doing anything. I came home from work one day to grab a quick bite to eat and Ken's* *in his underwear, his hair's all messed up because he had just woken up, and he's on the phone with some girl he wanted to take out.*

He turned around and saw my face. He knew I was plenty pissed off and hung up the phone. I told him, "This is my house and we all work in this house. I'm not going to allow you to live at home rent free while I'm out there working three jobs. You got three choices: You either go back to school, get a job, or join the service. What you ain't going to do is sit around in your underwear all day, run up my electricity bill, and talk to the girls. You got another think coming, boy!"

That's when Ken decided to join the Marines, because he was too lazy to get a job and pay rent.

Because both my father and I were stubborn and bullheaded, I found it hard to talk openly to him about my problems. In these instances, Al Rosenberger became my surrogate father because he could listen to me objectively without getting emotionally involved. I respected Al's advice, and when I broached the subject of joining the Marines, Al was all for it.

"If you get any kind of rank, Ken, it's a good career," he told me. "They also have the GI Bill, so that if you ever wanted to go back to school, it's paid for. You're covered on both ends." Al went to college on the GI Bill after World War II and then started his career in high school athletics. "The Marines are the best," Al declared.

A deep-seated fear had always lingered in the back of my mind: that I would be stuck in Jacksonville for the rest of my life. Now that I had had a taste of the outside world, I realized Jacksonville didn't provide many opportunities for a black man trying to advance himself. I saw it firsthand with my father, who had to work three jobs trying to make ends meet. He was armed with an 11th-grade education and eventually earned his graduate equivalency degree. Most white men in Jacksonville didn't have that much education. The best a black man could do in that town was work for the police or fire department. Incidentally, my father was the first black man to work for the Jacksonville Fire Department. He had to take a written test, which had been implemented because of the Civil Service Act, and he passed with flying colors.

Things in Jacksonville haven't changed much in 40 years. There's only one black police officer. That number doesn't reflect the population, which is half white and half black. To me, the town is still prejudiced; however, now it's just more subtle.

I had an overwhelming feeling of doom that if I stayed in Jacksonville, I'd find a menial 9-to-5 job, get married, raise a few kids, worry about a mortgage, pay my taxes, retire after 30 years, collect my pension, pick out my burial plot and casket, and take a dirt nap and never get the opportunity to leave Jacksonville. That's how millions of Americans live their lives, and some even consider it bliss, but to me, it would be a nightmare. I wanted something more for myself. I wanted an exciting life. I wanted adventure. I wanted to live a life where I called the shots; not be owned by the company store. I guess I was young and restless, but an inner voice told me that I had to follow my dream to break free from Jacksonville's hold on me.

I think that's when I decided to become Pvt. Norton of the United States Marines. It wasn't an easy decision to make. I knew the Marines were the biggest and the baddest men in uniform and were always the first to go to war. But more important, there was a special pride to them that I sensed and desperately sought, an inner security that had eluded me. Besides, my old man never thought I could hack it in the Marines, and maybe that's why I decided to join.

In my mind, it was time for me to grow up and become a man. Before I entered the Marines, I was just a boy in a man's body.

Chapter Three

A Means to an End

The year was 1964, the year the Beatles invaded the United States and played to a television audience of 70 million people on "The Ed Sullivan Show." It was the same year I joined the United States Marine Corps. I was all of 20 and it showed. Inside I was still the immature, spoiled wonder boy from Jacksonville. The Marines were going to re-educate my spoiled ways, but that's what I wanted. They didn't disappoint me, either. They never disappoint.

My entrance into the Marines began on a sour note: My precious and beloved Aunt Mary became very sick while I was sitting at the main bus terminal in St. Louis, waiting to be taken to Camp Pendleton in Oceanside, California.

Aunt Mary had developed adult-onset diabetes, which eventually led to her having her foot amputated, and then later on, her entire leg. This lady with such dignity was going out the worst way possible, slowly, and it hurt me deeply. I knew she was sick when I entered the corps, but I never imagined that her condition would deteriorate as fast as it did. Almost overnight she was in intensive care.

I received a phone call from my father telling me that Mary was in the hospital and wasn't going to make it through the night. I read between the lines; he was telling me that she was waiting to say goodbye to me before she made her peace with God. Not that she needed to make peace with God. I picture Mary vividly in Sunday church services, shaking her hands up high, singing as loud as she could with the choir, giving the Lord all she could offer to him.

The phone call upset me terribly, especially given the fact that I was going to be locked away in boot camp for the next 13 weeks. Fortunately, my mother called one of my superiors and explained the situation to him and I was granted permission to go back to Jacksonville until my personal affairs were finished. Jacksonville was 100 miles away from St. Louis and the next bus left in a few hours. It wasn't enough time to get back to Aunt Mary, and she passed away before I had a chance to say goodbye. I was crushed.

> **Ruth Norton:** *At that time in his life, Ken was closer to Aunt Mary than he was to me because he had spent more time with her growing up. She quietly slipped away before Ken had a chance to see her, and he was understandably upset. When Ken showed up at the hospital, he was a wreck. I called his commanding officer at Camp Pendleton and explained the situation, hoping that he wouldn't send a posse out after Ken.*
>
> *When Ken got out of control, nobody could talk any sense into him and I would have hated to see Ken in any kind of confrontation with the military police. He wouldn't have gone quietly, that's for sure. Luckily for Ken, his commanding officer was very understanding, but John and I had to force Ken to go back to basic training. There was nothing he could do for Mary now, but he said he'd go back after her funeral, so we reached a compromise, and Ken kept his word and headed back to Oceanside.*

It was the first time in my life that I had lost somebody so near to my heart. It was as if I lost a part of me, and I grieved for her as I had for no other. After Mary's funeral, friends and relatives gathered at her house and food was served. For some reason, it angered me that people came to her house to eat and I became upset, indignant, and belligerent. I ordered everyone out of the house and scared the shit out of all of the guests.

I was a young fool who had never dealt with death on such an intimate level before, and I think I became a little more serious that day. The days of innocent youth were behind me now. Aunt Mary's death took a long time for me to overcome, but that old cliché proved true: Time does have a way of healing pain.

I can look back and be thankful for the times we had together. Aunt Mary taught me the basics of life: respect for yourself, taking responsibility for your actions, the love of God, and how to treat people decently. Most important, she gave me the gifts of love and laughter. She taught me to take the time to laugh at myself and not take life too seriously. Aunt Mary had lived a full life, well into her 70s. She was surrounded by a family who loved and adored her. She was at peace with herself and knew where she was going. I can't think of a better way to go. It's been over 33 years since Aunt Mary left this earth, but I think of her often. Every time I do, it brings a smile to my face.

I had no illusions about joining the Marines: I knew it was going to be tough, but for me, that was good. Until I got on that bus that took me to Camp Pendleton, I was never responsible for anything I did. I could do anything in Jacksonville and people would just turn their heads because they wanted to keep me happy. The Marine Corps didn't care if I was happy or not. They just wanted to make a man out of me. In the Marines I learned I had to depend on myself. In time, I became the self-assured man I had always wanted to be. The Marines made me grow up.

To my surprise, boot camp was not that physically taxing for me. As a college athlete I was in excellent shape. And just as it had in school, my athletic ability brought me respectability in the corps. My drill instructor saw me as a natural leader, something I did not see in myself. He made me the squad leader of my platoon, and soon I learned how to lead people. I also learned how to follow people when necessary. Boot camp pushed me to my mental and physical limits—something that had never happened before.

During boot camp, the day began at 5 a.m. sharp with our drill instructor yelling, cursing, and making occasional comments about our mothers' overactive sex lives. It gave new meaning to "rude awakening."

Now awake, each man had to make his bed so that the drill instructor could bounce a quarter off of it and catch it. Sometimes I tried to make my bed too fast so that I could be the first one out of the barracks, but that meant I didn't make the bed too well. I got my ass handed to me for breakfast on those days. The drill sergeant was careful not to show any preferences, so the squad leader got disciplined, too. It helped me become a better person, a better man.

Once the beds were made, our shoes and belt buckles had to be spit-polished, shined to perfection. For those on kitchen patrol, or KP, the toilets, floors, and showers had to be scrubbed and cleaned spotless. I'll never forget the time the drill sergeant yelled at the top of his lungs, "I want this crapper to be so clean that the Virgin Mary would be proud to come in here and take a dump!" I got the shakes from laughing so hard I had to contain myself before the drill instructor asked me what was so funny. I ended up punching myself in the stomach a few times to bring me back to a more serious state of mind. One thing about those drill instructors: they have the funniest lines!

Actually, I took to life as a Marine extremely well. Hey, coming from Jacksonville, this new life was exciting and adventurous. I liked the discipline the Marines instilled. It gave me a sense of pride I had never felt before. Sure, I was proud of my athletic achievements, but that was nothing compared to being presented with a bleak, harsh situation, and realizing that you can move mountains if you focus your efforts on attaining a goal.

For example, when I first got to boot camp, I thought there was no way in hell I was going to make it through 13 weeks of rigorous training, making my bed, perfectly polishing my shoes, with drill instructors in my face every time I messed up or answered incorrectly. What they actually were doing was tearing down the old Ken Norton by breaking down those bad habits while building up the new Marine Norton. You can't rebuild something on a solid foundation without first tearing down the old. That is what the Marines did with me and it worked. Many of the things I learned in the corps are still with me today.

I would later explore the area of positive thinking when I became a professional boxer, but I believe the Marine way of life and thinking was the genesis of positive thinking for me. It's just like that old saying: What the mind can conceive, the body can achieve.

After my 13 weeks in boot camp, I was assigned to Pensacola, Florida, to communications school to learn Morse code. The powers that be felt that I would be most beneficial to the Marines if I became a radioman. Actually, they pegged me pretty good because I had a great instinct for Morse code and could send out or receive 500 words a minute.

I had it all: an ocean-side view, a paying job that I liked, travel, three square meals a day, a roof over my head, and a cake job to boot. I could get to liking this, but there had to be a catch, right?

I soon discovered in a combat situation, the radioman is hunted down first because he gives coordinates to the artillery command as to where the enemy might be lurking. The radioman wields the most power in that given situation. If you take him out, all firing power is eliminated. That was the catch, and if you ask me, it wasn't the catch of the day. I'd prefer to throw that one back in the ocean, thank you very much.

I could see it now: All 6-foot-3 and 205 pounds of me driving around in a jeep full of radio equipment on a dirt road in Vietnam. I might as well have painted a bull's-eye on my helmet for all of the snipers to see. There was no doubt in my mind that as soon as I got my shipping orders, I would be a dead man.

In my mind, shipping orders were just a prelude to a death certificate. The North Vietnamese were extremely mysterious people and they didn't play by the conventional rules of war. These people strapped bombs to their own children and sent them inside a tent to blow up American soldiers. Men, women, and children all came at you.

It was my personal opinion that these people weren't playing with a full deck, and I wasn't going to be anybody's Joker. That, and the fact that the United States had no business in this crazy man's war, made me dread going to Vietnam.

I think most people have this vision of military people as fanatical mercenary types hell-bent on starting wars. Nothing could be further from the truth. Prevention is the key word. We want to prevent what may happen to this great country of ours and often that means having to take a stand. Yes, I wanted to defend my country if called upon, but that didn't mean I wasn't scared. I didn't want to die. Bombs going off in the distance, bullets whizzing by, or watching a buddy from the front row get blown into a thousand pieces stepping on a land mine wasn't my idea of a good time. People who have seen the horrors of combat firsthand never want to go back and give a repeat performance.

When my 13 weeks of basic training in Pensacola were finished, I had a month off before heading to Camp Lejeune, North Carolina, for my first assignment. I returned to Jacksonville to spend some time with my parents. I could see in their eyes that they were pleased with the choice I had made regarding the Marines. Their boy was finally a man.

Then I went out and did something stupid that proved I wasn't as mature as I thought. I got a girl pregnant.

I hadn't seen a member of the female persuasion for 13 weeks, a lifetime of purgatory. Too much male testosterone in one place is definitely not good. How did I spell relief? W-O-M-A-N!

Careva Woods and I had grown up together in Jacksonville and when I came home on leave, she had grown into a beautiful young woman. Getting a woman pregnant was something I never thought much about. Back in the early '60s, it wasn't dealt with as openly as it is today. While having a child out of wedlock was not unheard of, it did come with a social stigma. My mother was living proof of that. I was so naive regarding birth control that when I found out the news from Careva, I pleaded in ignorance: "But we only did it once!"

My father taught me that if you start a fire, you put it out. Rather than run away from my responsibility, I offered to marry Careva, even though we didn't love each other. Given that we weren't in love, and I was in the military and would soon be moving to North Carolina to start my career, Careva wisely declined my offer of matrimony and courageously raised the baby by herself. She married my cousin, Gilbert Banks, a few years later, so at least she kept it in the family!

My son, Keith Anthony Norton, was born on November 2, 1965, in Jacksonville, Illinois. Keith is an exceptional man today, something for which I can take no credit. I was ready to have sex, but I wasn't ready for the responsibility that came with it. As a result, for many years, Keith knew Ken Norton was his biological father, but he never knew Ken Norton as a real father.

Today Keith and I enjoy a wonderful relationship. He's a former Marine and works in an executive position in the business sector in Miami. He was a great kid who has matured into a well-adjusted adult. It simply amazes me when he was growing up that he never held a grudge against me for not being there for him. When we resumed our relationship a few years ago, he immediately accepted me with open arms and genuine warmth. In retrospect, it was I who missed out on Keith. Fortunately, we have our best days in front of us.

Keith Norton (Ken's son): *My mother let me know who my father was when I was around seven or eight; that's when I first got to know Ken. I knew who he was before he was a celebrity. I would visit Ken in the summers when I was in junior high, and during the school year we stayed in touch over the phone. When I was in the Marines and stationed at Twentynine Palms, California, we became very close.*

I've learned a lot from my father over the years, even when we weren't together. He would teach me things over the telephone and give me encouraging advice. He stressed working hard and staying focused. I remember him telling me at a very young age to have positive thoughts about everything I did. He was a role model I could look up to. Whenever he had a fight on television, I would always know that he was my dad.

My dad is a great guy: warm, thoughtful, and playful. To achieve what he has achieved, that is really something special. If I can accomplish half the things my dad has, I will feel that I have accomplished a lot.

I was shipped out to Camp Lejeune, North Carolina, in the fall of 1964. I became adjusted to living in the south quite easily. The people in North Carolina were friendly and hospitable. However, reveille at 5 a.m. was the one thing I could do without. I became friendly with a gentleman at Camp Lejeune named Art Redden. One day I asked Art if he knew of any loopholes, anything at all, to get out of reveille.

"There are two ways I can think of right off the top of my head," Art said. Answers, I liked answers. "If you play football or box, and become good enough, you could tour the country. You get up later, no reveille, you get to keep your liberty card and get served better food," he said.

But there had to be a catch, right? There's always a catch involved.

"Hey look, it's great PR for the Marines," Art told me. "If the football team is winning and you're on the team, you don't have to go get your head blown off by some Vietcong in a rice paddy. It's a win-win situation for everyone involved, but you have to be good enough to make the team."

I didn't think that would be a problem. My broken collarbone had finally healed properly, so that wasn't going to be a hindrance. And I missed football, so this would be a double blessing. I would get to play football and get special treatment. Ah, how I enjoyed the perks of life.

When I introduced myself to the football coach, he was ecstatic. One look at me and he knew I was a ballplayer. When I told him that I had played college ball at Northeast Missouri State, he looked toward the sky and said, "Thank you, God!" and then he looked at me and said, "I knew going to church with my wife was going to pay off in the long run." We both laughed at his candor, and I knew this was a good situation. It just felt right.

"What position do you play, son?"

"Halfback," I replied. The coach shifted uncomfortably in his stance and I perceived something to be wrong. "Halfback, huh?"

"Yes, sir," I said with supreme confidence.

"Well," the coach said, "there's another person on the team who's kinda attached to that position, but if you really want to play halfback, you'll have to go head to head with him. You're not opposed to trying out for that position, are you?"

I assured the coach that I was not opposed to competing for the position. That was the name of the game in football. Nothing was given to you. May the best man win. Besides, competition always motivated me. I was actually looking forward to it. What I didn't count on was military rank being pulled, but that's exactly what happened. In football you wear shoulder pads on the playing field, not medals. Everyone is the same rank once those cleats touch the grass.

The gentleman at halfback, and I use that term loosely, was a white officer, actually a captain, who held the highest rank on the team. He was an adequate running back, but in all honesty, he didn't hold a candle to me. In terms of physical ability, there was no match. I ran around tacklers, busted through the line, charged for touchdowns, blocked like a tackle, and pummeled defenders into the ground who dared to get in my way.

Unfortunately, the coach decided on the captain as the starting halfback. He seemed to be intimidated by this officer and let him have his way. Other guys on the team grumbled under their breath, but no one stepped forward to stick up for me. I wasn't going to be labeled a complainer, and I chose not to say anything. I was relegated to the bench for half the season until a fateful day in practice.

Keep in mind that one of the reasons why I didn't complain to the coach was that I was on the gravy train with biscuits for wheels. The football players were routinely fed steak and potatoes, we had our own hours for practice, which meant my duty was cut short and I didn't have to wake up at the ungodly hour of 5 a.m. for reveille with all of the other chumps. I had it good, all the athletes in the Marines did, and I was not about to rock the boat.

In practice, the first and the second team scrimmaged each other daily, and on one particular day the second-team offense was going against the first-team defense. The first-string halfback, Capt. No Talent, was playing defensive back. A sweep was called to the right side of the field, exactly where he was going to be a sitting duck. The quarterback took the snap from the center and spun around to pitch the ball to the other running back in the backfield. I was the lead blocker and was to take out the first member of the defense who got in the way. Imagine my surprise when Capt. No Talent slipped through his man's block and planted himself right in my path.

I had already gathered up a full head of steam and was at the peak of my stride when I saw my golden opportunity to flatten his ass into a pancake. Our eyes met right before the moment of impact, and he could tell in that instant that I was nothing less than overjoyed. My eyes got big and my mouth watered. He planted his feet and didn't move. I was running at him with my arms pumping up and down, plus, I had a good 40 pounds on the guy. It was payback time for pulling rank.

When our bodies crashed, I lowered my head and planted my helmet right on his numbers. I lifted him in the air and bucked him like a bull catching a matador by his horns. He was lifted off the ground and thrown violently to the grass with a thud. He was not only tossed aside like a rag doll, but humiliated as well.

When the whistle had blown, the good captain dusted himself off and headed my way.

"You really think you're hot shit, don'tcha, nigger? the captain snorted.

I had him just where I wanted him. Anything I was going to say was going to piss him off, so I had better choose my words carefully. Now we were nose to nose with sweat dripping off.

I smiled at him and said coolly, "No, sir. What I was thinking is you're an asshole, sir." I just couldn't leave well enough alone.

The coach stepped between us, both of his arms outstretched with the palms of his hands touching our chests. "Hold on, Norton!"

"I'm fine, coach," I said. "Running him up to command for calling me a nigger or kicking his ass ain't gonna change anything. He'll still be an asshole. I don't need this shit, coach. You can take your team and . . ." I hesitated for a moment, then bit my tongue and remained silent. I decided if I had said any more to the coach, there might be some really serious repercussions.

As for the captain, he stood his ground with me. I told him, "Get out of my face, sir. You might make me mad." I knew this guy didn't have the guts to take a swing at me. I turned on my heel, and yanked off my chin strap and tore my helmet from my head. I slammed it down to the ground. In show biz, that's called a "grand exit." But I wasn't in show biz, at least, not yet. Then it hit me: My beloved steak and potatoes, my meatloaf, my rack of ribs, all of that was gone. I pictured a screaming drill sergeant waking me for reveille. The gravy train started to spin its biscuit wheels and run out of steam.

Then that scene was replaced with a vision of Private Norton peeling potatoes in the back of the kitchen surrounded by industrial-sized metal pots. I pictured cutting my hands several times with the potato peeler. A grim dose of reality set in.

As I made my way back to the field house, I walked across the gym to where the boxing team was working out. My friend, Art Redden was on the team. He had introduced me to a lot of the guys and once introduced me to the coach, Pappy Dawson. Pappy was a nice, older gentleman who was a former Marine. He had been a mainstay in Marine boxing for years.

I was an emotional wreck as I walked across the gym in my cleats and pads. My head was down and I wore a grimace on my face. Pappy spotted me and asked me what was wrong. He was a perceptive old man.

"I just quit the football team."

Pappy moved in for the kill. He asked no questions as to why, nor did he want to know. He probably knew that I was bummed out that I was going to lose out on all of those special privileges that the athletes become accustomed to. Pappy had only one question for me: "Would you be interested in boxing for the Marines?"

"I might as well," came the reply.

It wasn't as strong a response as he would have liked, but it would do for now. Pappy had just landed himself every boxing trainer's dream: a coachable heavyweight prospect with tons of athletic ability. A potential gold mine!

And that was my introduction to the sport of boxing.

Sure, as a kid I listened to "Gillette's Fight Night" on that radio Fridays. Boxing was an exciting spectator sport, and that's all I wanted it to be for me. I wanted to listen to it on the radio or watch it in the stands. There was no way on God's green earth I was going to risk anyone touching this pretty face. Muhammad Ali thought he was pretty, hey, he couldn't hold a candle to me. Sorry, Muhammad, but I was the one who eventually starred in a handful of movies (baring my backside in two of them!) and was asked to pose for a magazine. You might have been The Greatest, but in the department of good looks, I have taken it upon myself (modestly, of course) to declare myself the winner.

In addition to messing up my good looks, boxing simply was a sport that I wasn't attracted to. Track and field was my first true love, then football, basketball, and baseball. Boxing wasn't even a minor consideration. The only time the sport was ever brought up was during the Friday-night broadcasts, when my dad told me one time I'd be an excellent boxer.

"Boxing requires skill, athleticism, and brains," he told me, "and you've been blessed with all three."

As you will continue to read throughout this book, you will see that nothing was ever planned. I plodded through my life without a thought for tomorrow; things just happened. Some people may call it a lucky or charmed life, but that implies that there wasn't a struggle along the way. I've had plenty of struggles in my life, but I'd prefer to chalk it up to destiny; the way it was meant to be. Why spend your life wondering why it turned out the way it did or questioning why God chose to punish you? That's such a waste of time. Why not just accept fate, move on, and deal with it as best you can? Boxing for me was always a means to an end. Nothing more; nothing less.

Destiny had cleverly disguised itself as a pair of red leather boxing gloves.

Chapter Four

The Golden Boy

So the shoulder pads came off and the gloves got laced up. I knew next to nothing about boxing.

For the first time in my life, I didn't have a sport completely mastered. Boxing was as familiar to me as a diet was to Fat Albert.

I looked pitiful when I first tried to shadow box. The proper technique and footwork felt foreign to me. I was very self-conscious about myself in those days, and I refused to work out in front of the team. I jumped rope, shadow boxed, and hit the heavy bag in the dimly lit corner of the gym so that no one could see what I was doing. Pappy Dawson didn't push me in front of the others or force me to expose my awkwardness. He was just content to have me there. I was sure he would work his way to me in due time.

Pappy knew what he was doing, and he knew exactly how to treat me. He was a fight veteran for five decades, and part of the realm of a trainer is to know how to read a person. He knew I was very apprehensive, and he left me alone to get it together. I was excited at the prospect of learning the sport, but I needed to get over that hump of self-consciousness. If I could train myself to look competent, I could train in the open before the team. It would take three long months before I relented and came out from behind closed doors to work with the other fighters, but by then, it was too late. Pappy was killed in a freak automobile accident.

Pappy happened to be sitting on a bench at the local bus terminal, biding his time reading a paper while waiting for a city bus to take him home. The bus made a wild turn and came around the corner too fast, crushing Pappy up against the terminal's brick wall. I had only known him a few weeks.

From what I understood from the guys on the boxing team, Pappy had a vast knowledge of boxing and was one of the best trainers in the country on the amateur level. He was a good man and a proud Marine. I felt his loss strongly because I felt the one man who could teach me how to box properly was now gone. Art Redden would help me refine my technique, but I more or less taught myself how to box. I guess that's why boxing critics have always called my style "awkward." Personally, I prefer the word "unique."

The most traditional defense in boxing is to hold up both hands to your face at the cheek level. I basically covered up my face with my arms. This is commonly referred to as a "crab style," where the arms are in a horizontal position. To me, it was plain common sense not to leave your face wide open when a quick jab could penetrate the traditional defense.

I was obsessed about my face. Chalk it up to vanity, but I liked the face that God gave to me, and I wasn't going to get my nose broken or lose any teeth. Worst of all were cuts. Those mean ol' nasty scars stayed for life. No way was I going to let the silky smooth skin on my face get torn up. I'm sure there are people out there who like the "rugged he-man" look, but I wasn't one of them. My face was downright pretty, and I liked it. I liked me. I liked waking up in the morning and looking in the mirror and not looking like minced meat. I liked it so much, in fact, that I rubbed cocoa butter on my face every night before I went to bed. I did this because when I sweated during a fight, the cocoa butter would make my face so slick, a boxing glove would just slide. To this day, I have only one noticeable scar. No one ever taught me that trick; I learned it on my own. Pretty smart for a pretty boy.

I didn't develop a proper jab until later in my career. I did develop a devastating punch that made me famous in the boxing world. It was called the devastating looping overhand right, and I did it by taking a step with my left leg, cocking my right fist, and starting my swing behind my back. When I brought the swing around to the point of impact, it struck with such force that it was bound to do some damage. And if it connected to the face, it was "good night, Gracie." In time, I also became known for my left hook.

Critics will point out that I dragged my right foot behind my left as opposed to dancing around the ring like Muhammad Ali. That worked well for him, but it didn't work for me. Besides, I wasn't a dancer in the ring. I stalked my opponents. Boxing to me meant two men enter the ring, one man leaves. The winner is the one left standing up. It was that simple.

After three months of rigorous workouts, I was ready to test my skills in the ring. The team was taken over by an assistant coach, but I considered Art Redden the only man in my corner. My gut instinct also had played a big role in how I boxed.

I was incredibly nervous before my first amateur bout, but I must say, I was all about taking care of business. I knocked out my opponent in the first round, claiming my first ring victim.

Many boxers have said that there's nothing quite like the feeling of conquering another man in the ring. To pummel someone until they collapse brings out the ultimate beast in a man. An air of superiority emerges in that boxer for a few fleeting moments, and it's a feeling unlike anything else in the world.

I can honestly say that I never felt that way when I beat another man into the canvas. I never had a feeling of elation when I rendered a man unconscious. It was a brutal sport, and I knew it was vicious and ugly. On the one hand, I was happy in that I won, but I wasn't particularly proud of the mess I had left behind. In my hands lay the potential to kill someone for the sake of sport, and it wasn't something that I wanted to think about. I never worried for myself, but I always worried that someday, somehow, I would be responsible for ending another life. I vowed I would never become a vicious animal who savored the taste of blood in the ring.

During my first year in the Marine Corps I went 10-1, knocking out most of my opponents. All amateur fights are three rounds, and many fights are won on points. I didn't care for the amateur system of scoring points, because a cleanly landed light jab counted just as much as a landed power punch. I thought it was a stupid way to score a fight, and that's how I lost my first fight, on points.

Our team won the match, but I was very upset that I didn't contribute to our victory. Art Redden won his match, but I lost mine, and it bothered me something fierce. If you're smart in life, you learn from your losses. I learned quickly that I didn't like to lose. I also learned that slugging toe to toe wasn't necessarily going to win you fights. From that first loss, I was willing to learn how to box, not just trade punches.

Richard Steele (boxing referee): *I was stationed with Ken at Camp Pendleton and we sparred quite a bit. As an amateur, he was big and strong, but lacked style; he relied completely on brute strength. When we sparred together, I moved a lot and boxed instead*

*of trading punches with Ken. He hit so hard he would hurt you
without even knowing it, so I just tried to stay out of his way. When
he got out of the Marine Corps and turned pro, I couldn't box with
him anymore, he improved so much from the time he started to the
time he got out.*

I dedicated myself to honing my technique; not relying so much
on my brute strength, but rather focusing on my opponent's style. I won
the All-Marine Championship three years in a row and ran up a 24-2
record with 19 knockouts to my credit. As I developed as a boxer, I noticed that I received more attention both in and out of the ring.

The base newspaper began to cover my matches in detail, and I
enjoyed the attention. My boxing uniform was a bit on the flashy side. I
was decked out in sparkling gold trunks, headgear, shoes, and gloves. I
was so flashy, Elvis Presley would have envied my threads. The local media dubbed me the "Golden Boy," and the nickname stuck like glue, even
though all the other boxers on the team wore gold, too.

Heavyweights in boxing always get the most attention, and I became a local celebrity at Camp Lejeune. My picture was constantly splashed
on the front page of *The Camp Lejeune News*. The attention I received
made me work even harder. I guess that was always the core of my driving
force.

With attention came the perks. Many female admirers came looking for me, but one who did not was one Jeanette Brinson. She had no
idea who I was, and in a way, that appealed to me.

Jeanette was a gorgeous young lady when we met on a hot, muggy
summer day in 1965. Jeanette, then 19, was a slim 5-foot-6. She was also
equipped with tantalizing hazel eyes, silky smooth hair, and killer legs. In
an instant, I was smitten with her. Her father owned a nightclub not too
far from the base, and I approached her and asked her if she'd like to
dance. Although she said yes, I could tell that she was very shy. Later on,
I would discover that she was painfully shy. I, on the other hand, was the
exact opposite. We conversed quite easily. I did all the talking while she
just listened!

Given our different personalities, we rarely clashed. In fact, in a
short period of time, we fell in love. I was drawn to her physical beauty at
first, and then later, her inner beauty. She was very sensitive, and I think
she responded to the fact that I was a boxer and could protect her.

Jeanette had a son named Tommy who was two at the time. She
had gotten pregnant by a former boyfriend who took off when he found
out she was having a child. To make ends meet, she and Tommy lived
with her parents.

It wasn't too long after we started dating that Jeanette became pregnant. Even though I wasn't ready for marriage, I proposed because it was the honorable thing to do. Her mother was crazy about me and her father was a quiet guy, but we got along just fine. I'm sure they would have preferred their daughter marry a doctor or lawyer instead of a grunt in the Marines, but I didn't fly the coop like the previous guy who got her pregnant. I'm sure I won brownie points in her parents' eyes for sticking around.

Would I have married Jeanette if she hadn't gotten pregnant? Well, let's just say that we wouldn't have married so quickly. It might have happened, I don't really know for sure, but I cared a lot about her.

We were married in her parents' home in North Carolina. My boxing buddy from the boxing team, Art Redden, was best man. Both sets of parents attended, and it was a beautiful wedding.

Jeanette, Tommy, and I moved into an apartment on base and got along beautifully. I can't ever recall us having a fight or harsh words. She was quiet, but we talked to each other easily. A few months before she gave birth, I was transferred to Camp Pendleton near San Diego. While I got situated there, I asked Jeanette to move in with my parents in Jacksonville so that she could have my mother around to help her. I wanted Jeanette and my parents to connect, but things didn't go according to plan.

Quite frankly, Jeanette didn't take to them and they didn't take to her. She was so shy, so quiet, that they thought she was missing her tongue or something. She locked herself in her bedroom all day and wouldn't come out. If she said anything, they'd have to drag it out of her.

Looking back, sending her to Jacksonville was a mistake. I should have let her stay in North Carolina with her parents and have the baby in the comfort of her own surroundings. She was all of 19, pregnant, and had never left home before. Now she was in a different state, a different home, and without me or Tommy. She must have been frightened, but I didn't see it at the time.

On September 29, 1966, Jeanette gave birth to our son, Kenneth Howard Norton Jr., in Jacksonville. My mother called me with the news. "You have a son," she told me over the phone, "and he looks just like you." I could tell she was pleased.

I didn't have the opportunity to see my son until two months later when I finally had the chance to visit Jacksonville and bring Jeanette back to North Carolina so that her parents could see their new grandson.

When I first saw him, my heart just melted. I was so happy inside. I'm a big kid now, but I was a bigger kid then. When I saw Ken Jr. for the first time, I jumped up and down and hollered at the top of my lungs, "That's my boy! That's my boy!"

Ken Jr. was a big child; cute and cuddly. I developed a bond with him right away. I picked him up and held him high over my head.

"You and I will always be together, little man. Always. I'll never leave your side," I told him. And I meant every word.

During the trip to North Carolina, Jeanette told me that she wanted to stay at her parents' home for a while. She missed Tommy and her parents, but more than that, she just didn't want to leave North Carolina. The South has a mystique to it that makes people who were born there never want to leave. I admit, it did have a certain charm, but I wanted to see the world, not live in North Carolina the rest of my life.

"OK, but Kenny is going to California with me," I said in a tone that left no doubt.

"That's fine," she said, giving no hint that she had a problem with my demand. It was too easy, I thought. So off I went to Camp Pendleton with my son in tow, ready to make a new start, fully expecting Jeanette and Tommy to follow shortly behind me.

I was wrong.

She stayed in North Carolina for six long months.

San Diego has some of the most beautiful women in the world, and there I was in my early 20s, fresh from Jacksonville, Illinois, a country boy more or less. Every woman I spotted looked like a model. In those six months, I was very lonely and wanted companionship. I wanted my family. Jeanette was acting like child and wanted to stay with her parents. I wasn't the worst looking guy in the world, and so I embraced the single life again.

I never had a line *per se,* but I was always friendly and up front and the women responded to my honesty. I was not a womanizer or a user, but I began seeing a few ladies regularly, and it was hard to stop. Had Jeanette come out to California sooner, I think we could have lasted. Don't get me wrong, 90 percent of what went wrong with that marriage was my fault, and I'll take the full blame. I cheated on Jeanette, she didn't cheat on me. I just don't think a woman should ever leave a man alone for more than two weeks or she's asking for trouble.

In the six months that it was just Kenny and me, I grew more and more attached to him. As a parent, you're bound to develop a special bond with your child, but ours was a little deeper because I had changed his diapers, wiped his tush, prepared his food, and cleaned up after him. We were inseparable. There wasn't anything I wouldn't do for my son.

Because I was a single parent, I was Kenny's whole world. I was his mother, his father, his protector. He had a lot of his mother's traits, specifically her shyness, and he was very introspective and quiet. If some-one knocked on the front door, he would run and hide in the closet.

Jeanette and Tommy arrived in San Diego one day unannounced. She caught me talking to one of my girlfriends in a car, and my girlfriend swiftly made tracks. When Jeanette asked who she was, I didn't lie. The bright lights of California and the pretty ladies had put a distance be-tween us, and I no longer wanted to be married. There was no way I could go back to married life again. Any love between us had vanished in that six-month period, and we amicably agreed to go our separate ways. She agreed to take Tommy back to North Carolina and let me keep Kenny.

Why didn't Jeanette want Kenny, her own child? One reason was that she already had Tommy, and had a special relationship with him. A second reason was that she felt that no man would ever marry a woman with two kids, each one fathered by a different man. But the main reason, as far as I was concerned, was that she knew I would never give Kenny up. Never, never, never. I just wouldn't do it.

The bottom line was that she left without fighting for Kenny, and for years I told Kenny that I took him from his mother. I didn't want him to feel bad that Jeanette left with her other son. I let Kenny think that I was the bad guy because I didn't want him to hate his mother. I was always careful that I never said anything derogatory about his mother, but he now knows the truth. I wasn't going to give him up without a fight. Jeanette and I were married a little less than a year before she filed for divorce.

Growing up Kenny always wondered, "Where's my mother? Why did she leave?" Everyone else had a mother and he couldn't figure out where his was. I gave him a picture of Jeanette and he clung to it closely. Later on, the photo was a permanent fixture in his wallet. He always loved her.

My whole life changed now that it was just the two of us. I was forced to become more responsible. I was a lot different than my father, and in hindsight, I think that I might have made a mistake. You see, since it was just Kenny and me, I decided that I'd be his father and his friend. We grew up together as partners instead of as father and son, and because of that, I wasn't as strict with him. When the time came to give him a swat on the butt, he'd get mad at me and hold a grudge for a long time.

I wished to God I could have given Kenny the idyllic childhood that I had, but I couldn't afford to do the things I wanted for him. He missed out on a lot of things because I was too busy trying to make it on my meager salary in the Marines.

Kenny and I have had a few conversations about those days, and he remembers much more than I thought he would. He specifically remembers the days when all we had was to eat were hot dogs, mustard, and relish. Trust me, those were on good days.

What was even worse was that my days as a Marine were numbered. My four years were coming to an end, and I still didn't know what direction my life was going to take. That was especially scary because I had a son to support. I thought of going back to Jacksonville, but I dreaded it because of the lack of jobs.

They say that when God closes a door, he opens a window, and a window of opportunity presented itself on a silver platter my very last day as a Marine.

During the summer of 1967, I beat an opponent named Forrest Ward in the AAU Tournament. This tournament determined which boxer could advance to the Pan American Trials. Even though I beat Ward soundly, he had a group of backers with deep pockets who vetoed my going to the Pan American Trials. In their words, "Norton didn't have an international style of fighting." That's true, I didn't have an international style of fighting. I had a pro style.

Nevertheless, Norton was out and Ward was in. It was at those trials that I met a boxing referee named Art Rivkin. I liked him immensely, but forgot about him when the tournament was over. Luckily for me, Art did not forget about me. He put it in the back of his mind to approach me when I got discharged from the Marines.

Art also happened to work for a Coca-Cola distributorship and eventually became a minority owner of the San Diego Padres.

A week before I was discharged, I was out in a jeep in a large field of grass driving fast, doing wheelies, spinning the car around, and just plain having a ball. Somehow I managed to flip the jeep, along with $30,000 worth of radio equipment. Because of the damage to the equipment, the Marines wanted to punish me and keep me in the corps until I paid for the equipment. Some way, by the grace of God, I was given an honorable discharge in September 1967 and got out of the Marines without having to pay for the equipment I wrecked. Whew!

The day I was discharged, I finally had to face the music: I was going back to Jacksonville to become a police officer. The captain of police in Jacksonville had had his eye on me for years, and I was going to become the first black police officer in the city of Jacksonville. In that town, everyone was put in a slot and stayed there. I was doomed to stay there forever, and now that I had a taste of life outside of Jacksonville, it especially galled me to have to go back. Then something miraculous happened.

Art and his friend, Bob Biron, summoned me to a large, impressive meeting room at the Coca-Cola distributorship where Art worked. The two men had an interesting business proposition: The two of them, along with Lloyd Schunemann and A.B. Polansky, wanted me to turn pro in boxing and they would pay me $100 a week plus a share of any purses if I agreed. Would I be interested?

It took me all of 30 seconds to consider their proposition. I said yes.

They regaled me with stories of how rich I was going to be, the opportunities I was going to have, and that I would be able to meet Forrest Ward again as a pro to avenge my loss for not going to the Pan American Trials. Forrest Ward never did make the cut as a professional boxer and I never got the chance to box him again. But the picture Art painted for me was so vivid, I could just visualize all the money I'd be raking in.

What I made was zilch. What my son and I lived on was that $100 a week. For one hell of a long time.

In their defense, Art and Bob turned out to be two of the most influential and honorable men I ever met, but more important, they were savvy businessmen who could protect my financial interests if I hit it big.

Because Art was a high-level executive at a Coke distributorship, I felt that if my professional boxing career was a bust, I could always work my way up in the ranks at Coke. By turning pro, it opened up a few doors that were once closed. I didn't turn pro because I liked boxing; getting my face smashed in wasn't my first choice in how to earn a living. Plain and simple, I boxed to survive. I wasn't trained to do anything else other than Morse code, and there was no use for that in civilian life.

My time in the Marine Corps was nothing but a positive experience for me. I grew up, I learned responsibility, I learned how to lead, I learned how to follow, I learned how to be a team player, and I learned how to depend on myself. The Marines instilled in me a pride and confidence that has carried me through the tough times in life.

Most important, the Marines taught me who I was and made me proud to be black. For that, I am eternally grateful.

I didn't know it yet, but the journey to becoming the heavyweight champion of the world was now set in motion. That journey took me 10 years, and it didn't come without its share of blood, sweat, hard work, pain, heartache, and even a few tears to boot.

I was 24, a single father to a baby boy, newly divorced, and barely made enough money to feed my son and myself. My prospects were dim at best, but boxing provided an opportunity for a better way of life.

To the victor belong the spoils, and man, did I want to get spoiled!

Chapter Five

Becoming a Pro

San Diego wasn't exactly the mecca of boxing in the late '60s, and 30 years later it's no different. Although my backers lived in San Diego and I fought most of my early professional fights in the beautiful and enchanting city by the ocean, Ken Jr. and I moved to Los Angeles so I could train at the Hoover Street Gym. We lived in a three-room apartment off Manchester near Watts, where the infamous race riots took place in 1965. I went from base housing with an oceanside view in San Diego to Watts, where I could get a view of a man walking down the street with a television set on his shoulder that clearly wasn't his. Talk about your culture shock!

The Hoover Street Gym is a little hole in the wall on 78th and Hoover in south central Los Angeles. Henry Davidson of the Hoover Street Gym trained me for my first pro fight.

I soon found out that there was a big difference in training methods between the Marines and the pros. In the Marines, we trained and boxed for a three-round competition. The pros were six rounds, then graduated to 10 rounds, and then to 15 rounds for championship fights. In the '90s, most fighters start out with four-round fights, working their way up to bouts of six, eight, and 10 rounds. Championship fights have been reduced to 12 rounds, as opposed to the marathon 15-round fights I had to endure. As a pro, you're trained to fight longer, but not necessarily to go the distance. Most pro fighters look for the knockout.

Professional boxing stripped to its barest form is just entertainment. In the pro ranks, the premium form of entertainment is the knockout punch. I was always looking for the knockout because then I wouldn't have to proceed with the fight. Besides, boxing promoters and fans paid good money to watch the heavy hitters.

The pros emphasized a lot more sparring, mitt training, precision and combination punching than the Marines. I also did more abdominal work to prepare my body to go more rounds and handle the punishment more common in the pros. In the Marine Corps, I practiced the same amount of time on everything but never specialized in one area. Overall, my training as a Marine was helpful but nowhere near the intense physical workout that the professional boxing world demanded. The equation was simple: If I wanted to get anywhere a pro fighter, I had to work three times harder than when I was a Marine, and my laid-back nature dictated that I didn't like to work that hard. With a son to take care of, I reminded myself that every time I slacked off in training, I was cheating my son out of a better living. That motivated me on days that were especially hard.

Much to my dismay, I discovered that $100 a week wasn't going to cut it financially. I had a son to feed, a car to maintain, and rent due every month. I had no other choice than to get a day job and go to the gym after work. A cousin of mine, Charles McPike, managed to get me a job at the Ford Motor Co.

At Ford I worked on the assembly line and aligned the front end of the frames where the seats are placed. It was grueling work. In the mornings I would get up 5 a.m., run five miles, shower, shave, and have breakfast. At six I would then take Ken Jr. to his babysitters, a lovely couple named the Talberts. Then I'd drive to work by seven and work until 3 p.m. Right after work I'd head to the gym, work out hard until seven. By the time I'd pick up Ken Jr. at the Talberts, I'd head home dead tired. Then it would start all over again in the morning.

My debut as a professional boxer occurred on November 14, 1967, at the old downtown coliseum in San Diego when I fought Grady Brazell. Brazell was a very good boxer who moved well and had a pretty good jab, but he lacked power. I was hungrier for the win, and I overpowered him. I knocked him out in the third round, and my hand was raised in victory by the referee. Some record books list this as a ninth-round knockout victory, but my management team would have never thrown me in a 10-rounder for my debut.

My second fight also took place in San Diego, this time against Sam Wyatt on January 16, 1968. Wyatt hailed from Los Angeles and had already fought in 12 bouts, his record a not-so-impressive four wins and six defeats with two draws. He had been knocked out by Harold Dutra a month before we squared off. I would knock Dutra out in my next fight.

Wyatt was an elusive fighter, and I just couldn't knock him out. The fight was scheduled for six rounds, going the distance. My lack of experience showed in this match because I hadn't mastered my technique yet, and I was still learning how to cut off the ring to trap an opponent. Then again, the people I was matched with weren't cakewalks, either. I could easily have lost to a few of my early opponents had I taken them too lightly.

I met Harold Dutra on February 6, 1968, for my third professional fight. I was showing more promise, and I knocked him out in the third round. Dutra was another worthy opponent, and his strategy for the fight was to come straight at me. It wasn't a good fight plan for him, however; he was an easy target because he had no defense. If I could hit my opponent enough times, he was going to go down.

After my third fight, my trainer, Henry Davis, left for Germany to train another fighter. Eddie Futch would take his place as my trainer.

Eddie is without a doubt the greatest living trainer alive and probably the best of all time. He is a master psychologist and strategist who knows how to get the most out of his fighters. Starting in 1958 with welterweight Don Jordan, he has trained 22 world champions and numerous contenders. At one time or another, Eddie has worked with such champions as Joe Frazier, Larry Holmes, Michael Spinks, Alexis Arguello, and Riddick Bowe. It was Eddie, along with Yank Durham, who masterminded the strategy that Frazier used in his historic victory over Muhammad Ali on March 8, 1971, at Madison Square Garden in New York City. Eddie also would map out the game plan that led to Ali's second victory over me in March 1973.

Eddie was born August 9, 1911, in Mississippi to a sharecropper father, Valley Futch. Valley moved to Detroit to work in an automobile factory when Eddie was five. Eddie was a gifted athlete in track and eventually became an outstanding basketball player. He played forward for a Detroit all-star team that played a Chicago team called the Savoy Big Five, which was led by one of history's greatest ball handlers, the amazing Marques Haynes. The following season, the Savoy Big Five would change its name and become the first incarnation of the barnstorming Harlem Globetrotters.

Eddie's amateur boxing career started in the early 1930s at the Brewster Recreation Center in Detroit. There he would become the Detroit Golden Gloves lightweight champion in 1933. He also became a stable mate of the future heavyweight champion of the world, the legendary Brown Bomber, Joe Louis.

When Eddie met Louis, he was a light-heavyweight with only one amateur bout under his belt, that lone fight being a loss. There were several talented amateurs at Brewster's, and Joe used to struggle to win the club championship. Louis and Eddie used to spar together quite often, even though Louis outweighed Eddie by 40 pounds. Louis used to reason that if he could hit Eddie in the ring, he could hit anyone, and therefore he would be at his sharpest and ready for competition. Louis would eventually go on to become the national amateur light-heavyweight champion and then on to national fame, reigning an incredible 11 years as world heavyweight champion. Louis remained friends with Eddie until his death in April 1981.

By 1936, Eddie was set to turn professional after a successful amateur career of 37 victories and three defeats. He was married and had three children to boot. While taking his physical to enter the paid ranks, it was discovered that he had a heart murmur. Thus ended his dreams of becoming a professional fighter. He would soon turn to training boxers and distinguish himself among boxing's elite.

By 1951, Eddie had moved to California. Several fighters he had previously trained in Philadelphia moved to California to continue their training with him. The last of those transplanted fighters was "Smokin'" Joe Frazier.

By the time Futch started training Frazier in 1966, he also was training several other fighters who weren't exactly world class, and he had to take on odd jobs to pay the bills. He worked as a hotel waiter, a road laborer, a welder, a sheet-metal worker in an aircraft plant, and a distribution clerk for the Los Angeles Post Office. It wasn't until Joe Frazier's eighth professional fight that Eddie earned a decent-enough salary as a trainer and quit his other jobs so that he could devote himself full time to training boxers. He was still working at the post office when I first met him in 1968.

As a trainer, Eddie was a boxing tactician who possessed a brilliant mind. He knew every little detail about how a guy fought, his style, if he was trained properly before a fight. He covered all of the bases. In the gym, Eddie was a no-nonsense guy, and if he didn't feel you were serious enough about your career, he had no problem moving to the next guy who was. He was all business.

"It's just like the post office," Eddie once told an interviewer regarding his theory on boxing. "I have my prescribed system: The use of my fighter's strengths and the exploitation of his opponent's weaknesses. Then you put the pieces together."

I was a diamond in the rough when I met Eddie. My only real strength was raw power, but Eddie took me in and honed me, taught me how to box, taught me the fundamentals all over again, and then he fine-tuned me into the boxer he felt I could be.

Eddie Futch (Ken's trainer): *Ken came to the Hoover Street Gym in Los Angeles when he had three professional fights under his belt. He looked over several of the trainers, their services, their fees, and then he chose me. At the time, I had two other heavyweights under me. One was Joe Frazier and the other was Walter Moore, a former national AAU heavyweight champion. I was working at the post office at the time and didn't have much time to train other fighters, but Norton insisted on convincing his managers to have me take him over because he was so impressed with the way I worked.*

I had known his former trainer, Henry Davis, since he was a little boy. Henry trained fighters at the same gym. I made an arrangement for Henry to work with Ken, and I would assist whenever I could. Davis had to go to Germany, and when he came back, Norton went to San Diego to see his managers, and they fired Henry under pressure. Ken was very good to work with and he followed directions well. I saw definite potential in him and that's why I agreed to train him.

I learned more in my two years with Eddie than I did in all of my other years of boxing combined. He was the master teacher, and I was the willing pupil. I would have jumped through hoops of fire for Eddie; that's how much I respected the man.

In my eyes, he was the dean of trainers. The first thing Eddie taught me was how to cut off the ring to reach an opponent. It was essential to learn this technique to go with my natural aggressive style. I also had a few natural habits that I brought to the ring with me, and instead of trying to break me of those habits, Eddie incorporated them into my fight plan. For instance, I fought sideways and dragged my right leg behind me. Eddie also showed me how to fight each opponent. He made my sparring partners fight my opponent's style so that when I entered the ring I was prepared.

In my first fight under Eddie, I took on Wayne Kindred in San Diego. Kindred was a good, strong puncher—a real banger—and the best boxer I had fought to that point. The only weak point he had was that he fought with his chin out, and when I had the opportunity, I landed an overhand right and scored a sixth-round TKO. The victory was savored for a long five months, until I fought again.

At this point in my career, I was beginning to make a name for myself, and my reputation was getting a little ahead of me. People began to hear about Ken Norton, the Marine from San Diego. In boxing, you don't necessarily fight the best possible opponent. Even though this is a gladiator sport, some opponents, the smart ones, will avoid you at all costs if they know you're any good. A loss on a boxer's record is a serious blight and could severely damage his marketability. Unfortunately, that meant I was a fighter to be avoided at all costs until serious money was on the table. In essence, that meant fights were harder for me to come by. I won my next 11 fights, and my record was a sterling 16-0 when I entered the ring July 2, 1970, to fight Jose Luis Garcia.

Garcia fought most of his professional fights in his native Venezuela. He was tall, strong, slender, and a good boxer who packed a punch. Going into our first fight, he had boasted an impressive professional record of 11-2-1. One of his two losses had come against fellow Venezuelan Vincente Rondon via a 12-round decision loss in Caracas, Venezuela, in Garcia's 10th pro fight. At the time, Rondon was a veteran of 23 pro fights. Rondon would eventually go on to win the World Boxing Association light-heavyweight title. Garcia was certainly the next big test for me and the most experienced boxer I had fought since Kindred. Because he was from a foreign country, there wasn't any film available on him for me to study. That was crucial because I prided myself as a student of the sport.

I had been developing quite an ego and was getting way too cocky. Eddie had warned me several times about my attitude and my lack of intensity in working out, and I guess I needed someone to knock me on my behind to prove it.

The difference between confidence and overconfidence is not training properly and entering the ring against your opponent without any fear. Fear is a good thing if properly controlled, and for me, if I didn't enter the fight without any butterflies in my stomach, then I was overconfident. When I ducked under the ropes to enter the ring for that particular fight, I didn't have any butterflies.

Jose Luis Garcia knocked me out in the eighth round, and there was a picture in the paper the next day of me sprawled out on the canvas with my eyes glazed over, my opponent's hand raised in victory. The first time I went back to the gym, I opened my locker and found that picture, which Eddie had taped to the inside of my locker. When I looked around, there was Eddie laughing mischievously. He had a sense of humor when he chose to.

"Damn Norton, that photographer done got your best side in that picture. You gonna listen to me now?" Eddie laughed.

I don't know what hurt more, the actual knockout or Eddie's verbal taunts, but he taught me a valuable lesson: Never take any opponent for granted. In boxing, that could get you killed.

"All right, Eddie," I conceded, "you were right. I got a little over-confident and I'm sorry I didn't listen to you. I want to fight Garcia again."

"Hold your horses, Ken. We gotta start from the beginning. Don't worry, though, you'll get your chance, Sugar Britches," he laughed. That old man could really take the piss out of me, but he was right. I had to start from scratch.

My backers felt that I was too cocky and took Garcia for granted. I wasn't prepared mentally or physically, and they urged me to see a hypnotist, Dr. Michael Dean.

Dean, whose real name is Sanford I. Berman, held a doctorate in general semantics and effective communications at Northwestern University. Dean claimed that I wasn't listening to Eddie effectively, and that I didn't know the difference between self-confidence and overconfidence.

What Dr. Dean tried to instill in me was that the big difference between success and failure isn't all that big. It's only one-millionth of an inch. Can you imagine that?

Dr. Dean and I met once a week for a 45-minute session, usually on Fridays, and he would put me under hypnosis. He'd make sure I was relaxed before every fight, and a relaxed person is good at whatever he does. He made the point that all of the good executives are relaxed, and it is true in all walks of life.

For example, I told Dr. Dean that one of my problems was that my arms got so tired starting around the sixth round. He told me through autosuggestion that whenever my arms felt heavy or tired, I should step back from my opponent's range, roll my shoulders, relax and think, "I feel great," then come back fresh and continue to fight. It worked, and I used that technique in the first Ali fight.

Dr. Dean also prescribed some reading material and gave me a book that changed my life, Napoleon Hill's *Think and Grow Rich*, which basically embodies Dale Carnegie's formula of success. In his teachings, Hill states, "The only man who wins is the one who thinks he can." I must have read that book more than 100 times while in training, and I became a stronger person for it. Hill writes of everything in monetary terms, but it works outside of that as well. When I beat Ali in March 1973, I was not only the first black man ever to be honored with the Napoleon Hill Award for positive thinking, but also the first athlete to win, an achievement I'm very proud of.

The fight with Garcia wasn't my only setback: Money was also becoming a problem. I was still making the same amount per bout I had earned with my first fight, $200. Until my first Ali fight, my opponents always made more than I did, because my backers had to pay more to the other fighters to get them to fight me.

Bob Biron (in a 1975 interview): *At first I was content to just be one of the backers. Eddie Futch was doing a good job. In the beginning he handpicked the opponents, getting all the proven trial horses for Kenny to bang away on. But then, as his career progressed, it was apparent Ken needed my experience as a negotiator. At one point in Kenny's career, all the money was going to the opponents, to the James J. Woodys and the Jack O' Hallorans. We needed them, and it cost money to bring them from the East. To get opponents like that, all we could get from the promoter was a percentage of what was left over. And a lot of times that was nothing. A lot of times we'd have to dip into our own pockets and give Kenny $300 or $400 as a token purse.*

Plain and simple, the money I was making from fighting and the money I was earning from the Ford Motor Co. didn't make ends meet. In desperation, I even contemplated robbing a liquor store for some fast cash. The only thing that stopped me was my upbringing. I knew instinctively that it was the wrong thing to do and that if I ever got caught, I couldn't face them. If I got caught I don't think I would be able to forgive myself for the shame I would have brought to them.

There never seemed to be enough of anything: money, food, clothing. I'd leave Ken Jr. with the Talberts while I trained, and then I'd purposely stay late. I knew if I didn't come home, they'd feed him. The Talberts must have known what I was doing, but they never said a word. In fact, they treated Kenny like one of their own. When they bought their children clothes for Easter, they also bought clothes for Kenny. They were great people. A lot of people were awfully good to Kenny and me during those lean years.

In times of need I had always sought my father's advice, but this time I was ready to pack it in. This lifestyle was too hard and painful. All of my life I had managed to avoid going back to Jacksonville, but this time I was ready to pack it in and move back to become a police officer. I dialed the number to my parents' to inform them of my choice. My father answered the phone.

"Hi, Dad, it's Ken," I said, sounding dejected.

"Yes, son."

"Dad, do you think you can send me some money?" I asked, totally embarrassed because I had never before called him for money in my whole adult life. "Dad, I can't make it here. I want to come home."

His answer stunned me.

"No," he said. There were a few seconds of uncomfortable silence, then he spoke again, "Ken, if you quit now, the next hard thing that comes along you'll quit, too. No, you stick with it. You've got to finish something. Finish this."

Looking back, had my father sent me that money, I would be in Jacksonville today, most likely a retired policeman collecting a pension. My old man was smart for denying my request. He made me tough it out, and I'm glad he did, because good fortune was just around the corner.

From 1967 to 1970, Muhammad Ali was officially banned from boxing because of his stance against the Vietnam War. He was drafted and refused to serve. Ali claimed that he was protected by his freedom of religion, as he was now a minister in the Muslim faith.

Ali was visiting Los Angeles in January 1970 and looking for a good workout while in the City of Angels. Although Ali was still officially in pugilistic exile, he kept in shape, hoping that one day boxing might take him back. He knew that Eddie was living in L.A. and could show him some promising young guys to spar with, so he came to the Hoover Street Gym. Ali kept a pair of boxing gloves and his workout gear in the trunk of his car. His name always drew a big crowd, and the word got around that he was coming to the Hoover Street Gym. The place was usually occupied by the fighters and the people who worked there, but it was wall-to-wall fans when Ali walked through the doors.

Working out with me were two other heavyweights, Scrap Iron Johnson and Howard Smith, as well as welterweight Hedgemon Lewis. Ali boxed with each one of them, and then Eddie told him that he had a young heavyweight he was trying to break in—me. I'll let Eddie tell the story from here because his memory is better than mine.

Eddie Futch: *Ali didn't even know Ken's name. Ali looked at me and said, "How about working a round with your guy?" I said, "OK." I took Ken aside and told him, "Don't try to be a wise guy. Just be smart. Go out there and work along with him and try to learn something. If it gets rough in there, take care of yourself. But just try and work along with him." The first round went like that, but Ken was never a smooth-looking fighter. He didn't have a classic style. Ali had looked him over pretty good. I guess he decided that the kid couldn't fight much. So with this enthusiastic crowd there, Ali decided he's going to give 'em a show.*

Near the end of the round, Ali stepped back and announced to Ken and the crowd, "OK, boy, I'm through playing with you. I'm going to put something on you." Ali really starts punching, but Ken goes right with him. What a round that was, a wild round.

The thing was, Ali didn't think Ken could counter, but Ken had only been working along with him earlier. And when Ali started punching harder, Ken countered. Ken embarrassed him, and Ali didn't expect that. Ali didn't like that at all. The next day Ali walked into the gym screaming, "I want that Norton, where's that Norton?" But I had told Ken to stay in his street clothes.

Ali looked over and saw Norton standing around in his street clothes. "Ain't he going to work today?" Ali asked.

"No," I said.

He said, "Why not?"

I said, "Yesterday you came in here looking for a workout. Today you came in here looking for a fight. When this kid fights you, he's going to get paid. And paid well."

Ali left the gym in a huff. He had gotten a taste of Eddie's wisdom and didn't like it when someone got the better of him.

When the door slammed behind Ali, Eddie turned to me and said, "Now you can beat Ali!" and proceeded to tell me how I could beat The Greatest. Eddie had me believing that I could beat the world champion, but the time, the place, and the money had to be right. Ali actually called Eddie that night and made an offer of $25,000 to fight me, but Eddie turned him down.

"Why?" Ali demanded to know.

"He's not ready yet," Eddie said patiently.

"Eddie, I'm going to give him $25,000. That's probably more money than he ever saw in his life," and Ali was right. It was the most money I'd ever been offered up to that time, and I would have fought him for that amount, but Eddie was the master.

"Yeah, three times as much as he's ever seen. But that's not nearly as much as what he's gonna see when he fights you later." Eddie turned down the offer flat. It would be another two and a half years before Ali made a second offer.

I wasn't mad at Eddie for turning down all of that money. I had nothing but complete trust in his judgment. Sure, the $25,000 would have made my life easier, but Eddie was looking at the big picture. He told me like he told Ali, "You ain't ready yet, son, but when you are, watch out, world!"

At the very least, Ali now knew who I was, and it definitely wouldn't be the last time The Greatest would have difficulty with me in the squared circle.

Chapter Six

The Road to Ali

I had taken on The Greatest and gotten the better of him. Word got around about our little battle, and my stock rose dramatically. Eddie Futch told Yank Durham, Joe Frazier's manager and trainer, that I had embarrassed Muhammad Ali in the ring.

Good sparring partners are heavily in demand in boxing, and Eddie convinced Yank to give me a chance to be a sparring partner for Frazier, who was then the undisputed and undefeated heavyweight champion of the world. Frazier would get a good sparring partner for his upcoming fight with Jimmy Ellis, and I would be able to learn and improve on my technique from one of the hardest hitters of all time, "Smokin'" Joe Frazier. It was a win-win situation, and the money wasn't bad, either. Frazier paid me a handsome $500 a week to spar with him, but let me tell you, I earned every cent for some of the shots I took.

Going to Frazier's camp was my introduction to the big time. Joe was then, as he is now, a very fun-loving guy, but he trained in the gym very hard. Once the gloves were on, he didn't mess around. You made no mistakes with Joe or you lost your head. At the very least, he could break your ribs.

Frazier grew up with little education in South Carolina. He wanted a better life for himself and realized boxing was his ticket to prosperity, so he was willing to pay the price and trained hard to get to the top. When I sparred with him in 1970, he was in his prime. He had every intention of staying at the top, and he trained even harder than before.

Frazier beat me hard the first time I climbed into the ring with him. I made the unfortunate mistake of going out drinking the night before, and I almost got killed. He caught me with that lethal left hook, and I just went numb. The second time we sparred, there was a crowd on hand, and we didn't hold anything back. After three rounds with Frazier, boxing Godzilla for 10 rounds was nothing!

Joe Frazier (former heavyweight champion): *Ken was a different fighter for me. I could tell he had the potential right away to eventually become the heavyweight champion of the world. He was a Marine and a tough son of a bitch. He had a different style, and you had to mix it up with him to get close and throw a good punch. He warned me off pretty good and gave me a lot of problems in the gym. I tried to take him out, but he had a laid-back style; his right hand stayed up, but his left hand stayed down. And he was bouncing in and out, whereas I was always coming at him. He was a very good fighter and was not an easy guy to hit.*

This was the kind of guy Yank wanted me to beat. His style was so unique. He was more of a counterpuncher. We worked together and sparred, but that's as far as I wanted to go with him. In training, I only wanted one round with him. Eddie or Yank might have wanted two or three rounds, but I only wanted one round with him. There were days when I called in sick because I knew I had to spar with him that day. I didn't want to fight Ken; I wanted no part of him.

He wasn't sure if he could kick my ass, and I wasn't sure if I could kick his ass, so we just remained buddies and never fought each other. We figured that unless the money got to that breaking point, it was best to remain friends. It would have been a rough fight, and I don't really know if I would have won; but let's just say I probably have a little more use of my brain today because I didn't have to fight Ken Norton.

It was rumored that Frazier and I made a pact never to fight each other because we were such good friends. That simply was not true. The reality was that if we had been offered the right amount of money, we would have fought each other. However, after two years of sparring with each other, we knew each other's style so well and had formed a mutual respect for each other's abilities.

All in all, working with Joe was a fantastic experience. My defense got better, my boxing knowledge improved, and most important, my confidence shot up 100 percent. After going to Frazier's camp, everything else was a breeze. It was a boost that I couldn't have gotten anywhere else, and I will always be thankful to him for advancing my career.

Frazier's training camp boosted my confidence by helping me see that I could tangle with the big boys, but it was his first fight with Ali in Madison Square Garden on March 8, 1971, that made me want to stay in boxing.

Actually, I was supposed to be on the undercard for that landmark fight, but it was canceled at the last minute. That was fine by me. I got a great seat! The hype, the excitement and all of the hoopla sent chills up and down my spine, and I finally realized that this was what I had been searching for all of my life. A world heavyweight boxing championship fight is what I yearned for.

Ali must be credited for making that fight a historic turning point in sports. He turned the fight into a piece of work that P.T. Barnum would have been proud of. In addition to all of the media attention, he managed to land $2.5 million for both him and Joe Frazier, an astronomical amount of money for a boxing match in those days.

Ali can take sole credit for bringing boxing into the big leagues and big money. I would even go so far as to say that Ali brought not just boxing but the whole sports world into the 20th century, as far as salaries are concerned. Luckily for both Ali and Frazier, that fight lived up to all of its expectations and was worth every bit of that $2.5 million.

I knew in my heart that I could beat Ali, and I hung around to get a piece of the pie, although it got frustrating at times. I saw my friend Hedgemon Lewis, who also trained with Eddie, move steadily up the ladder to the big money in championship fights, and wondered why the same thing wasn't happening to me. Lewis fought in five championship bouts and held a world welterweight title recognized by the New York Athletic Commission. Eddie kept telling me to be patient. He pointed out that Archie Moore had to wait 16 years for a title shot, and even Sugar Ray Robinson had to wait seven. Eddie said I had to stay in shape, because the chance might come on short notice.

Ever since my fight with Jose Luis Garcia, I never again took anyone lightly, and because I learned so much sparring with Frazier, I now was pounding my opponents into the canvas. My record was 21-1 when I took on Henry Clark on November 21, 1972, in Stateline, Nevada, near Lake Tahoe. This fight was on the undercard of the Ali vs. Bob Foster fight in which Foster, the undisputed light-heavyweight champ, lost to Ali in the eighth round for the North American Boxing Federation title.

Clark was the California state heavyweight champion and certainly no pushover. He was a beautiful boxer with a great chin and was also a classy gentleman. Our fight went nine rounds before I knocked him out. As a by-product of our battle, both of his eyes swelled shut. After the fight, which was held outside of the casino, Clark stopped off at the craps table and spent his entire paycheck of $3,000 with his eyes swollen shut, still in his boxing gear. I guess you could say he spent that money with his eyes closed!

Foster and I became good friends. After my fight with Clark, Foster told me, "You can beat Ali." I never forgot his words of encouragement and they stayed in my head. When I beat Ali, Foster was the first person I called, and I reminded him of what he had told me and how it had given me such a mental boost.

Throughout the Ali-Foster fight, Ali kept looking over at me and tried to flash me intimidating looks and an occasional taunt.

"I want you next, Norton!"

I thought his taunts were out of desperation—as if he needed to build himself up—and I laughed loudly and proudly, which seemed to infuriate him even more. He didn't intimidate me one bit, and I was flattered by all of the attention he was giving me. It made me feel as if I were the new kid on the block, and he was waiting for me to come and get him. At the very least, he was letting me know I was now on his fighting level.

After the fight, Ali and I ran into each other in the casino. We didn't have what constituted a great friendship in the first place, and looking back, I guess I stole his thunder in front of the ladies—a big no-no in his book. Not only did Ali fancy himself as the greatest fighter in the world, he also fancied himself as the greatest lover in the world.

Bill Slayton (Ken's trainer): *That night in the casino, all of the women checked out Kenny and told him what a fantastic build he had. Muhammad started talking trash to him. Kenny wasn't saying much, but Ali hollered up a storm about how he could whip Kenny. Ali was a little jealous because Kenny was getting all of that attention from the women. Ali said, "Oh, so you women think that Norton has such a great body? A better build than me? I'll show him."*

Like clockwork, Eddie got the phone call from Ali, begging him to fight me, and this time Eddie didn't pass. He had a figure of $50,000 in his head and Ali matched it. The largest payday I had seen up to that time was $8,000. Bob Biron and Art Rivkin made the generous gesture of letting me keep the entire amount because they didn't need it.

I bought a tract home in a better section of Los Angeles with the money. Ken Jr. and I had a real place to call home, and finally, I quit the Ford plant to prepare for Ali. I laughingly told the press, "For $50,000 I'll fight the Russian Army." (Ali received a guaranteed $210,000 for his efforts.)

Come March 31, 1973, it was official: Ali and I were set to rumble in San Diego.

Before I took on The Greatest, and I say that with all due respect because Ali is the greatest boxer of all time, I had one more opponent in Charlie Reno, a tough club fighter. We fought in the San Diego Sports Arena on December 13, 1972, and once again I had my work cut out for me. Reno was a journeyman who had 14 fights to his credit, and his record was an unimpressive 7-6. He had previously been stopped by heavyweight contender Jerry Quarry in five rounds. Reno was a light puncher who had not recorded a single knockout going into our match. It was a fight, I'll give that to Reno, and it took me 10 rounds to dispose of him with a knockout.

Once that fight was out of the way, I had three months to concentrate on the Ali fight. I had slowly crept up the ranks in the heavyweight division, and I was ranked seventh nationally by the boxing governing bodies. Still, I was mostly unheard of by the national media and boxing press. The press had a field day with Ali's new opponent, and I was tagged a 5-to-1 underdog. That was fine by me, because I wanted to be the underdog. As a matter of fact, I thrived on it.

I was labeled a "ham-and-egg fighter" by several self-anointed boxing experts. The question that lingered in their minds was, "Who did Norton ever beat?" Even sportscaster extraordinaire Howard Cosell, who eventually became a good friend, got into the act by boldly proclaiming the upcoming fight "the worst mismatch in boxing history; a disgrace. Whomever put that boy in there with Muhammad Ali ought to have his license revoked." Cosell was the broadcaster for the fight, and he got to see firsthand how mismatched the fight was. I made him eat his words.

Angelo Dundee, Ali's trainer, also had a few choice words for me on viewing my 31-inch waist and bodybuilder's physique. "Ali will break him in half," Angelo coolly predicted. Ali had vowed to the press he was gonna "whup" me, even specifying that I would go down in round seven.

A few weeks before the fight was aired on "ABC's Wide World of Sports," Bob Arum, the fight promoter, phoned Bob Biron, expressing some concern.

"Hey, can your guy last more than two rounds?" Arum asked. "If not, the fight on ABC is going to make me look silly."

Bob Biron smiled ruefully and replied, "Mr. Arum, I think Ken's going to surprise a lot of people; and to answer your question, yes, he'll definitely last more than two rounds."

A lot was riding on this fight for Ali, as it was the first time in more than three years that one of his bouts was going to be on national television. His other fights had been shown exclusively on closed-circuit, and both Ali and ABC-TV had a lot to lose if the fight wasn't a success. Ali more so because he was in a no-win situation: If he won the fight, well, he was fighting an unknown ham-and-egg fighter who had never fought a contender. If he lost to this unknown on national television, even worse. I give Ali a lot of credit for taking the fight.

At the time, Ali had lost only once, having been decisioned by my friend and sparring partner, Joe Frazier, in their first bout. Frazier remained the undisputed world champion until George Foreman knocked him out in two brutal rounds in Kingston, Jamaica, on January 22, 1973. Foreman knocked Frazier down six times in two rounds. Foreman then became the champ, and frankly, Big George frightened the daylights out of Ali. Hell, Big George frightened everyone!

Ali had been hoping to win the title back from Frazier in a rematch; however, Foreman now entered the picture, and Ali was bravely making the quest to challenge George Foreman for the title. Ali was victorious in his next 10 fights after his loss to Frazier and won the vacant NABF title against Jimmy Ellis. It was at that point that Ali began calling himself "The People's Champion."

The NABF title is a lightly regarded regional title that garners a fighter some recognition, but mainly was created so that a match can be billed as a "title fight" for marketing purposes. Ali was looking at me as a stepping stone to the fight with Foreman. I made sure that Ali stubbed his big toe.

The fight with Ali was the opportunity of a lifetime, and I dedicated myself to training for three months. I stayed in a place called, ironically, the Massacre Canyon Inn, which is located in Gilman Hot Springs, California, about 100 miles south of Los Angeles in the San Jacinto Valley. The weather was hot and arid, 105 degrees in the shade. It was the perfect weather to train in for a fight. I requested no air conditioning in the gym, and all the doors had to be closed. I was very focused and determined.

I gave my body and soul to Eddie, whom I trusted completely because he had been in Frazier's corner when Frazier beat Ali. Eddie had a special fight plan developed for Ali's style, and he told me the first day of training exactly how we were going to execute the plan.

"The jab is Ali's best weapon," Eddie told me, "but it's also his flaw. When he throws it, he carries his right hand out a little way from his face, instead of right up against his cheek. When everyone else fights Ali, they try to slip his jab, or try to block it and counter, but Ali's so quick that by the time they do that, he's gone. Ken, you must always keep your right hand pressed to your face as he's jabbing at you—that's when he's open. Two jabs and he'll be back against the ropes. Now, when you get him there, don't go to the head with the left hook like all the others do; he'll only lean against the ropes and stretch back. He's got that quickness. You'll miss him, and you'll be off balance; that's when he'll flurry. Hit him in the body with both hands. This will make him try to protect the body, which will make him bring his head down toward you. Then go to the head with the hook." Sage words from a master.

While I trained for the biggest fight of my career, it's been said by Ali's entourage that he undertrained for that first fight with me. I'd like to take issue with that point.

First and foremost, I embarrassed Ali in the Hoover Street Gym nearly three years before our first match. Ali knew what I was capable of in the ring and I got his attention and respect. Second, he saw what I could do when we met up again when he fought Foster and I was an undercard for that fight. Third, I had Eddie in my corner, which Ali had to respect. If Eddie was behind the strategy for the fight, don't you think Ali would have had to stand and take notice of Ken Norton? Lastly, I was going to have the hometown advantage; we were fighting on my turf.

If Ali did undertrain for this fight, that was his fault. My personal belief is that his people made excuses for him when he lost, and it made a great reason to have a rematch.

Two other factors came into play that the Ali crowd always mention about our first fight.

Factor No. 1: He had sprained an ankle 11 days before we fought, when he took a wild swing while teeing off on the golf course and stepped on a golf ball. I think the word *sprain* might be an exaggeration. Most likely, he twisted the ankle, because he was quite agile in the ring with me those first few rounds. What the heck was Ali doing playing a round of golf 11 days before a nationally televised fight against a ranked contender? Why couldn't he have waited until after the fight to play golf?

Training camp should be like boot camp: Get up at 5 a.m., go for a run, eat a big breakfast, study films of your opponent, train and spar in the gym, abstain from sex, and lights out by 9 p.m. No if, ands, or buts.

Factor No. 2: The boxing media claimed Ali was no longer in his prime and was on the downside of his career. Let me remind all of the boxing historians that almost a year and a half later, after our first fight, Ali challenged and successfully defeated Foreman in October 1974 to reclaim the heavyweight title. In addition to that, Ali held on to that title until he retired in late 1978, four years after he defeated Big George. He wasn't called The Greatest for nothing!

I trained for the Ali fight with an intensity that, sadly, I never matched again in my professional career. I knew this was my one shot at greatness and I gave it my all. I took training camp very seriously; eating, breathing, and sleeping boxing. I became obsessed with the fight, training my body and feeding my mind with only positive thoughts. Come March 31, 1973, I would raise my hand in victory and stun the boxing world by defeating the greatest boxer who ever lived. I visualized that scene over and over again in my mind until I believed it was going to happen.

Most of Ali's fights were not just mere boxing matches, they were events of epic proportions—milestones in sports—representing much more than the sport of boxing. For example, Ali made his first fight with Frazier into a race issue. He claimed Frazier was the "white people's champion" and even went so far as to call him an Uncle Tom. When Ali fought Foreman in Zaire, Africa, he charmed the pants off that country and claimed that the people of Africa were his people. This is where Ali, in my opinion, was a marketing and promotional genius.

Our fight was labeled by the media (maybe at Ali's insistence) as the "Draft Dodger vs. The Former Marine." At that time in our country's history, Richard Nixon was president, a staunch Republican at that, and San Diego was a conservative naval town. Ali insisted we fight in San Diego, knowing that the city would instinctively rally behind its hometown hero who hadn't ducked out on his responsibility to his country, serving proudly in the Marines.

The media and the public bought it hook, line, and sinker, but I wasn't offended when Muhammad Ali declined to serve in the military; quite the contrary. I respected the fact that he spoke out against the Vietnam War because, after all, that was his right as a citizen of the United States. His religious convictions have always been genuine, and time has proven him right. I can't think of a man other than Billy Graham who is so devoted to his fellow man and to his religion. Ali never hid behind his religion to duck out of going to war. His dedication was truly inspiring, and I never doubted his convictions. Ali will go down in history as one of the world's greatest humanitarians and diplomats. I can personally attest that the accolade is well deserved and long overdue.

Ali could charm the birds from the trees, and he maintained a great relationship with the media because he was so quotable. He had to hype the fights because not many other boxers did, especially in the heavy-weight division. Ali had a ton of charisma and the gift of gab. I always treated the media with respect, and they returned the same respect to me, but that didn't mean I wanted to befriend them. There was one exception: a writer by the name of Buford Green.

Buford was the sports editor for the *Jacksonville Journal Courier* when I first met him in 1967. My high school coach, Al Rosenberger, brought me to the office where Buford was working. I was just beginning my boxing career and needed all the press I could get. Buford and I hit it off immediately, and he covered my career from its inception to my retire-ment. I made sure that Buford received a free ticket to every one of my fights—I wanted to ensure that my parents could read about me in the local paper.

Buford Green (journalist): *I knew of Ken Norton's feats when I was in high school. I was a year ahead of Ken, but our paths never crossed until Al Rosenberger brought him into my office. We hit it off right away, and I kept tabs on Ken through Al and Ken's parents. Our paper ran a news item on him for every one of his fights.*

For the first Ali fight, I was invited by Ken and Bob Biron to hang out, watch the fight in person, and write a piece for the paper. That was the first bout I had ever seen in my life. I was given a ringside ticket, and it was quite an eye opener. Bob Biron welcomed me with open arms and took care of all of the accommoda-tions, and I even ate at the training table with Ken.

I got to a chance to talk to Ken the night before the fight, and he began opening up to me. I could definitely sense that his future was tomorrow afternoon. This was his chance to shine, and I remember him saying something to the effect of, "I know I'm going to get hit tomorrow. I don't like it, but I've got to do it." He also ex-pressed confidence that he could win the fight when virtually no one else did, with the exception of the people in his camp, and, by God, he did it!

I liked having my parents with me when I fought. My father was already a boxing fan, and he was delighted to watch my fights. It was a different story with my mother. Her nervous system couldn't take the tension, and it became a ritual for her to stay in the hotel room at the time of the match. She would wait by the phone for confirmation not that I had won or lost, but that I had come out alive. It was her biggest nightmare that there would be one phone call that might say otherwise. When I fought Gerry Cooney in 1981, my mother's nightmare almost became a reality. I got caught up in the ropes early in the first round, and I couldn't fall to the canvas. Cooney kept punching away because he didn't get any signal from the referee to quit. Finally, when the referee did step in, the fight doctor proclaimed me four seconds away from death.

While I was getting my hands taped for my initial bout with Ali, my father came over to me and shared a few words of wisdom. Even though I radiated an inner calm and confidence, he wanted me to know a few things.

"Son, no matter how things go out there tonight, your mother and I want you to know how proud we are of you," my father said. Whether you win or lose, we'll always be very proud of what you've accomplished."

He then put his arms around me and gave me a hug. My father was not a demonstrative man, but something must have come over him that night. Having him there that night was an extra boost for me. My father then stepped aside and let Eddie take over.

Eddie was all business. "Now you know what you have to do out there, right?"

"Yes," I said.

"All right, then, let's go over the fight plan."

"Ali's main offensive weapon is the jab," I recited. "When he jabs with his left, he carries his right hand out to the side. When he starts to throw the jab, I keep the right hand high, his jab will pop into the middle of my right glove and as I step forward, my left jab will hit him right down the pipe in the middle of his face."

"And how are you going to know his punch is coming?" asked Eddie.

"By looking at his pecs. If they start to move, that'll tip me off that the jab is coming."

"Good, Kenny. It'll take you three moves to get Ali on the ropes. Once you get him there, don't do like all the other guys do. Don't throw your hook to the head. He'll pull back against the ropes and when you're off balance, he'll pepper you with counterpunches. When he's on the ropes, instead of going to the head with the left hook, start banging his body with both hands. I don't care whether you land or not. Make him protect his body by bringing his elbows and head down. That will give you a clear shot to his head. Kenny, if you execute this plan exactly as I tell you, you will win this fight. Ali ain't gonna know what hit him. If you don't follow this plan to the letter, you will lose, and you've come too far to lose."

With that, Eddie left me alone. There was little noise in the locker room: the sound of tape being stretched and snipped, the faint noise of the crowd filling out the arena. Bob Biron and Dr. Michael Dean both wished me well.

The night before the fight, Dr. Dean had told the press that hypnosis would be accepted as a boon to humanity 100 years from now, and that if I beat Ali, it would be a tremendous boost.

"Show business is a means to an end, to gain attention for something very serious," said Dr. Dean. Much to my dismay, Dr. Dean was looked upon by the boxing media as a weirdo in a three-ring circus. To the contrary, he was a generous man concerned with helping people realize their full potential in business, education, and athletics. The concept of hypnotism was new to boxing, and boxing was a very traditional sport with a rigid mind-set. Dr. Dean was correct in his prediction that it would take 100 years for hypnotism to be accepted. Nearly 25 years later, Dr. Dean's work with me is still looked upon as an experiment.

It was a tradition for me to have a few moments of solitude in the dark to relax and meditate. These precious minutes of quiet time were invaluable to me. Before Eddie closed the taping room door so that I could be alone in my thoughts, Dr. Dean reminded me to meditate on the last stanza of my favorite poem from Napoleon Hill's *Think and Grow Rich*. These words were the final inspiration in my victory over Ali:

> *Life's battles don't always go*
> *To the stronger or faster man*
> *But sooner or later the man who wins*
> *Is the man who thinks he can.*

Chapter Seven

Beating the Greatest

Muhammad Ali entered the ring in the San Diego Sports Arena that afternoon like a king taking to his throne. His entourage numbered between 30 and 40 people, and they guarded Ali like a tigress protecting her cubs. As they made their way to the ring, I stood against the ropes, witnessing this spectacle in amazement. I had never seen such a group in my life. My people consisted of a trainer, a manager, and a few sparring partners. We were definitely a contrast in lifestyles.

Buford Green: *I had my doubts about Ali's group. It wasn't the kind of people I saw in Ken's camp, but you have to remember, I viewed this with prejudiced eyes. I saw a lot of good people around Ken, whereas with Ali there were a lot of hot dogs and ballyhoo, your typical big-time entourage with a lot of hangers-on, people who raised my suspicions. I'll say this about Ali: I've always liked him. He was a great showman and a pretty good guy to talk to if you were away from all of the hype.*

Ali sported a beautiful white robe given to him by Elvis Presley that cost somewhere in the neighborhood of $3,000. The robe contained many jewels, and inscribed on the back in blue lettering was, "People's Choice." It has been said by many of Presley's associates that he was a great admirer of Ali's; specifically of his sense of flair, style, and his ability to promote himself.

When it came time for the referee to instruct us in the ring, Ali and I finally faced each other. Ali stared at me and bit his bottom lip with his upper teeth, the pose that he is so famous for. I kept my head down and stared at the canvas below me, ignoring whatever he might be doing to take my mind off my fight plan.

I knew that Ali got to other boxers by his behavior in the ring: talking trash, making funny faces, finding a way to get his opponent mentally off balance—anything to get that little edge. I must admit, Ali was a master at it. Joe Frazier definitely let Ali's antics frustrate him, and he took a lot of things personally. Joe was in the locker room with me before the fight and told me, "Don't listen to him. He'll play games with you, but you just take care of business. OK?"

I never let any of that stuff bother me because it was all mental. I admired him tremendously growing up, so it was hard for me to hate him. Later, when I got to know Ali on a personal level, I admired him even more.

When the referee finished instructing us and asked us to touch gloves, Ali smiled at me and said, "You're gonna get a lesson in boxing today, Mr. Norton."

Under the North American Boxing Federation rules, it was agreed that we would fight with 10-ounce gloves, not the usual 8-ounce gloves used in championship fights. That was good for Ali because he would have felt my punches even more had we used lighter gloves.

I was ranked No.7 in the world, I weighed in at a svelte 210 pounds, and had a record of 30-1, with 24 knockouts to my credit. Ali looked a bit overweight and out of shape at 221 pounds, a good 10 pounds over his best fighting weight.

Nevertheless, he held an impressive record of 41-1 and had never been knocked out by an opponent. Joe Frazier had knocked him down, but couldn't finish him. Ali's will to win was the most impressive trait about him as a boxer. Before the fight began, I was listed as a 5-1 underdog by oddsmakers. I would prove the experts wrong.

I waited silently in my corner for the bell to ring. For five years I had been eeking out a living barely above the poverty level, I was raising a son by myself, held down two jobs, and trained every day at the gym under the watchful eye of Eddie Futch. My life had boiled down to this very moment, down to this very ring of the bell. It was time.

At the bell, Ali came out moving, and I quickly began circling and pursuing him, cutting off the ring. We exchanged a few meaningless jabs and were feeling each other out in the ring. The experts had labeled me unorthodox because of my jerky rhythm and the way I carried my right hand against the left side of my face while dragging my back leg. I've always thought my style was a sound tactical defensive strategy. It totally baffled Ali; he had never seen anything quite like it. Near the end of the first round, I landed the first meaningful combination of the fight.

In round two, I stuck to my fight plan and continued not to show Ali any respect. Ali's left jab, considered by many to be one of the finest in the history of the sport, was equalized by my stiff left jabs to his face. I was leading with my left jab and throwing it at Ali's head and body. At times I was able to double up on my shots to his face. I also was able to connect with a few lead rights. Near the end of the second round, I threw a left that connected to Ali's body. I followed it with a punishing overhand right to his jaw. Ali was against the ropes. Many people think that this is the punch that broke Muhammad Ali's jaw and catapulted me into the national spotlight. But more about the broken jaw later.

For round three, the champ came out of his corner much more tentatively; he also stopped talking trash. I think he was starting to take me serious. I kept the pressure on, but Ali kept dancing, staying out of harm's way. Ali kept on his bicycle, flicking out soft jabs while I kept cutting off the ring in hopes of catching him with a nice punch. I did finally catch him on the ropes, firing combinations and alternating punches to the head and body. At the end of the round, we exchanged punches, with me doing most of the damage. In a show to the crowd, Ali waved me on for some more.

A minute into round four I began connecting both upstairs to Ali's head and downstairs to his body. I landed more than a dozen overhand rights to his face, most of them hitting his chin. Ali kept dancing around the ring, but never punched or showed any kind of offense. He basically gave the round away.

I came out firing in the fifth round. Ali's jab was still ineffective, and I kept picking it off with my right hand. I'd counter by stepping in with my left and giving him good stiff jabs to the face. Eddie taught me a neat trick that enabled me to block Ali's shots effectively. If you ever watch a tape of the fight, you'll notice that I never look directly at Ali's face. I focused solely on his pectoral muscles. Whenever he was ready to throw a punch, I'd see his pecs tighten and move, which signaled to me if he was getting ready to throw a left or right hand. This tactic worked perfectly, because I knew exactly what to expect.

We had a few more exchanges in that round. Eddie's fight plan was working to at—he had me mixing up my punches and combinations with lead rights and lefts to the body. My constant head and upper-body movement also befuddled Ali, letting me slip and block many of his punches. While I was in the corner waiting for the bell for the sixth round,

I told Eddie, "Boss, I can beat this dude."

Ever the cautious taskmaster, Eddie answered, "You can do it if you do as you're told." Eddie didn't want me to get too cocky and reckless, but there was no denying my confidence was picking up with each round. I had been pursuing Ali the entire bout and the adopted hometown crowd was beginning to smell an upset.

I connected with a series of jabs at the start of round six, also catching Ali with a couple of rights, I noticed he had stopped talking to me. Imagine Muhammad Ali at a loss for words! In the last minute of the round, Ali began to come on strong with a flurry of shots. That display of energy took a lot out of him, and for the rest of the fight, he looked sluggish. His jabs and punches had no sting left to them.

I decided to turn the tables on Ali in the seventh round by talking a little trash to him. I chided him, "Whip it on. C'mon, gimmee a fight! Is that all you got? C'mon sucker, give me a fight!" While he stood there bewildered, I warned him, "Watch it, here it comes," and then I threw a sweeping left hook to his jaw followed by an overhand right. I finished with two hard left jabs that knocked him off balance. I completely dominated the round.

For round eight, Ali came out dancing and I kept chasing him, jabbing and scoring. By this time, Ali's corner gave him an ultimatum: Either start fighting back or we're going to stop this fight, because you're obviously tired and taking a beating. At the end of the round, Ali connected with a series of punches, but they had no effect. I was still standing there in his face when he finished this spurt of punches.

In round nine, it was more bad news for Ali. In the first 20 seconds of the round, I landed some solid body shots with a few roundhouses thrown in. When I got him in the corner of the ring, I went to town punching his face and body with everything I had. All he could do was cover up and pray. When we got close, he put a hand on my head to keep me away and so I grabbed him at the waist and lifted him in the air, showing him that I still had a reservoir of energy to burn. I was hoping to intimidate him a little. Round nine was all mine.

In the first seconds of round 10, I landed a couple of thunderous rights that drew a standing ovation from the crowd. Sensing the crowd was on my side, Ali decided to go toe-to-toe with me. We exchanged a fair share of punches, but I was clearly in command.

At the end of the 10th, Ali was slumped over in his corner, panting, "Give me some water. Give me some water." He was taking huge gulps of oxygen while I sat upright on my corner stool, breathing methodically, glaring at him. I gained an inner strength by watching him gasp for air. Ali was exhausted, but I admired his will to continue the fight.

Before the 11th round, Eddie warned me to keep the pressure on but not to get careless. It seemed evident by now that Ali needed a knock-out to win the fight. At the bell, Ali sensed that he was behind and picked up the tempo by throwing multiple combinations in hopes of catching me and ending the fight. Ali was scoring well, but I eventually pinned him to the ropes and landed some ferocious shots, including the punch that I think broke his jaw. Ali managed to work his way back to the center of the ring, launching a volley of combinations at me. To his credit, he ended the round strong, moving and jabbing, occasionally planting his feet to fire off a combination.

Why do I think that this was the round in which I broke Ali's jaw and not the second? For the plain and simple reason that if I had broken his jaw in the second round, he would not have been able to sustain the constant shots to his chin that I put on him. Many doctors have told me that when the jaw is fractured, your mind takes over and you pass out from the pain.

In addition, Ali fought a lot more tentatively in the last round of the fight. He didn't cover up in rounds three through 11; he fought very aggressively. He didn't in the 12th round.

Not to put Ali down, but I think the round-two broken jaw rumor was started by people in Ali's camp. Angelo Dundee will swear until he goes to the grave that I broke his jaw in the first round. I love Angelo and think he's one of the classier guys in this sport, but I think he's wrong in his assessment of when the jaw was broken, but I'll let him speak his piece for the record.

Angelo Dundee (Ali's trainer): *I knew Muhammad was in trouble in between the first and second rounds, and I considered stopping the fight. I told him that I thought his jaw was broken and that maybe we should stop the fight. He adamantly said, "No! You stop this fight, and I am gonna knock you out!" Once we knew the jaw was broken we kept a cool head; nobody blew their cork. Howard Cosell was seated near us announcing the fight at ringside and he kept asking me what was wrong with Muhammad. He knew something was up. I told him it was nothing serious, but that Muhammad's gum was bleeding and that was all.*

Even Dr. Ferdie Pacheco, Ali's personal ringside physician, stated in his book, "The jaw was broken in the second round. Ali was missing a tooth at the point of fracture, and that, plus the pressure from Norton's punch, broke his jaw. He could move the bone with his tongue and I felt the separation with my fingertips at the end of the second round."

It's interesting to note that during the fight, Ferdie Pacheco kept insisting to the television crew that Ali was fine. He yelled over to Howard Cosell in the 12th round that Ali had bleeding gums and a loose tooth. If Pacheco really believed that Ali's jaw was broken in the second round, then why did he let his fighter continue to get his jaw bashed for 10 more rounds?

I think stories get embellished and legends are born as time goes on and that this particular story was embellished to show that Ali was tough as nails. There's no doubt about it: Muhammad Ali was a very tough fighter who took a good deal of punishment throughout the years. However, X rays showed that when I broke his jaw, it was a clean break with a quarter-inch separation. How could a man endure 10 rounds of constant punishment, including direct hits to the chin, and not pass out from the excruciating pain? The trouble with beating living legends is that nobody believes you did it even after it happened.

Eddie Futch: *Nobody seems to know for sure just when Ken broke Ali's jaw in that fight. But with all the shots Ali took, if his jaw had been broken that early, it would have been shattered by the time Ken got the 12-round decision. In my opinion, Ali's jaw was broken in the 11th round with one very good right hand that Ken threw when he caught Ali on the ropes. I've always thought that was the punch. In watching the videotape, Ali's expression every time he got hit on the jaw was pretty normal until he got hit in the 11th round.*

That fight will go down in history as Ali going the distance in a valiant fight with a broken jaw, but I don't buy it. I'll always believe it happened in the 11th round. Angelo Dundee is a very smart man. He made it appear that Ali had stayed in there like a warrior in the second round. No way. He got hit with so many right hands on that jaw that if it had been in the second round, the jaw would have been in splinters. The jaw was broken in the 11th round when Ali got hit by a beautiful shot with the right. After watching replays over and over again, I still say that's when the jaw went.

The judges had the fight scored even going into the 12th round, although in my mind I was way ahead. At the bell we both raised our left gloves and touched them, a gesture of goodwill. Ali came out moving, jabbing, and trying in vain to finish the fight. I landed the first strong lead right of the round while Ali kept moving away from me, avoiding any kind of punishment. He even held the back of my head with his glove, a move that was illegal but which bought him some precious rest time. I was relentless in my pursuit, however.

With about a minute to go, I backed Ali into the ropes and tossed a series of powerful left hooks to his head and body. Ali was reeling and hanging on for dear life. In the last 30 seconds, Ali was vainly trying to fight back, but he was spent. It was at this point that I swarmed all over him and landed a damaging overhand right that sent him staggering to the nearest corner. I chased him down and rained punches on him as the final seconds ticked away. I was going for the knockout and all 11,800 fans were on their feet. Ali was barely able to stay on his feet.

I felt I ended the fight with an exclamation point when I threw the last punch of the round. The final bell sounded, and I knew in my heart I had just defeated the greatest fighter in boxing in front of my sold-out hometown crowd. I couldn't have dreamed of a better ending.

I went back to my corner elated. Eddie smiled broadly, opening his arms wide for a congratulatory hug.

"You did me real proud out there, son. You just beat Muhammad Ali."

I cried tears of joy and was on a natural high, higher than any I'd ever felt before or since. The emotions and feelings from a victory of that magnitude are hard to put into words. My jaw muscles ached the next day from smiling so much—my smile could have lit up the Las Vegas Strip and served as backup power to the Hoover Dam! At that point, the judge's decisions weren't in, and I waited nervously for the results. In boxing you can never tell, now matter how much of a margin there is. I held my breath in anticipation as the ring announcer grabbed the microphone.

"May I have your attention, please. The judge's results are in. Referee Frank Rustich scored the fight 7-4-1 for Norton. Judge Fred Hayes scored it 6-5-1 for Ali, and Judge Hal Rickards scored it 7-4-1 for the winner by split decision, Ken Norton!"

As the announcer declared me the victor, 11,800 shrieking fans cheered enthusiastically for me. The referee raised my hand in victory, just as I had visualized for weeks, but the real thing was 100 times sweeter than anything in my imagination.

To his credit, Ali didn't leave the ring mad or act as if he had been wronged. He sat in his corner quietly, his gloves now off, leaning back against the ropes and catching his breath. I walked over to the man who was my hero as a kid and as an adult, and offered my hand to him. He stood up from his chair, took my hand and squeezed it warmly. I said to him looking directly into his eyes, "I hope this doesn't affect our friendship." We were never really friends before the fight—I had only seen him twice before—but those were the only words I could think of to say. I meant what I said, but I felt a little awkward saying it to him. He didn't respond because of his broken jaw, but I never gave his silence a second thought. I've always felt that Ali was valiant in defeat. It increased my respect for him even more.

It was at that point that Ali was whisked away by his people to Clairmont General Hospital, where he underwent 90 minutes of surgery to repair the broken jaw. The X rays confirmed the jaw was broken cleanly, a fourth of an inch wide.

The media descended into the ring. ABC's Howard Cosell got first dibs to interview me. Despite what has been said and written about Howard, he always was very good to me, and I respected the fact he apologized to me on the air for his comment that the fight was "the worst mismatch in the history of boxing."

Howard's first words were, "Kenny, you made me look silly."

"That's OK, Howard," I teased, "you always look silly."

Howard laughed, not taking offense. From that moment, I became lifelong friends with him and his lovely wife, Emmy. Howard always treated me with the utmost respect, and he instantly became one of my biggest boosters. When I think of Howard Cosell, the word "classy" comes to mind.

Ali's people were classy as well, and gracious in defeat. When pressed for a reason why Ali lost the fight to a relative unknown, trainer Angelo Dundee replied, "We've had our share of the good days, and you have to be able to take the bad with the good. This day belonged to Ken Norton and to the people of San Diego. It was a great win for both!"

The reality that I had defeated one of the all-time legends in sports took a few days to sink in. That didn't stop me from celebrating in high fashion. I pinched myself more than a few times to make sure I was not dreaming. While I was in the midst of my victory lap, Ali was recovering from defeat in the hospital, tending to his fractured jaw.

Dr. Gary Manchester wired Ali's jaw together and said of the break on the left side, "The bone which was broken had three or four jagged edges and they kept poking into his cheek and mouth. It was a very bad break."

The day after the fight, I visited with Ali at the hospital and we had a nice conversation. Seeing him bedridden, my heart went out to him. His jaw was wired shut, but that didn't stop him from talking. The first thing out of his wired mouth was, "I want to fight you again, Norton." I laughed because I had just broken the man's jaw, and he was crazy enough to tell me he wanted to fight me again. You had to admire his courage, the courage of a lion.

"You got it, champ," I told him with a smile on my face. We shook hands, and Ali's manner eased considerably. I like to believe that we became friends then and there in that hospital room.

"Pull up a seat," he told me, "Visit with me awhile." Ali then steered the conversation to the aftermath of the fight.

"You know, now that you beat me, and the world now knows who you are, there are going to be temptations for you. Beware of spending your money too fast, fast women, and hangers-on. People are going to come out of the woodwork to get at you, and you have to be able to decide who's your friend and who's out to get something from you."

His words of wisdom touched me deeply because he was concerned about the possible route my life might take. In public when we had fights to promote, he enjoyed teasing me, making comments about how he had created a media monster, but in reality, he truly cared for my well-being.

As I left, we shook hands again. He looked at me with a mischievous grin and said, "Now Norton, just because we had this nice talk and all, don't think I'm gonna just sit here and take it. I'm gonna have to teach you a lesson when we get back in the ring, and let me tell ya, it ain't gonna be pretty!" Even with a wired jaw, the man had me in stitches. I was holding my insides as I left the room, chuckling to myself the whole way home. Then it struck me: Only Muhammad Ali could lift someone's spirits while he was in the hospital!

I had entered an exclusive club with a membership of two: Frazier and I were the only human beings ever to beat Muhammad Ali in a professional boxing match. That number would grow to five by the end of Ali's career, but Frazier and I were the only fighters to beat Ali in his prime.

My first fight with Muhammad Ali would go down in history as one of the greatest upsets of all time, but I never had a doubt that I could beat him. My world changed completely overnight. I was 29, the new North American Boxing Federation heavyweight champion, and could now write my own ticket.

The years of hard work, dedication, and struggle had paid off, but mostly, I have Muhammad Ali to thank for giving me the opportunity to fight him. It changed the course of my life.

Chapter Eight

Fame and Fortune

Ali's words of caution kept coming back to me. I was the No. 1 sports story across the nation that night and all of the next day. I was the cover story in the sports sections of all the major newspapers including the *New York Times*, the *Los Angeles Times*, and of course, the *San Diego Journal*.

What they say about overnight fame is true: it is literally "overnight." Suddenly, everybody knew who I was. The day before, I could walk down any street in San Diego or Los Angeles and nobody paid attention to who I was. That all changed in the blink of an eye. After defeating Ali, I became an instant celebrity. Doors were opened, the handshakes were a little stronger, the greetings a little warmer, the ladies were definitely a lot prettier! The world was handed to me on a silver platter. This new way of life was easy to get used to, but that's where I had to take stock of Ali's warning, especially when it came to raising Ken Jr. I wouldn't allow my fame to affect his upbringing, and I tried as best I could to raise him in a normal, loving environment.

Ken Norton Jr.: *After the first Muhammad Ali fight, my father took extra precautions to shield me from the boxing world. He didn't want me to follow in his footsteps because boxing was a rough sport in and out of the ring. At the time, I was too young to understand what was happening to my father. The one thing that affected* *me deeply because of my father's newfound fame was the fact that we moved to a better neighborhood almost immediately. I had become attached to my classmates at my old school, but other than that, my father's fame didn't affect me that much.*

I was shy as a kid and never brought up who my father was. If you knew me on an intimate level or was a neighbor, only then would someone know that I was Ken Norton's son. My father did a good job raising me; making sure not to spoil me and always going out of his way to let me know that he loved me. I can't really say I grew up with the usual stigma of having a famous father. I was just a regular kid growing up, doing normal things that kids do, like riding bikes, playing sports, and hanging out with friends.

I had been dating several women since the first Ali fight, and I enjoyed the spoils of success, but once the women found out I had a son, things became different. They still liked me, but they would shy away and our relationship wouldn't make it to the next level. That is, until I met Jackie Halton.

I knew Jackie's cousin, Karen, and she had told me about her attractive cousin who was a secretary at Motown Records. I spoke to Jackie on the phone several times, but never got the opportunity to meet her. We both had very busy schedules, and we canceled a few dates. We would arrange to go out, then something would pop up.

After a few months of playing cat and mouse, Jackie and I finally met, and I wasn't disappointed. She was tall, had great features, was intelligent, and had an easy manner about her. She also was a single mother. It was easy for us to understand each other because we were both single parents who loved their children. Jackie had a five-year-old son named Brandon from a previous marriage. He would eventually become my son.

Minutes after our first fight, as Ali sat in the locker room, a brown paper bag was handed to him. On the back of the paper bag was a message from an anonymous, not-so-adoring fan. His taunt read: "The butterfly has lost its wings. The bee has lost its sting. You are through, you loud-mouthed braggart. Your mouth has been shut up for all time. It's a great day for America. You are finished!"

Ali taped the bag on the wall of his gym so he could see it every day. When his jaw healed, he began training for our second fight, which was scheduled for September 10, 1973, in Los Angeles. I wish that fan had kept his big feelings to himself. It's true what they say: The pen is mightier than the sword!

The press was a factor in motivating Ali: it proclaimed him all but washed up. For years, Ali had charmed the close-knit group of boxing journalists and spoon fed them helping after helping of quotable remarks, making their jobs that much easier. I'm sure from Ali's point of view, they had turned on him. Ali got testier, shorter, and more ornery.

"There is a great deal of interest in Muhammad Ali. Is he through or is he not?" Ali lashed out. "Is he still the fastest and most beautiful man in the world, or is he growing old and slow? Well, it shows you what they think of Ali that this question would come up.

"They never talked about Floyd Patterson like this," Ali raged on. "Old Floyd's been whipped 99 times, and he's still in business. Joe Frazier got slaughtered, and he's still fighting. But Muhammad Ali is so great that people don't think he should lose even when his jaw is broke, his ankle is twisted, and his hand is hurt, like what was wrong when he fought Norton last time. What happened is Muhammad Ali ate a lot of ice cream and cake, and he didn't do his running, he didn't punch the heavy bag. And still he almost won. If he hadn't been clowning around with his mouth open and got himself hit with an uppercut, he would have beaten Norton that first time.

"I took a nobody and created a monster. I put him on 'The Dating Game.' I gave him glory. Now I have to punish him bad."

This certainly didn't sound like the Ali of old, laughing and clowning around, predicting what round he was gonna knock me out in. For the moment, it appeared as if Ali had lost his sense of humor and his patience with the media.

Our second fight was being billed as "Ali's Revenge," and revenge was definitely what he was seeking. I think he was embarrassed by several things regarding our first fight in San Diego: I was an unknown fighter who came out of no-man's-land to beat him; his defeat was a nationally televised event for the whole country to see; he did not take me seriously and trained poorly for the first fight; I broke his jaw; and I had more female admirers than the Champ!

I knew Ali was taking our second fight a bit more seriously when he stepped into the ring at 212 pounds. He weighed nine pounds less than he had in our previous fight and was the lightest he'd been for a fight in eight years, when he fought Sonny Liston. His muscle tone was also more defined for the second encounter.

Rather than enter the ring with his usual attitude of putting on a show for the people, Ali entered looking determined, confident, and serious. He had spent 15 weeks in seclusion, training at his camp in Deer

Lake, Pennsylvania. Except for a few shuffles in the early rounds of the match, there was no clowning around. When we met in the ring for the referee's instructions, he wasn't making faces, talking trash about my mother, or trying to psyche me out. He was strictly business.

When the bell for round one sounded, Ali came out moving and dancing at a fast pace. The weight loss made him noticeably quicker. He scored the first punch when he fired a quick left jab followed by a right. It was obvious to me that his game plan was to keep moving and jabbing, avoiding any kind of confrontation where he'd have to stand and trade punches. I was pursuing him without throwing any punches, trying to address his much-improved speed. Finally, I began pushing forward, getting in a few jabs. Because of my head movement and jerky rhythm, I slipped past a good majority of his jabs; however, I couldn't throw any punches back, because his rapid movement still had me confused. Right before the bell, I threw a wild left hook that missed, and Ali walked confidently back to his corner.

In a show of force, Ali chose to stand in his corner as opposed to sitting on a stool, suggesting that he was in top fighting condition. When the bell sounded for round two, I jumped up off my stool and charged at Ali, who once again continued to move and circle. It was a lot more difficult to cut off the ring this time because of Ali's perpetual motion, and once again I wasn't able to land any punches. I did manage to get a few left jabs and hooks in, but Ali followed his fight plan to the letter and controlled the tempo of the fight.

In round three Ali wanted to get the glitzy Los Angeles crowd on his side, and he came out dancing on his toes, giving them a patented Ali shuffle for an encore. The crowd loved it. I did a little better this round, because I was successfully cutting off the ring, slipping his punches, and even returning a few of my own. I was frustrated because I was in constant pursuit of Ali but was unable to back him into the ropes, where I could do my best work against him. Ali was scoring with harmless jabs that had no effect on me. I started to sense that The Greatest was slowing down a bit and was unable to keep up the blazing pace he had set for himself in the first two rounds. However, the judges still thought he did enough to win the round. Now he was up on me three rounds to none.

After the fourth round, Ali chose to sit down on his stool in between rounds. His fight plan was starting to wear him down physically. In the fifth round, I finally caught up with him, but he effectively tied me up and we had to break. In effect, that meant that he was free and clear to avoid me once more. Round five was my breakthrough. I landed a couple of big shots to the head and body, taking my first round of the fight. I was down four rounds to one, and Ali was sitting pretty on a nice three-round lead.

About a minute into round six, I landed two nice left hooks. Again, Ali was showing signs of fatigue, and I began reaching him with stiff straight lefts. I stalked him, encouraging him to trade punches with me. He took the bait and we exchanged punches, but mine did more damage. I wanted him to trade punches with me because I truly believed his couldn't hurt me; they lacked any real power. In our entire three-fight series, Ali caught me with some good punches, but I was never in serious trouble. On the other hand, I believed that I could inflict serious damage on him if I caught him with one good solid punch. Slowly but surely, the tide of the fight was turning.

In round seven, Ali tried once more to dance around on his toes, but it was apparent to me that he lacked the speed or zip in his legs that he had shown in the earlier rounds. He continued to move as I pressured him, flicking out jabs that I easily picked off. I managed to get him against the ropes and landed a good combination that included a couple of hard left hooks. Ali broke free and went back to moving and jabbing, but his fight plan was no longer working. Every time he'd attempt a jab, I countered by blocking with my right glove and at the same time I stepped in, firing stiff left jabs that were catching him in the face. Again, I pinned him against the ropes and reeled off several vicious head and body shots.

Anytime we were tangled in a clutch, Ali held on to me to catch a breather while the referee tried to separate us. He was panting, and I knew he was in trouble. I caught him with a solid left hook to the jaw that rocked his world. I pressured him with punches right to the end of the round. As I sat down in my corner, Eddie and his assistant corner man, Thell Torrance, told me that I was trailing only by a round, and they instructed me to stay on the offensive and take the fight to Ali.

I kept the pressure on in the eighth round, but as I was attempting to cut off the ring, I was greeted by a left hook. A few seconds later, I pinned Ali against the ropes and peppered him with hard punches. We traded punches, and each of us landed a few respectable shots, but as we clinched, Ali held me once more to catch his breath. I caught him at the bell with a big overhand right, ensuring the round went in my favor. We were now dead even at four rounds apiece.

Ali looked sluggish as the bell sounded for round nine. I immediately began stalking him, realizing from his body language that he was tired. I caught him on the ropes early in the round and fired some heavy punches. One of my stiff jabs snapped Ali's head back, but then he answered back with punches of his own. In the last 60 seconds of the round, Ali stood flat-footed and traded punches with me, landing a powerful right hand in the process. We exchanged punches right to the end, but his last shot scored big with the judges, and the round went to Ali.

In between the ninth and 10th rounds, Bob Biron felt I needed to be rejuvenated and asked that Eddie Futch splash some water on my face. Eddie ignored Bob and began talking strategy. Bob felt as if Eddie didn't do anything to help me and that bothered him. This incident haunted Eddie and me later in the ensuing months because Bob never forgot it.

Surprisingly, Ali came out moving and jabbing in round 10, even circling and trying to pressure me. Halfway through the round, I caught Ali with some good punches against the ropes and connected with a hard left hook to his head. I continued to pin him against the ropes with punches. Near the bell, I landed one last left hook to ensure the round went to me. Eddie said the fight was dead even and up for grabs and that I needed to win the last two rounds to guarantee victory.

Round 11 was the wild card of the fight. Again, I kept the pressure on, hunting down Ali, and missed him with a wild left hook. Ali decided to trade punches with me, and we both landed a few bombs. Then I chased him into the ropes and connected with a couple of vicious body shots. In the last 30 seconds of the round, Ali spun me around. My back was against the ropes for the first time in the fight. He landed a few punches at the sound of the bell and the round was called even.

Right before the start of the 12th bell, we both were showing signs of fatigue, but we also knew that it all boiled down to this final round. Whoever won the round won the fight; it was up for grabs. At the bell, the two of us met in the middle of the ring to tap gloves, and then Ali caught me with a left followed by a right, but I blocked both punches. I don't know how he had the strength, but Ali got up on his toes and started moving again. When he stopped moving, he fired off a rapid combination, catching me with a few of his blows. As I was moving in pursuit, Ali stopped and planted his feet, getting off the occasional jab.

With about a minute to go, Ali caught me with a huge right uppercut that snapped my head back, but I kept pressing forward. That last punch cost me the fight. I began pursuing Ali in hopes of attempting to land an equally damaging blow, but Ali kept moving, not daring to stop and trade punches with me. As the final bell rang, the two of us stopped to look at each other and embraced.

Once the battle ended, I paced the ring frantically waiting for the decision. Several rounds had been extremely close and one particular blow in a given round could have been enough to sway the judges. This go-round was closer than our initial encounter. I felt I did enough to pull it off, but it was in the hands of the judges.

It's a strange phenomenon in boxing, but once that final bell rings, any hatred boxers might feel for one another is instantly replaced by a certain respect and brotherhood, and that's why we hug each other after trying to knock each other's block off. Make sense to you? It hardly makes sense to me, but there you have it.

In regard to Ali, there was never a moment in my life where I hated him for even one iota of a second. He is the man who gave my career a big boost by picking me as an opponent in our first encounter. I liked him, I laughed with him, I respected him as a man and for what he did for boxing, but all of that went out the window once we got into the ring. When we were facing each other for the same prize, only one of us would grab the brass ring.

This time, Ali grabbed the brass ring. The three judges scored a split decision 6-5-1 for Ali, 6-5-1 for me, and 7-5 for Ali.

Eddie Futch: *In that second fight with Ali, Ken went out and suddenly decided to fight Ali like Joe Frazier had fought him two years earlier. Ken bobbed and weaved. The trouble was, Ken didn't know what to do from that position, so Ali won the first four rounds. I finally got Ken going in the fifth round, and he started to come on. By the 11th round I thought he was pulling even, maybe a little ahead. But then Ali, being the great con man that he was, knew that he had to win the last round. He marshaled his strength in the early part of the 12th round and stole the fight with a strong finish. Despite that, I still think Ken won the fight. I think Ken won all three fights with Ali."*

Thell Torrance (corner man): *I thought Ken won the fight. He may have trained too hard, he wanted it that bad. Ken weighed in about five pounds less than their first fight, and he looked sharp in training camp. He was confident and ready. Muhammad Ali was the only guy I knew who could dance and move without landing solid punches for 12 rounds and still get points for it and win rounds in the judges' eyes.*

Buford Green: *I was at that second Ali fight and maybe Ken did lose that one. He was not as bitter the second fight as he was in the third fight in Yankee Stadium, that's for sure.*

The loss to Ali hurt, but I knew it had not been a convincing redemption for Ali. In retrospect, it did little to hinder the progress in my career. If anything, it increased my stock as a contender. The decision could have gone either way, and this time Ali had no excuses like poor conditioning or a broken jaw to fall back on. My convincing performance eventually led to a crack at a world title, but I suffered a terrible blow when master strategist Eddie was dismissed shortly after the second Ali fight.

Eddie Futch: *I started working with Joe Frazier in 1966, and Joe's manager, Yancy [Yank] Durham and I were close. Yank used to say, "If anything ever happens to me, I want you to take my fighters. Eight weeks later I was in California getting Ken ready for his second fight with Ali. Bobby Goodman, who was the Madison Square Garden matchmaker, and I had gone over to Las Vegas to see Jerry Quarry fight. When we got back to our training camp at the Massacre Canyon resort the next morning, Bobby checked his messages. He was in the room next to mine. I could hear him talking on the telephone. The next thing I knew, he was knocking on my door to tell me Yank had suffered a stroke. About an hour later Bobby told me Yank was on a life-support system. Later that night, after we had heard that Yank had died at 51, Joe Frazier called to ask what I was going to do. Joe said, "Yank's gone, Eddie. What are you going to do?" I went to Philadelphia, where I met with Joe and Bruce Wright, the head of the Cloverlay syndicate behind Joe, and we worked out a deal for me to take over as manager. Two weeks later, right after the second Norton-Ali fight, I moved to Philadelphia to manage Joe.*

Personally, I didn't have a problem with Eddie becoming Frazier's manager, because Eddie was just keeping his word to his late friend, Yank Durham. Eddie was my mentor and took me in when I was a raw youngster and molded me into a world-champion contender. The man was a genius, and the way I had it figured, some of Eddie was better than no Eddie. Moreover, Frazier was a good friend to me. He was in dire straits because Yank was the only manager he'd ever had. I didn't mind sharing Eddie with Frazier. Unfortunately, Bob Biron felt it was a conflict of interest for Eddie to be in both Frazier's and my corner at the same time.

Bob told Eddie right up front, "If you leave to train Frazier, we have to do something to protect Norton's interests. Eddie, remember one thing, you have left us, we have not left you. We would be happy to have you continue."

Bob was a decent and honorable person. We were like father and son. He was generous and made sure I was taken care of in every respect. Bob not only felt the conflict of interest was enough to dismiss Eddie, but he also reminded me about the incident between the ninth and 10th rounds, when he felt Eddie should have doused my face with water to rejuvenate me.

Additionally, Bob felt Eddie had overtrained me for the fight because I came in five pounds lighter than in the first fight with Ali, causing me to tire in the last round, the round that determined the winner.

Eddie lashed out: "Ken being overtrained—that is too much! All of a sudden, you're an expert, second-guessing me?"

Even though I didn't want to, I had to go along with Bob's wishes because he was the man in charge of everything—my career, my finances, my investments—and there was no doubt in my mind that he had my best interests at heart. He was forever looking out for me. With that said and hindsight being 20/20, letting Eddie Futch go was the biggest mistake of my career. I should have fought harder on Eddie's behalf and insisted to Bob that Eddie stay in my corner. I never questioned Bob regarding anything, and I quietly went along with what he wanted, never wanting to rock the boat.

You couldn't tell me that it was a mistake back then, but I realize that as a fighter who hadn't fully matured, I would have been 25 percent better than I was at my peak if Eddie Futch had still been in my corner. It's the single greatest regret I have regarding my boxing career, and if I could take it back today, I would do it in a flash.

Eddie's dismissal from our camp soon got out, and when the press got wind of what happened, it got ugly. For three weeks the story was quelled, but boxing scribe Bill Weurding of the *San Diego Evening Tribune* asked Eddie for confirmation.

Eddie admitted it was true. "After five years of guiding Norton's career and bringing him to the threshold of the world title, I've been informed that my services are no longer needed. If it weren't so tragic, I could think of it as somewhat amusing. I do find the whole thing most ironic, to have come this far with Norton, and then be told that I am no longer of importance.

"The truth of the matter is that Bob Biron and Art Rivkin are getting outside advice. There is always somebody in this business trying to jump in at the top. The same thing happened to me many years ago when I took Don Jordan all the way to the world welterweight title. If this were the first time it had happened to me, yes, I'd be bitter. But this is nothing that I haven't been through before."

Once Eddie spoke his mind to this reporter—and it was evident from his words that he had bitter feelings toward all of us for questioning his integrity—there was no turning back for any of us. I'd lost Eddie for good.

As for my comments to the press, I told them, "Personally, I hope this can be resolved. I would feel bad, because, after all, Eddie and I have been through a lot together, and it wouldn't seem right if he was not in my corner when I win the title.

"But Bob Biron has always done the right thing by me, and I'll have to go along with what he says. Bob is my great white father. He's my manager for my boxing career and my personal finances. I never have to worry about Bob giving me the shuffle."

Eddie retorted back in print, "I'm disappointed in Ken because I've had fighters that I expected less of who did more. But if he goes along with them [Biron and Rivkin], I don't have a leg to stand on. Ken is not the type of individual you can turn loose to just anybody and everybody. There's so much you have to know about him and his personality. He's a very strong-minded individual, and you have to have complete control over him to get results."

I must admit, Eddie's words hurt me deeply, but I could certainly see where he was coming from. I should have backed him all the way when I had the power.

Ironically, Bob and Art also dismissed Dr. Michael Dean from our camp, citing the same reasons as for dismissing Eddie; that after losing to Ali, he was no longer needed. Two decades later, I realize that both Eddie Futch and Dr. Dean were given the shuffle by my manager.

As a result of my second impressive showing against Ali, I was offered a shot against George Foreman for the world title. I was going into the most important fight of my career with a stranger in my corner.

Chapter Nine

Shattered Hopes

Without Eddie in my corner, I pondered my future in the ring. Eddie moved me from a raw talent to a world contender, but I still felt I had more to learn. I knew I hadn't reached my full potential as a fighter.

As a corner man, Eddie had only one peer in the business, and that was Angelo Dundee. Dundee was spoken for by Muhammad Ali, and that's who his loyalty went to first and foremost. George Foreman had Dick Sadler in his corner, along with former light-heavyweight champion Archie Moore training him. Joe Frazier had just inherited Eddie. I was left in the cold. I was in a mad rush to look for a world-class trainer to get me prepared for Foreman, the most intimidating and ferocious fighter since Sonny Liston. I was between a rock and a hard place.

As Bob Biron and I ticked off the names of trainers who were available, one name kept coming up: Bill Slayton.

At the time, Bill was a little-known Los Angeles trainer who enjoyed life to the fullest. He wasn't one of the people on the fringes of boxing hoping to latch on to a boxer to hitch his star to. He had been a longtime amateur and professional trainer.

Bill was a Los Angeles native and a former semipro football player. The tall, lanky athlete was the son of a city maintenance worker. He later boxed in the Army while in the Pacific during World War II. When he got back from the war, he worked as a truck driver and a yard foreman, but boxing was still his passion, and he loved to teach the sport to any young buck who was willing to learn.

"I just loved boxing," Bill told me after I got to know him better. "I had guys like Adolph Pruitt; he fought for the title four times. But whatever money I made, I gave it right back. I'd buy equipment for the gym, things like that."

Bill Slayton (Ken's trainer): *Back in 1970, my fighter Chuck Leslie lost a 10-round decision to Ken Norton. I didn't speak to Kenny; he didn't speak to me. I thought he was an arrogant, cocky guy who acted like he was better than everyone. But I later learned that he's a beautiful guy. He'd do anything in the world for a friend.*

In 1974, he and Bob Biron were looking for a trainer for Kenny, because Eddie Futch had left him. But when Kenny talked to me about the job, he was very sarcastic. He didn't know much about me, and he was very off to himself. Kenny only kept a few very close friends. He's a Leo, you know. Leos don't get too close to people, but if Kenny's your friend, you've got a true friend for life.

Anyway, Kenny asked me about 150 questions about how we would train together, and finally I said, "Wait a minute. We can play this cat-and-mouse game all you want, but I'll tell you what we can do. We can train for two weeks, and if you like what I'm doing, we'll go from there, and if you don't like the way I work, I'm outta there and you won't owe me a thing." Kenny said, "OK, sounds great." That's how we got affiliated, and after that, everything worked out.

As it turned out, I liked Bill a lot. He and Eddie had completely different personalities, and the two of us got along well. Bill was much more laid back than Eddie. Eddie was from the old school and was a strict disciplinarian who brooked no bullshit. Bill was brilliant from a tactical point of view, but chose to stress the positive points rather than focus on what I was doing wrong. With Bill I could crack a joke every once in a while, but with Eddie it was all business. I needed the change of pace mentally, but Eddie's no-nonsense approach for preparing me for a fight got the most out of me.

I also learned that I could get away with more with Bill than I could with Eddie. It was always my nature to take the easiest path, and that's where Eddie was a great help. With Bill, I could turn on the charm and wear him down, eventually getting him to see things my way. Of course, that only hurt me in the long run.

After I decided that Bill would be my trainer, I had just six weeks to get ready for my heavyweight title shot against George Foreman in Caracas, Venezuela, tentatively scheduled for March 26, 1974. Between fights I always stayed close to fighting condition. I never let myself get out of shape, so six weeks was enough time to get into decent fighting shape.

Bill Slayton: *When Kenny started training with me, he didn't like what I had to say because he doubted it. But I had patience, and I learned how to reverse things on him, make him feel it was his idea. I'd tell him, "Man, the way you were throwing your hook today, that was beautiful." Then he'd do it more because he figured it was his idea. He didn't want to do anything I suggested, but if he thought it was his idea, he'd do it forever.*

That's how I learned that you had to give Kenny the positive points before you bring in the negatives. I'd always praise him first. After that I could tell him all the bad things he did, and he would accept them. These are things you have to learn about guys to get the most out of them. The cocky guy, you have to knock him down in front of people, you have to embarrass him in front of people. But if you did that to Kenny, he'd sulk for months.

Despite the fact that he had only six weeks to get ready for his title shot, Kenny got into good shape. Kenny trained harder than any fighter I ever had.

Foreman and I made the formal announcement about our fight on January 30, 1974, in New York City. We were set to square off March 26, 1974, in the exotic locale of Caracas, Venezuela.

Big George was guaranteed a generous $700,000 against 40 percent of all income from the fight, while I was guaranteed $200,000 against 20 percent of all income.

The press tried to engage us in conversation, but Foreman just scowled, never smiling or shaking my hand. It was a big intimidation act that worked effectively with other fighters, but not with me. I wasn't intimidated by him and answered a few questions from the press with open praise for him. When asked what the difference between Ali and Foreman was, I replied, "Fighting Ali was like a game of chess. Ali has tremendous speed. With Foreman, it's just the opposite. Ali is a boxer. Foreman is a classic slugger. I've got to try to find a way to nullify his power. He's very strong."

Foreman responded by telling the media, "Norton knows what I'm gonna try to do," and left it at that. Before we left the podium, I stuck out my hand to wish Big George good luck and say may the best man win. George looked at me stone-faced and showed no signs of wanting to shake my hand. The reporters picked up on it immediately and booed Big George for his lack of sportsmanship. George defiantly stood his ground.

"There is no way I'm gonna be laughing and shaking Ken Norton's hand right now," he said.

Foreman's slight toward me was all an act for the press in the exact opposite way Ali approached hyping a fight. I couldn't be mad at the guy because he was giving me a shot at the world heavyweight title.

We were to fight in a new coliseum that seated 14,000. Ironically, its name was El Poliedro, Spanish for "many faces." It was a hint of the disastrous events to come.

Bob suggested our camp fly out to Caracas a week before the fight to get acclimated to the altitude. Caracas was 3,000 feet above sea level. The flight wasn't bad. Departing from New York's Kennedy Airport, it only took us five hours to reach Venezuela.

As our plane descended, I peered out the window to get a good look at Caracas. Beautiful, majestic mountains outlined the city as if they were protecting this jewel in the Caribbean. The ice blue water was edged by pure white beaches, and the radiant tropical sun beamed down. I thought I had arrived in Paradise. Looks can be deceiving.

From the airport we were hustled to the Caracas Hilton, headquarters for both camps. The ride to the Hilton took us over mountains and rugged, red dirt roads. We had only the green jungle of the rain forest to watch from the windows. Once in a while we passed a house, if you could call them that. They were small, squat, unshaded structures made mostly of red clay blocks, salvaged lumber and sheet metal. They were nothing more than tin huts, shanty dwellings, which the natives called home. One-third of the Caracas population of two million lived in these shacks. I had never seen such poverty before. *"Why on earth did Don King pick this place for the heavyweight championship of the world?,"* I thought to myself.

When Bob checked us in at the front desk, the clerk solemnly told him that the reserved rooms were no longer confirmed, but for $50 he might be able to do something about the inconvenience. It was later discovered that all of the clerks had pulled the same number on all of the guests related to the fight.

The room clerks weren't the only ones to put the squeeze on us. When Don King first struck a deal with the Venezuelan government, it was while President Caladra was still in power. Caladra welcomed the fight as a way to attract tourists to his country, and this was a grand opportunity to extol the virtues of his country. By the time the fight took place, Carlos Andres Perez had been elected president, and a new set of rules was applied to everyone surrounding the fight. The new president was out to squeeze every dime he could out of the "rich" Americans.

As we unpacked and settled into our rooms, I looked out of the window of my suite and saw that the clouds had turned dark and gray. A violent storm was brewing, and I'm not just talking about the rain.

If I could pinpoint the first of many things that went awry in Caracas, it had to be the debate over which referee would work the fight. The contract with the promoters stated that the rules and officials for the fight would be jointly agreed upon by the Caracas Boxing Commission, the World Boxing Association, and the World Boxing Council. The WBA and the WBC were and still are rival associations and have produced over the years many questionable champions in several divisions. The Caracas Boxing Association, which was affiliated with the WBA, was not a signatory on the contract but was insisting on its right to officiate the fight.

While this heated debate was going on, Foreman's trainer, Dick Sadler, brought his own referee, Jimmy Rondeau, to Caracas. Jimmy had officiated the Frazier-Foreman fight in Kingston, Jamaica, and Bob felt that Rondeau had let Foreman run the show with his brutal style of fighting. During that fight, Rondeau had let Foreman push, hold, grab, and manhandle Frazier. Bob wanted to ensure we had a referee who wasn't partial to either fighter, and in his mind, Rondeau was definitely out of the question. Ever the statesman, Bob said he believed in the competence and integrity of the Venezuelans and was against importing any referees. He pointed out that the country had hosted eight title fights. While this controversy didn't get resolved until fight time, another more serious matter reared its ugly head.

While all of the parties were trying to hammer out a compromise about a partial referee, Henry Schwartz called a press conference to announce that he had signed Ali and Foreman to fight in Zaire, Africa, in late September 1974. But here was the doozy: Each fighter was to receive $5 million apiece, making it the biggest fight of all time. The reporters went bonkers and fired away a million questions. The timing of Henry's press conference couldn't have been any worse; it took the focus and edge off this fight.

Bob pulled Henry aside and scolded him: "I would have appreciated if you'd consulted with us and waited until this fight was over before making your announcement." Henry apologized and told Bob that news of the fight had leaked to the press and he had to head it off at the pass. Those leaks were made by none other than Don King, who was positioning himself to become the biggest promoter in boxing. It would be his grand entrance into the big leagues and his *coup de grace* at the same time.

The debate regarding the referee resumed and went on for three days until Dick threatened to pull out of the fight altogether. Hell, he had bigger fish to fry now that his fighter and Ali were going to "Rumble In The Jungle" for $5 million. Why risk losing this fight with me for chump change? A lot was riding on this fight for Foreman.

"I'm not trying to get my own referee," said Dick. "I just want what I'm entitled to. Frazier always had his own referee. I could blow my title on a misinterpretation by somebody that don't speak the language. There's no question about these guys being honest, but what about incompetence?"

All discussion came to an end when it was put point blank that unless we agreed to let Jimmy ref the fight, Dick was going to pull out and go home and prepare Foreman for Ali in September.

When the press got wind of what was going on, they naturally sided with our camp. It was only then that Dick came up with the excuse that Foreman possibly might have sprained his knee and the fight might be off.

Chris Dundee, a promoter and trainer out of Miami and Angelo Dundee's brother, was a man who pulled no punches and had little patience when it came to games. In an attempt to get the truth out of Dick, Chris put Dick on the spot. He asked the question that the media wanted to ask but were afraid to for fear of reprisal: "Is the fight on or off?" he asked loudly.

Taken aback by his aggressive tone, Dick replied, "The fight is going to be on or off as the decision's made today."

"It'll be a fine draw," Chris thundered back. "I'm a promoter. I have four closed-circuit fights. My people are waiting to hear in the States. Tell us yes or no."

"So you got four closed circuits, and I got $5 million coming," Dick boasted.

So there it was. It all boiled down to money.

Tired of Dick's bullshit, Chris roared back, "Tell us yes or no!"

"Find out from the commission doctor who has the charge of that. I'm broke. I'm broke. If you ask me, I say, yeah, he's going to fight. I don't need no official. It's out of my hands." Dick then marched out Foreman's personal doctor, Peter Hacker, who told the media in a very shy manner, "Mr. Foreman has sustained an injury. He either has a serious sprain or muscle spasm in his knee. I am unable to tell at this time if he'll be able to fight."

When the reporters began booing, Dick chimed in, "The doctors said it's an old injury. We have been nursing it. We have been unable to run here for one whole week, and we have been getting a ton of ice from the kitchen."

Dr. Hacker (honest, that was his last name!) came to life and spoke into the microphone, "My recommendation is to wait and see."

The reporters by now were in a frenzy and fired away. Once again, Chris' voice boomed the loudest and he asked, "But don't you have a deadline?"

"I would imagine fight time," replied Hacker, in a sincere and yet naive tone. The conference was quickly turning into a mob scene of yells and screams, and Chris brought it to a halt.

"Hold it, hold it down!" For once, I thought Chris was going to be the voice of reason. "Let's give credit to Dick Sadler for being a super salesman." Man, talk about lowering the boom.

Dick pounded the table where he was sitting and was infuriated. "There is swelling in the X rays, so any goddamn fool knows the fighter can't fight if his leg's messed up!" With that, Dick and Dr. Hacker popped up from their chairs and huffed off, leaving everyone confused.

The burning question on everyone's mind (especially mine!) remained, "Is the fight on or off?"

While I had that question to worry about, I had a more serious and personal issue to deal with when my parents arrived.

I flew in my parents from Jacksonville for all of my fights. I should have used better judgment than to fly them to Venezuela.

Once it was discovered that my parents were in Caracas, a nasty rumor swept both fight camps that my parents were going to be kidnapped by local thugs and held for a hefty ransom. It really put the meaning of world-title shot in proper perspective; the safety of my parents was truly all that mattered for the moment.

My parents were everything to me then and everything to me now. I treated this particular threat very seriously, so seriously, in fact, that we hired bodyguards and moved our training headquarters from the Caracas Hilton to a hideaway in the woods a few miles out of the city.

Buford Green: *Caracas brings back such awful memories. The city was a shantytown. Terrible place. The whole fight ordeal was bad enough, but this was an added distraction, and Ken had his hands full. George Foreman was known as being invincible and he certainly was at that time. He was a machine. Ken knew he didn't need the extra distraction that hit men were out to get him and his parents.*

I remember getting off the plane with John and Ruth Norton at three in the morning a few days before the fight and we were greeted by soldiers with submachine guns. When we entered the terminal, I heard over the loudspeaker, "Señor Buford Green, please pick up a courtesy phone." It was one of Ken's bodyguards. He didn't want to tip off anyone and use John or Ruth's names, so Ken advised them to contact me instead.

When Ken moved his training camp into the woods, body-guards armed with Uzis were placed in and around it and in the hills. There were roadblocks placed halfway up the mountain, and we traveled in a limo. One night, a bunch of young kids were jacking around and one of the bodyguards pulled out a rifle and pointed it at them, but the clip fell out. He pulled their car over and told the kids that they were lucky they weren't killed because of the rumors. I also heard that some of Ken's bodyguards were hired privately from Interpol. Bob Biron made sure that Ken and his family were safe, and he pulled out all the stops. That fight should have never taken place, given the emotional duress Ken was under.

To say that I wasn't mentally prepared for the fight would be a classic understatement. I was an emotional wreck. When I trained for the fight, it was done halfheartedly because of all of the distractions; no one knew if Foreman was going to show up or if the referee situation was going to be resolved. I stuck it out because I didn't want to forfeit the $200,000 purse or be the cause of a legal entanglement because I didn't follow through on my contract.

Big George acted as if he didn't have a care in the world, but then again, he didn't have his parents' lives threatened. In regard to the referee controversy, he told the press, "I don't care if three little old ladies judge the fight." Foreman's fight plan was to come out swinging. "He don't know what I'm gonna do, but he can pretty well guess. Wherever he goes, there's gonna be George Foreman, right in his face."

My plan was to box Foreman, because I knew he was going to be coming straight at me right from the bell. When he did, I would move away from him and make him think about strategy, eventually wear him down and move in on him in the later rounds, much like Ali did when they later fought. At least, that was the original plan. When I jumped in the ring the night of the fight, I blew those plans all to hell.

Mentally, I was drained way before the bell rang because of all of the extenuating circumstances. It all came to a head on fight day.

On the morning of the fight, the issue of who would referee the fight was still not resolved. Foreman claimed that his knee went out on him the day before when he paid a social visit to the local police chief. In front of everyone, he limped out of the hotel supported under his left shoulder by one of his trainers and headed for the local hospital to X-ray his right knee. An hour later he limped back to the hotel; this time supported by the same trainer under his right shoulder. Old George couldn't even keep his lies straight.

For the rest of the day, rumors swirled furiously that Foreman could or could not fight. One rumor had it that the knee was an old football injury. Another was that it was a pinched nerve, but Dr. Hacker claimed that it was a strained muscle. After the fight, Dr. Hacker told the media of his miracle cure: a shot of cortisone and novocaine. When asked about the shot, Foreman and his camp got their bullshit wires crossed again when he admitted, "I didn't get no shot. I hate needles."

By 5 p.m., the referee controversy had been resolved when Bob finally relented and gave in to Dick's request that Jimmy officiate. What actually happened was that Schwartz pulled Bob aside and told him point blank, "If you don't agree to Rondeau, Sadler's going to call off the fight." Bob was confident that I could beat Foreman and he figured that if we didn't agree to their terms, who knows when I might get another shot at the title? Once the announcement was made that Jimmy was the referee, Foreman's limp mysteriously disappeared. He moved with more speed, grace, and agility than I ever recalled him having.

Bill Slayton: *When we made the move out of the Caracas Hilton and into the woods, the only place where Ken could train was this little aerobics gym that had a mat but no ring. We had to spend a week and a half sparring on this mat. This was a world championship fight he was training for! Then we came into town and we had this hassle about Foreman threatening to call the fight off because of a bad knee. Everybody knew he was faking the injury.*

It got worse the night of the fight. Bob Biron told me, "Don't say anything to Ken, but don't leave the hotel until I call you." Now we're waiting for Bob to call. Ken's family is waiting with us. We're still waiting in the hotel when the undercard comes on television. We haven't even left for the arena, and the early fights on the undercard are already on television. We're supposed to be in the ring at 10:10 p.m., and now it's after nine, but we were still in the hotel waiting for Bob to call. Hedgemon Lewis, who was working with me, kept telling me, "Ken is going out of his mind." I knew I couldn't wait any longer and so we took off for the arena.

We had a van for Ken's family and a limo for Kenny, Hedgemon, three city policemen, and me. We told the driver we were in a hurry, so around corners he's going up on the sidewalk on the curb, passing vehicles, driving like a maniac. The arena was only about three miles from our hotel, but our guy was just nuts. We're not

even there and Ken is terribly upset because it's now 9:55 p.m. and
we are supposed to be in the ring by no later than 10:15 p.m.

When we finally get to the arena, we don't know where the
dressing room is, but we see Bob and he says, "I've been trying to get
you guys on the phone, but it was tied up." By now Kenny is walking
stiffly. The great Joe Louis greeted us in the dressing room and shook
Kenny's hand to wish him luck. Kenny was very, very down. We rushed
to tape his hands and he looked at me with a frown on his face and
just shook his head in disgust. Kenny had no time to meditate. I
always talk to my fighters in the dark before a fight so they are totally
relaxed, then I leave the room so that they can meditate. I could tell
by Kenny's lack of enthusiasm that he never had a chance to get prop-
erly mentally prepared.

Once my hands were taped and my gloves were laced, I was rushed
into the ring by Bill, Bob, Art Rivkin, and Hedgemon Lewis. Before I
knew what even hit me, I was standing in the corner of the ring in front of
8,000 screaming Venezuelans. Bill was trying to give me some last-minute
pointers but my head was somewhere else. *Were my parents safe? Would I*
make it out of this country alive? Would I make it out of this ring in one piece?
Would this nightmare ever end? All of those questions plagued me as I
prepared to go into battle against one of boxing's fiercest warriors.

"Remember the fight plan," Bill told me once again. "You have
to box the man, Kenny. Don't try to trade punches with him or you'll
lose." I shook my head and blankly stared into space.

A few minutes before the bell, Joe Louis stepped into the ring to
wish both of the fighters well. When Louis approached Foreman, he smiled
at him and whispered, "Remember, you're the champ—be cool." Foreman later reminisced, "I remembered that more than anything else during the fight," and that one sentence of wisdom from The Brown Bomber
inspired him to go after me in the ring and come out swinging.

Foreman was 39-0 with 36 KOs going into our fight and had
been inactive for six months. Foreman's personal life at the time was in
shambles and he needed time to sort out his much-publicized troubles.
His inactivity outside of the ring was a big advantage to me, even though
he was heavily favored 3-1 in the odds. Our fight was his second title
defense, and before I left for Caracas, I was sure I would come out the
victor.

Right before the bell rang, Foreman stared me down and smacked
the tips of his gloves together as if he were going to kill me, but I never
returned his stare.

Ali was sitting ringside doing TV commentary when Foreman shifted his icy glare from me to Ali. Ali taunted back: "If you behave like that, my African friends will put you in a pot," referring to their upcoming fight.

The bell sounded, and Big George stalked me down while I circled to my left, pumping out an occasional left jab. When I saw a slight opening in his defense, I attempted a right hook but missed wildly. Foreman then caught me with a few left jabs of his own and forced me into the ropes.

A minute into the round, he landed a clubbing right uppercut that shook my foundations. Sensing this, he attempted to pick up the attack when I retreated by getting out of the ropes and back into the center of the ring. We began to trade jabs when he landed a jackhammer-like left to my face. With time running out, Foreman pursued me with wild bombs until the bell ended round one. Even though I knew Foreman's strategy was to come straight for me, his ferocity scared the living daylights out of me. I had just experienced three minutes of sheer terror.

Back in my corner, Bill tried to build up my confidence by telling me I was doing fine and to stick to the fight plan and everything else would fall into place. Foreman's punches didn't do any damage as far as wearing me down; in fact, they were a shot of adrenaline that jump-started my nerves.

The bell for round two sounded, and I came out boxing wisely, jabbing and methodically looking for a chink in his armor. I threw and connected a fierce right uppercut that drew a major reaction from the crowd, but Foreman just kept coming at me, not even backing off for a second. He slowly pushed me against the ropes and let loose a volley of punches with knockout intention. One of his punches, a hard right, caught me as I was breaking free of the ropes. My knees buckled and I wobbled. Foreman sensed my lethargy, and like a shark smelling blood, he swarmed all over me, landing a series of thundering right uppercuts that sent me toward the canvas. The ropes caught me and broke my fall.

Jimmy Rondeau immediately gave me a mandatory standing eight- count and waved us to continue fighting. Foreman went on the offensive and landed two right uppercuts followed by a vicious right uppercut, then followed that up with a pulverizing overhand right, and finally, a left hook that dumped me on the seat of my boxing trunks. As they say in boxing, I was on Queer Street.

I tried to rise before the referee's count of 10, but Bill didn't even let Jimmy finish his eight count before he jumped up on the ring apron to call off the fight.

My first quest for the heavyweight title had been quashed.

Chapter Ten

The Perfect Fight

My nightmare in Caracas didn't end with my humiliating loss to George Foreman. Not by a long shot.

I headed to the locker room dejected, but on the other hand I was happy that I was going home in one piece. I would quickly erase my defeat from my mind, but leaving the country wasn't going to be as easy as I thought.

When our party arrived at the ticket counter at the airport, we thought we were home free. In a surprise move, the new Venezuelan government under President Perez decided to collect a healthy share of the purse of the fight by slapping an 18 percent tax on both George Foreman and me. To ensure payment, our flight was barred from leaving. That meant the government wanted roughly $47,000 from me, preferably in cash. Most of the members of my camp had posted a $60,000 bond, but Bill Slayton, Bob Biron, and I had to stay until the matter was resolved. Foreman got stung for an even bigger amount; he was presented with a bill for $126,000.

Henry Schwartz piped in the fight all over the world via satellite and was losing $50,000 dollars a day because his video equipment was being detained at the airport as well. The equipment was worth well over a million dollars. He contended, "It is our position that we are not responsible for taxes. This was a pure sell to El Poliedro Coliseum. The fighters did not earn any money in Venezuela, so they shouldn't be liable for taxes there. If there are any taxes to be paid, they should be paid by the arena." Then Henry got adamant, "Show me in the contract where it says I have to pay the taxes and I'll pay them."

Henry was right on the money with his view, but he wasn't sitting in the Maiquetia International detained by local tax inspectors armed to the teeth with the nastiest looking machine guns I've ever seen. No, Henry was back in his cushy New York office in the land of the free where he could say such things that were guaranteed under our Constitution. He wasn't in Venezuela twiddling his thumbs, wondering if he was ever going to see his family again. He could afford to say such things.

Our flight was delayed until the next day, a Saturday, and I wondered if we were ever going to get out of Caracas alive. I don't know exactly if Bob Biron promised the new dictator of Venezuela a lump sum of money or managed to wire him the $36,000 he wanted, but Bob did manage to get our party out of there on Saturday.

It was a fitting end to the ultimate boxing nightmare. Adios and good riddance, Caracas, Venezuela, and viva de los United States!

The experience in Venezuela left me totally drained. Even though I always managed to stay in fighting shape in between fights, I did not step inside of a boxing ring for three months.

After my defeat at the hands of Foreman, I did a lot of soul-searching and asked myself if I still wanted to stay in boxing. Did I really want the world heavyweight title badly enough? Was I willing to make the sacrifices to get myself into top-notch condition? Was Foreman the better man that night in the ring, or was it the circumstances in Caracas that prevented me from winning the world title? If I left boxing, how would I provide for my family?

Those questions plagued me every day during my three months off. After much soul-searching, I decided that I still had something to prove in the ring. It wasn't in my character to abruptly quit something that I hadn't mastered. I still felt that I was in the learning process, and that one day I would become the champ. Besides, boxing could lead to other things: color commentary, product endorsements, and movie contracts. None of these things would be possible if I left boxing, and so I stayed.

Bill Slayton: *As soon as Kenny was knocked down by George Foreman in the second round and I threw in the towel, I thought, well, there goes my chance to be this guy's trainer. When we got back to L.A., Kenny told Bob Biron, "I didn't follow Bill's battle plan. Bill told me things, and I just didn't do them." That took me off the hook, but it also took a lot of class to say those things because most* *boxers like to blame everyone but themselves because they are so pampered. Kenny was different in that he was grounded and could accept responsibility for his own actions.*

That's when I received an offer to fight 10th-ranked Boone Kirkman, a great white hope from the state of Washington. The fight was set for June 25, 1974, in Seattle. On paper this looked very risky, since it was my first fight since Foreman. Kirkman was built up like Superman in the Seattle, Spokane, and Portland areas, where most of his bouts had taken place. He had an inflated record of 32-3 and 23 KOs. He was a big guy at 212 pounds, with a courageous fighting heart, a decent punch, and a glass jaw. All three of his defeats had come via knockout. His boxing résumé was filled with more pretenders than contenders. In the biggest fight of his career, he also had been knocked out by Foreman in the second round in New York City on November 18, 1970.

While Kirkman was viewed as the baddest thing to ever come out of Seattle, I was viewed as a dying horse on his last legs, so it was a risky fight for me. Bob, Art Rivkin, and Bill felt that Kirkman was just an overhyped white contender who had been fed a steady diet of fringe contenders.

As expected, the fight, which took place at the Seattle Coliseum, was an immediate sellout, as the city rallied around the hometown hero. The fight was scheduled for 10 rounds, and if I lost this one, my career would be as good as over. There would be no more soul-searching or big paydays if I let this fight get away from me.

By the third round, I took a commanding lead, striking and pressing Kirkman with jabs and effective hooks. I bloodied my opponent's nose in the fourth round and inflicted a cut over his right eye in the fifth. Although Kirkman was physically strong, he left himself open many times and was easy to hit.

In the seventh round, I caught him with a monstrous overhand right, and he fell to the canvas headfirst. Technically he was saved by the bell, but referee Pat McMurty ruled that Kirkman had had enough after a severe pounding and wouldn't permit the game Northwesterner to come out for the eighth. My victory was ruled a technical knockout. After the fight, a lot of Kirkman's people came into my dressing room telling me that I would be champion of the world someday and that I looked sharper than ever.

Buford Green: *I think the fight with Kirkman was a confidence builder for Ken. I forgot what Kirkman said to Ken, but it* *was something that ticked Ken off. In my opinion, Ken carried him a couple of rounds before he put him away. He really wanted to beat the hell out of Kirkman before he knocked him out. Ken dominated this guy and I sensed his confidence was back and that he was headed for better things.*

After the Kirkman fight, Bob was contacted by movie producer Dino De Laurentis, who was screen testing for a part in his new film *Mandingo*. De Laurentis had produced several hit movies. Among his credits were *Serpico* starring Al Pacino, and *Death Wish* with Charles Bronson. I learned years later that O.J. Simpson tested for the part, but De Laurentis decided to go with me for the role of Mede. Simpson's hopes for playing Mede weren't dashed, and he recovered quickly and was cast as a security guard in *The Towering Inferno*, the biggest-grossing movie of 1974.

To be honest, I never had any acting ambitions, never thought of it in any respect and, in fact, never went to the movies much. I was too busy playing sports and chasing the girls. Back in those days, acting was for sissies, but this movie was altogether different.

Mandingo was a departure, as far as slave pictures go. It dared to illustrate the seedy, sexual side of black-white relations in the antebellum South. The movie was based on the enormously popular novel by Kyle Onstott. My part was that of a towering black slave named Mede whose taut muscles vibrate with power and sensuality. When I read the script, my first scene had me placed in the middle of a city square where I was to be sold. A potential owner, a white woman, wanted to "take a look under the hood," so to speak, and unzipped my fly to get a gander at my dander. She wasn't disappointed!

The movie's cast was respectable by Hollywood standards, and Richard Fleischer was a top-notch director with more than 50 films to his credit. Among those were *20,000 Leagues under the Sea*, *Tora! Tora! Tora!*, *The Vikings*, and *10 Rillington Place*. James Mason headed up the roster of seasoned actors, which also included Perry King, Susan George, Richard Ward, and Brenda Sykes. I was a newcomer, but everyone in the cast was eager to lend a helping hand, except for maybe Yaphet Kotto.

Yaphet today is a well-respected actor who stars on the NBC drama "Homicide." He had a reputation for being competitive, especially when another actor got more screen time. Yaphet was a little jealous that I seemed to be getting more attention from the females in the cast, and when it came time for our fight scene, he pulled no punches. In fact, he was supposed to throw a punch that grazed my chin, but it actually connected.

Luckily for him, it didn't do any serious damage, but I did get mad and warned him, "Yaphet, if you do that again, I'm going to kick your ass." While Yaphet gave me acting lessons I was willing to take, I'm not so sure he would have liked the boxing lessons I could have offered him.

Before I had even set foot on the set, the director, Richard Fleischer, recommended that I practice with acting coach Bob Modica, who at the time was considered the best around. I worked with Bob for six weeks going over technique, delivery, acting for the camera, hitting my marks, speech, and inflection. I found that with acting, you have to psyche yourself up just as you would for a boxing match, but the difference is that with acting you have to find something to relate to, to put you in a certain mood. One scene required me to cry. To get in touch with those feelings, I thought of my Aunt Mary and how proud she would have been of me. Thinking of Aunt Mary always brought a tear to my eye.

In another scene, Susan George seduced me; but after you get seduced 12 hours a day, two days straight, it's kind of hard to like it. The tedium of filming was worse than I had ever expected, but I found the creative aspect of acting rewarding. I learned firsthand that it took one day's worth of work to film two minutes of onscreen acting.

The critics were kind to me when *Mandingo* was released, but they savaged the movie for its explicit sexual content. Despite the horrible reviews, the movie did gangbusters business at the box office. So much so that I was asked back by Dino De Laurentis to make its sequel, *Drum* a year later with Pamela Grier.

A final note about *Mandingo*; "Saturday Night Live" did a stinging take-off of the movie with O.J. Simpson portraying me and Bill Murray as my love interest. They went all out, French kissing each other. Then it got really wild. Murray started French kissing a live cow!

After *Mandingo*, movie offers started flooding Bob's office. I liked working in movies, but I felt as if it was a career that I could return to once my boxing career was over. Besides, I made a lot more money in the ring. It was time to get back to work. My next fight was with Rico Brooks.

Bill Slayton: *After the Kirkman fight, Kenny had a long layoff, so I told Bob Biron, "We've got to get Kenny a fight where he can really get his confidence back, even if it's against a lightly regarded competitor. You don't set anything up, but you get him somebody you know he can destroy.*

I found the ideal guy, Rico Brooks. He had upset Ron Stander. I was there when he did it. He was a tough fighter, but he was 34 or 35 at the time, and he was thinking of retiring. I told him, "Rico, *how would you like to make yourself $3,500?" He said, "Fighting who?" I said, "Fighting Norton." He said, "Oh, man, no. I'm going to retire." I said, "Look, Rico, you do what you want to do, man, but you got a chance to make $3,500."*

I didn't tell Rico what to do. All I said was, "You got a chance to make some easy money before you retire, Rico; you got nothing to lose, man." He finally agreed.

The Brooks fight took place March 4, 1975, in Oklahoma City. The fight was basically a tune-up for a bout I had scheduled with Jerry Quarry just 20 days later, on March 24.

Brooks was a club fighter who entered the ring with an unimpressive 5-9-1 record, although he fought a lot of tough contenders. That roster included George Chuvalo, Ron Stander, Jimmy Ellis, and both Bobick brothers, Rodney and Duane.

The idea was that Brooks was supposed to provide me with a few rounds of work to help me get rid of the rust from my inactivity. Things didn't go according to plan. In the first round, I hit Brooks with a ferocious left jab that sent him straight to the canvas.

Bill Slayton: *When Ken hit Rico with that jab, everybody jumped in the ring. Kenny was ecstatic. Nobody seemed mad that it was the first round; however, I was concerned about Rico. But when I went over to see him, he said, "How'd I do?" I said, "Aw, man, I thought you might be hurt." He said, "He hit me pretty good, but I could've got up." That was Rico's last fight. He took his $3,500 and went back home.*

In boxing, it's known as getting an opponent. You can't say anything to fix it. But a guy can go in there on his own, and he'll go so long and then he'll say to himself, aw, man, why should I take a beating? You don't tell a guy to lay down. You don't tell a guy nothing. But you get a guy as an opponent who you're expecting will lose so that your fighter will get that confidence he needs. At that time, Ken Norton needed that confidence.

I continued on the comeback trail in hopes of getting another shot at Ali. Jerry Quarry, a legitimate contender, was next on my hit parade. Ali verbally promised me that if I beat Jerry Quarry, he would give me one more shot at taking his title away from him.

In the late '60s and the early part of the '70s, Quarry was a top-10 contender who was regarded as the best white heavyweight since Rocky

Marciano. He was a brawling Irishman who threw a devastating left hook, and had underrated boxing skills, but left himself open for a lot of good shots. He also was a notorious bleeder. Later on, unfortunately, it was discovered that he took way too many shots.

Quarry hailed from Oklahoma and spent most of his childhood living in a tent. He was one of five children with two brothers and two sisters. His brothers followed his path into the professional fight game. Jerry's father, Jack, moved his family from Oklahoma to Orange County. Many times I'd run into Jerry, and I got the distinct feeling from him that he didn't like me.

I'll admit freely that I did not like him. Quarry was the only man whom I fought in anger, and I went in to punish him. With most matches, I was out to do my job and win the fight. With Quarry, I wanted to pick him apart, savage him with body punches, snap his head back with jabs, and cut up his face. I wanted Quarry to be carried out on a stretcher. And so I trained for the Quarry fight as if I were training for the heavyweight championship of the world.

Bill Slayton: *I trained Quarry as an amateur and in his first five pro fights in the late '60s. At that time, he was good enough to have Rocky Marciano thinking about buying his contract for $50,000, which was big money then. I almost became his trainer, but we always remained good friends. Several times in passing he'd tell me, "If I would have stayed with you, I could've done this, I could've done that."*

For the fight with Ken, the press conference was held at Grossinger's in the Catskills. Quarry's whole family was there, so I went over to give Jerry a hug and say hello to his family. Kenny was upset about me giving Jerry a hug. Kenny asked me, "What are you doing talking to him?" I said, "Hey, man, I've known the guy for years. We're friends. I wasn't telling him any secrets. This is what boxing is all about. Fight tonight. Friends tomorrow."

So after we hashed out my talking to the Quarry family, Kenny said, "I'm going to kick his ass." I said, "I want you to knock him out. That's what we're here for." Kenny had other ideas.

On March 24, 1975, at Madison Square Garden, Quarry and I finally got to solve our differences in the ring. Our 12-round heavyweight fight was nationally televised on closed circuit as the main preliminary fight to the main event—the Ali-Wepner fight, which was actually held in Cleveland.

Quarry had been the first fighter to face Muhammad Ali since his return from his 3 1/2-year exile on October 26, 1970. He was sliced up and stopped by Ali in three bloody rounds. When Quarry fought, he plodded straight ahead and was prone to cuts. He challenged Ali again June 27, 1972, for his North American Boxing Federation title in Las Vegas and was stopped in the seventh round. It was part of a two-fight doubleheader in which Quarry's brother, Mike, challenged Bob Foster for the light-heavyweight title and was knocked out by Foster in the fourth round. The twin bill was promoted as the Quarry Brothers vs. the Soul Brothers!

Quarry also had been beaten by Ali and had been stopped by Joe Frazier in five rounds on two separate occasions. Our match represented Quarry's last legitimate shot at the undisputed heavyweight title. To make things even more interesting, Quarry promised he would retire if I defeated him. According to *The New York Times,* Quarry was confident that I was going to be a walk in the park.

"There's no ifs about it. When I win, I want to fight the champion," said a cocksure Quarry.

That night, Ali stopped the outclassed, but courageous, club fighter Chuck Wepner in the 15th round. An unknown actor, Sylvester Stallone, watched their fight on closed-circuit TV and was touched by Wepner's gutsy challenge. Wepner took a beating for the entire bout but hung on until the referee stopped the match in the final round. Stallone was so inspired by Wepner's courage that he went home and penned the Academy Award winning *Rocky.*

My fight with Quarry actually was the fight everyone wanted to watch, because on paper, our bout was considered by the experts as the more evenly matched of the two.

Anger fueled me when I first stepped into the ring. Quarry came out winging his trademark left hook, but missed. I countered his hooks by circling, then landed a stiff left jab to his face. In the middle of the round, Quarry caught me with a solid left hook to my midsection, sending me reeling into the ropes. I recovered quickly, sticking him with a solid right uppercut. I went back to circling him, trying to get him out of position, still popping him with my left jab. Quarry attempted to throw a few combinations, but they missed as round one ended.

At the beginning of round two, we charged toward each other and clashed heads. I noticed that Quarry's left eye was beginning to swell. My left jabs, followed with straight right hands, kept connecting, even though Quarry fought back, throwing potent left hooks. One of his hooks connected, and it stung! I launched a counter attack, and one particular right hand stopped Quarry in his tracks. Quarry rebounded and landed a few solid body shots, but every time he came within range, I pummeled him with right uppercuts.

Both of us came out circling and jabbing in round three. I fired off a three-punch combination that opened up a cut on Quarry's right eye. With my back against the ropes, a desperate and bleeding Quarry threw wild bombs in hopes of catching me with a Hail Mary shot. He was aggressive, but I kept pecking away, hitting him every time he missed a punch. Technically this round was judged as Quarry's because he was on the offensive and threw more punches, but I cut him badly, and he took some solid shots from me. At the end of round three, Quarry appeared beaten, while I looked very fresh. A doctor appeared in Quarry's corner to examine his cut right eye, but he allowed him to continue.

By round four, I sensed that Quarry was in big trouble and I began to aggressively take the fight to him. Quarry took a beating, as all of my head and body shots found their mark. Quarry's solid chin and huge heart were the only things keeping him upright. I continued battering him, landing solid uppercuts, left hooks, and looping right hands. Quarry's right eye was gushing blood, and he continued to absorb serious punishment up to the end of the round. Once again, the fight doctor examined Quarry in his corner, but allowed the poor guy to continue.

A battered and bruised Quarry valiantly came out swinging to begin round five; however, his punches were telegraphed and lacked steam. I easily avoided his attack by slipping his punches or catching them on my shoulders. By all appearances, the fight was now target practice on Quarry's head, but a courageous Quarry would not give up. It was time for the referee to jump in, and he did so, wisely stopping the fight. Quarry protested, but it was an effort in futility.

For five rounds, every jab I threw connected, every body shot landed; everything I threw at Quarry found its way to his face and body. I fought the perfect fight, and that night in Madison Square Garden was, without a doubt, the best fight of my pro career.

When it was over, we walked toward each other and hugged. Any animosity I had toward Quarry had vanished. The man had heart and he fought until the very end.

Bill Slayton: *It was definitely the best fight Kenny ever fought. Afterward I went over to Jerry's room. The doctors had him on the table because he was busted up. He asked me, "Did I disgrace myself?" I said, "You fought like a true Irishman."*

Quarry promised to retire if he lost to me, and he kept that promise for two years until his comeback fight against Lorenzo Zanon, on November 5, 1977, which he won by knockout in the ninth round. Quarry continued to bounce in and out of retirement, even taking a fight when he was 47, losing a six-round decision against an obscure opponent named Ron Cramer. He took a beating in that last fight but refused to give up or go down, just like he did in our fight.

Years later, the many punches that Quarry took in the ring took their toll on the Irishman. Quarry suffered from severe memory loss and brain damage due to the punishing blows he took during his career. I have often been asked if somehow I might feel responsible for contributing to his condition. That's a fair question, because he took many hard punches to the face that night in 1975 from me, and yes, as a human being, a part of me does feel responsible for his condition. However, if the shoe were on the other foot and I was the one suffering from brain damage, I would have to take some responsibility as a boxer for entering the ring and choosing boxing as my livelihood. Brain injuries are an occupational hazard in boxing, and I knew that from day one.

Did we know as boxers that taking too many shots could lead to "punchiness"? Of course we did back in the '70s and '80s. I had seen more than my fair share of punch-drunk former boxers. But you know what? That still didn't dissuade me from fighting. The subject of "pugilistic dementia" didn't become politically correct until it was suspected that Muhammad Ali might be suffering from it. He believes it's simply Parkinson's disease.

Sadly, Jerry Quarry passed away on January 3, 1999, at 53. He should have been enjoying the profits that come to world-class athletes in their twilight years. Instead, he spent his last years unable to care for himself or recognize his family members. He had been virtually a dead man walking for his final three years. According to Quarry's neurologist, his brain "resembled a grapefruit that had been repeatedly dropped."

The official cause of his death was cardiac arrest. How ironic: in life, the one part of Jerry Quarry that refused to quit was his heart.

After the finest display of my career against Quarry, I planned to exact a little revenge while upping my status. That was a tall order, but I was ready to carry it out with a rematch with former nemesis Jose Luis Garcia. I had now attained a No. 3 ranking by the World Boxing Council, and an impressive victory over Garcia could enhance that lofty position. The return bout with Garcia was set for August 14, 1975, in St. Paul, Minnesota.

Local heavyweight prospect Scott LeDoux was booked on the same bill. The promoters were hyping an all-Minnesota shootout if LeDoux defeated trial horse George "Scrap Iron" Johnson on the undercard. My main-event bout with Garcia was to be filmed for national television distribution at a later date.

It had been more than five years since I suffered my first taste of defeat in losing to Garcia. In my subsequent 19 contests, I had gained immense knowledge and defeated some of boxing's finest competitors. I was a totally different fighter, as Garcia would find out.

The first two rounds of my rematch with Garcia had been competitive, but my brutal body attack started to take its toll by the third round. I dropped Garcia in the third and fourth stanzas with perfectly executed left hooks to the midsection. I ended the event with another blow to the solar plexus in the fifth round, which sent Garcia down for the count. I landed the punch just above the stomach, which has a paralyzing effect. I wanted Garcia to pay for our first encounter. It was a convincing victory that led to my bout with another Venezuelan, Pedro Lovell.

Like me, Lovell also had some experience on the silver screen. Lovell recently had relocated to the United States to enhance his movie career and to seek out a higher grade of heavyweight competition. For his sake, I hoped he had talent as an actor, because I planned to derail his climb up the heavyweight ranks.

The Norton Express kept on rolling and didn't plan on stopping until it met up with Ali for a rubber match.

Chapter Eleven

The Norton Express

Whenever I reflect back on my boxing career, an incident in the Pedro Lovell scrap always stirs my memory.

"I'm going to destroy this man!" I boasted to Shirley Norman of *The Ring* boxing magazine regarding my upcoming fight with Lovell on January 10, 1976, at the Las Vegas Convention Center. Now that I was the No. 1 contender in the world, I was beginning to get a little cocky.

Lovell had only one defeat in 18 bouts with several knockouts to his credit. Many boxing experts thought for $100,000 I was taking a major risk in fighting Lovell, even though I was a 5-1 favorite. Personally, I felt that I was going at the right pace and trajectory for my career in hopes of catching Muhammad Ali again. It had been, after all, five months since my last fight.

At the prefight weigh-in, I noticed Pedro was concerned with his physical appearance. Too concerned. For some bizarre reason, his hair stood out, and I remember thinking to myself that it looked too perfect. It wasn't until the final round of our contest that my curiosity concerning Lovell's hair was satisfied.

When I showed up in the ring, I employed a little psychological warfare on Lovell. I diverted his attention to my trunks because they were loose and pulled up to my mid-section. It's a little trick that usually works on most fighters but you have to know when to use it. For example, you couldn't pull that on Ali—he was way too smart.

I boxed Lovell for the first round, employing a sound defensive strategy, feeling him out to gauge his strength. Near the end of round, I landed one good left hook, and the judges awarded the round to me.

In round two, which was Pedro's best and perhaps only winning round, he caught me with some nice shots, but nothing that put the fear of God in me.

I continued stalking Lovell in round three, hitting him with several hard left hooks early on. Lovell escaped from the corner and hit me with a good right hand and a solid left hook. That left the fight even on all three judges' cards.

By round four, I picked up my attack and gave Pedro a savage combination of punches, using him for target practice and hitting him at will. I had him cornered and pinned against the ropes several times and appeared to have him all but knocked out.

His face was puffy in several places and both of his eyes started to close; in addition, he had many facial cuts. You could say that I was at my ferocious best. Round four was definitely mine, which meant that I was one point ahead on the judges' scorecards.

Lovell gamely answered the fifth bell, but barely. This round provided some comic relief. During the middle of the fifth, I caught Lovell with a punishing uppercut. Lo and behold, his hair flew straight up in the air without his body and landed safely back on top of his head. Lovell was sporting a hairpiece, but his hairpiece wasn't too sporting!

The rest of the round was more of the same punishment I had dealt out in round four. I stunned Pedro twice before landing a solid left hook to his head, which literally spun him around. Lovell staggered and turned to his corner, and I chose not to go after him, which I easily could have done. The referee, Fred Hernandez, stopped the fight at 1:40 of the fifth round and awarded me a technical knockout victory. I winked at the press and said, "I'm glad you got to see me work out today. The next time you'll get to see me fight! I'm meant to be the next heavyweight champion of the world. That's the next thing that's going to happen to me. You just watch!" Like I told you, I was getting cocky.

The Norton express was moving along full-steam ahead. I had looked impressive in all five of my post-George Foreman outings. If I continued to devour meaningful competition, I would once again receive my just desserts. Next on my hit parade was a high-profile fight against rugged Ron Stander. It was a nationally televised co-feature to a world title fight.

The bout with Stander took place April 30, 1976, at the Capital Centre in Landover, Maryland, 15 miles north of Washington, D.C. Our fight was on the undercard of one of Ali's title defenses, a disputed win over Jimmy Young. Although Ali was given the decision, many in the crowd and in the media felt that Young had won the fight. I knew the exact feeling.

Stander was a rough-and-tumble fighter who was prone to cuts. (By last count, he had more than 60 stitches!) He had a decent punch but no defense whatsoever. Stander was a star running back in high school and he fought like a football player; no real boxing technique, just a brawling flat-footed fighter. Stander's nickname was the "Bluffs Butcher" because of his hometown of Council Bluffs, Iowa. Most of his professional bouts took place in Omaha, Nebraska, which is located directly across the Missouri River from Council Bluffs. In his 10th professional fight, May 11, 1970, Stander knocked out the hard-punching Earnie Shavers.

Stander challenged undefeated heavyweight champion Joe Frazier in Omaha, May 25, 1972, where he absorbed a lot of punishment and suffered some severe cuts before being stopped in the fifth round. In a classic observation, Stander's wife, Darlene, said that her husband going up against the likes of Frazier was like "a Volkswagen entering the Indy 500."

Despite being a colorful character, Stander had a more-than-respectable record of 28-6-2 and feared no man when he entered the ring. Crazy white boy! At this point in his career, Stander was a 31-year-old journeyman fighter. His dreams of becoming a champion were almost evaporated, and he was hoping for an upset over me to rejuvenate his career.

Stander weighed in at a rotund (and I'm being kind) 247 pounds, and he was much shorter than I was, so it made him look even flabbier. He might have looked soft, but he came out swinging in the first round with a face-first offense. Both of us traded punches until I got my jab working, snapping his face back with hammer-like left jabs. Stander came at me, charging recklessly, missing with wide, arching punches. I countered his misses with pinpoint combinations. Stander was covering up on defense but was leaving himself wide open with his kamikaze-style rushes at me. At the end of the round, he made one more mad dash at me, and I caught him with some nice solid uppercuts that snapped his head back.

In round two, Stander again charged at me head first and backed me into the ropes. Then he did something that even surprised me: He fired two intentional low blows. There is nothing more life affirming or painful than getting hit below the belt with a wallop that can only be thrown by a boxer. I was furious. Halfway through the second, I caught him with a series of vicious uppercuts that definitely had him wobbling. I had to give it to this guy, he had a jaw made of granite. I was landing pulverizing uppercuts and throwing bombs at this guy's leaky defense, and he was still standing at the end of the bell.

Stander didn't charge any more in the third round. Instead, he covered up passively as I circled him, firing off straight left jabs at his jaw. When we met in the center of the ring, we traded a few punches and then I retreated to the ropes, where I connected on a series of uppercuts. His left eye was cut, and the blood was pouring out, affecting his vision. He looked more like a drunken, brawling sailor than a fringe contender. Round three ended with more telling blows to Stander's head.

Stander went back on the offensive in round four, looking to trade punches with me. I caught him with a series of left hooks and uppercuts to his head and body. The cut over his left eye was reopened and bled profusely. Stander tried to clinch with me to buy himself some time, then occasionally threw a wild punch at me. So far, the entire fight was nothing but target practice for me. I sensed the end of the fight was nearing.

By round five, the blood was flowing into both of his eyes, seriously hampering his vision. I had to give it to this guy. He was still trying to chase after me, but he was sloppy, often stumbling and tasting many of my counterpunches. Then I landed a vicious right uppercut. Every punch I threw connected to this poor guy's face; first, an overhand right, then two right uppercuts, and finally, a looping overhand right. With that last punch, the referee finally stepped in and stopped the one-way slaughter. Still I have to give Stander credit for not going down. Some boxers are like that; you can brutally pound them at will and outscore them by a hundred points, but they just won't go down.

Bill Slayton: *Kenny just pounded on him. He was a rough, tough dude, but no defense. Ron Stander's head was his defense!*

On June 25, 1976, in probably the most controversial move of his career, Ali took on professional wrestler Antonio Inoki in Japan. It was nothing more than a sideshow circus act, and Ali did it was strictly for the money. He was guaranteed an astronomical purse of $6 million, one million more than he was paid to fight Foreman.

The original script of how the fight was supposed to end was scrapped at the last minute by Ali, who felt the public deserved a real bout. Inoki fought the entire match on his back in a crab-like position kicking at Ali's legs. The result was a boring farce. Ali's legs were so badly bruised from the kicks, he had to be hospitalized. Blood clots may have formed, and Ali had to be monitored by the staff at St. John's Riverside Hospital in Santa Monica, California.

I visited Ali in the hospital. Irving Rudd, Ali's and my fight pub-
licist, saw a grand opportunity to turn my visit into a media spectacle.
Hell, I didn't mind. The man was doing his job, and if he could get me in
to see Ali, so be it if I had to pose for a few pictures. All I wanted to do
was to shake the champ's hand and make sure he was OK.

"Bring that sucker up here tomorrow," Ali told Irving, "but I don't
want no press around when you do. No press. Ya hear?" The words went
in one ear and out the other.

Irving made a deal with Ali: The press would stay in the recep-
tion area of the hospital, where Irving could give them a report of the
meeting.

I drove 100 miles from Massacre Canyon to Santa Monica with
Irving in tow. When we arrived at the hospital, the media was waiting for
us. Right away, they were asking Irving to take them to Ali's room to cover
this historic meeting. Irving shifted into high gear and ran into the gift
shop and bought a huge Snoopy doll, handed it off to me like a fullback,
and instructed the photographers to snap away to their little hearts' content. Great! Now I looked like a complete idiot holding this damn dog.

When they finished taking pictures, Irving took me up a secret
corridor, up one wing, across another corridor, down another wing, up a
flight of stairs, and then finally we arrived at his room. There sitting on
the edge of his hospital bed was The Champ, sporting pajamas and a bath
robe.

The two of us looked at each other and smiled. I offered my hand
and Ali took it warmly in his and we gripped firm and hard. It was a
handshake of friendship.

"Hey, Ken, baby, nice to see ya!" said Ali.

"How ya doing, Muhammad. How are they treating you?"

"I can't complain, man. Can't complain."

Ali seemed a little antsy, if my perception was on target, after we
chatted for about five minutes. I don't think Ali liked being pinned down,
especially in a place like a hospital. It wasn't his style. Ali needed to breathe.

Ali turned to Irving and asked, "Where's the press?"

"Downstairs someplace. They're all waiting for your statement,"
Irving answered him. I'm sure Irving figured that Ali would just give a
statement for him to pass along to the reporters, but Ali, knowing the
boxing media was downstairs in full force, sensed an opportunity.

"C'mon," Ali said turning toward me, "let's go down and see the
press. How about we show these mothers we're still alive!"

I couldn't believe the transformation that took place before my
very eyes. One moment he's in a hospital bed, the next minute he's like an

excited kid ready to play a prank. Ali sat in a wheelchair and began to roll himself toward the elevator. He looked over at me with a mischievous grin on his face and asked, "What am I gonna call you? I know—Drum." He was referring to the name of my second film, the sequel to *Mandingo*. Then Ali changed his mind again.

"I know. I'm gonna call you Mandingo! That's what I'm gonna call you."

I was less than thrilled. Ali had a way of humiliating someone that was hard to respond to. Joe Frazier didn't like his teasing, but I knew it was all a part of his game, so I went along with it.

When we got off the elevator, I knew something was up. Ali wheeled himself into the thick of things, and as soon as the TV lights went on, he started his prime-time act. He was now center stage and he shouted at me, "Bring him here! Bring that sucker over here!"

Then Ali got up out of his wheelchair, hobbled over toward me and said out loud, "Let's see what you got!" Then he threw a real punch at me, even though he intended to miss. Ali had me in a no-win situation. If I defended myself, I would look like a man beating up a guy in a wheelchair. No doubt about it, Ali was one wily dude!

It was only when Irving stepped in between—all of 5-foot-5 and 135 pounds of him—that the fight between us was officially over. Ali made it appear to the press that there was some bad blood between us. Meanwhile, the press and the photographers are eating this up and Ali was shouting out at the top of his lungs that when we met for real in Yankee Stadium, my ass would be grass. The pens were moving a mile a minute, and the press were all thinking they had an honest-to-goodness bloodbath on their hands.

Ali ran off at the mouth: "I want a mike in the ring when we fight," he bellowed at me. "I want you to talk. We'll fight and we'll talk, and I'll destroy you."

I was chewing a piece of gum, interrupting my rhythm long enough to manage a straight man's smile. I was Dean Martin to his Jerry Lewis.

Then in unison, the microphones whipped over in my direction for a response. I didn't let them down.

"Every time he takes a breath," I said, "I'm going to put a fist in his face."

"Hear that?" Irving chimed in, sounding like a poor man's version of Mickey Rooney. "Ken's really working up a hatred for this guy. It's a vendetta."

Vendetta, my ass! I repeatedly told the press that I was thankful to Ali because I would be getting a guaranteed million dollars. If this freak show was going to sell a few more tickets to the fight, so be it. But deep in the back of my mind, I was going to pay back The Champ in spades for this little ruckus.

When we got back to his room, Ali's wife, Veronica, and her sister were sitting there. Veronica was a former model and her little sister wasn't half bad herself. Both women were stunning. Now was payback time.

I walked over to Veronica's sister and put my arm around her, all the while looking Ali straight in the eye with a menacing smile.

I whispered in the young lady's ear and crooned sweetly, "Hey Puddin', you and I gonna make it good, honey."

Ali went ballistic. "Hey, Norton, what you doin', sucker?" I kept up the charade, but Ali was too tired to fend me off. I knew I had his goat, and so did he. We laughed it off and shook hands once more.

"Get well soon, Champ," I told him.

As I left the room, Ali received a call from some guy at a radio station wanting to plug our fight. One minute he was calm, placid, tired; now he's screaming into the phone, "I'LL DESTROY NORTON! YOU HEAR WHAT I SAY? I'LL DESTROY THAT MAN!"

They broke the mold with Muhammad. They broke the mold.

The original rubber match between Ali and me was supposed to take place on July 4, 1976, in Yankee Stadium, but those plans fell through. Instead, I took on a risky tune-up fight with Larry Middleton in San Diego on July 10, 1976. It was a gamble, because if I lost, the third battle with Ali would be called off.

The bout was promoted as the "Battle of the Jaw Breakers." Earlier in his career, Middleton had broken Joe Bugner's jaw in London in 1971. At the time we met in the ring, Middleton was a durable journeyman who started his career in 1965 in Baltimore and had accumulated a professional record of 25-8-2. He was just coming off of a loss from red-hot prospect Duane Bobick. I was hoping to use the Middleton fight to sharpen my skills for the promised fall encounter with Ali, now with the bout set for September 28, 1976.

I entered the fight at my heaviest weight ever, tipping the scales at a sluggish 222 pounds, 12 pounds over my best fighting weight. Middleton weighed in at a trim 207 pounds.

I couldn't get a clear shot at Middleton the first four rounds of the fight as he circled, weaved, and danced out of range. Then in round five, I unleashed a heavy body attack, mixing it with some solid combinations to the head with some particularly nice left hooks. At the end of the fifth, I had Middleton sagging on the ropes and didn't think it seemed likely that he'd answer the bell for the sixth, but, miraculously, he did. Middleton had a head as hard as rock and withstood some of the most severe punishment I ever dealt out in one round.

Middleton dominated the first 2:30 of the sixth round, but then I came on strong, and he absorbed another brutal attack of body shots. I failed to capitalize in rounds seven and eight and plodded through the rounds with little enthusiasm, while Middleton continued to dodge me.

In the ninth, Middleton finally hit the canvas, but it was a slip. When he got back up, I worked him over with an assortment of shots that started taking a toll.

Round 10 saw Middleton hit the canvas one more time—another slip. I was frustrated with his repeated slips because I didn't know if he was doing it on purpose to prevent getting hit. When we were ordered to fight again, I caught Middleton with an overpowering overhand right, practically knocking him out on his feet. I pounced all over him, hitting him at will. I wondered why the referee wasn't calling to end it. Middleton's lip was cut up and his mouth was full of blood. He'd had enough.

Two minutes, seven seconds into the 10th round, referee Rudy Jordan pulled me off Middleton and proclaimed the fight over. Surprisingly, the fans, my hometown fans, didn't agree with Jordan's decision and booed him heartily. Middleton didn't agree with Jordan and told the press afterward, "No way was I hurt. I've taken too many devastating punches from too many fighters to be hurt. Jerry Quarry hit me harder than Norton did . . . so did a lot of fighters."

But I could see in the ring that Middleton's eyes were rolling around, and he was really hurt. The referee made the correct decision to end the match. True, I didn't look my best and Bill Slayton wanted me to go 10 rounds because he felt I needed the work. For the Ali fight, I promised the media, "I'll be faster, stronger, quicker, and my reflexes will be better." And I kept my promise.

Bill Slayton: *For the Middleton fight, Kenny didn't need to be at his peak two months before the third Ali fight. He needed the work. We took off one week after the Middleton fight and went back to work at Gilman Hot Springs for eight weeks of serious training. The Stander and Middleton fights were tune-ups, and they were not* *the type of opponents who brought out the best in Norton. He either respects a guy or under-respects him. It was all mental with him in the ring. With Ali, he always felt that he could beat him, so mentally, he was fine. I made sure that Kenny would weigh 215 pounds and be in the best condition of his life for the Yankee Stadium fight with Ali.*

I trained like a man possessed for the third Ali fight. I wanted to fight Ali hard for three minutes every round. I wasn't expecting an easy fight, and my public workouts showed my steely determination. One spectator was taken aback by my drive and stood up and yelled, "Stop it, Ken! You're pushing yourself too hard. Stop!"

"I want that title and I plan to take it!" I shouted back.

I planned to fight for 15 hard rounds, and if Ali tried his rope-a-dope, I trained specifically to break right through it. In all, I sparred 225 rounds, 125 more rounds than Ali did for this fight, and did more calisthenics and roadwork than I normally do. Right up to a week before the fight I was sparring eight rounds a day, plus 10 rounds of floor work and five miles of running. I'm proud to say that I was at the peak of my condition, and I was as ready as anybody who had ever made a challenge for the heavyweight title.

The official weigh-in for the fight took place September 23, 1976, at Grossinger's Hotel in the Catskills, 90 miles northwest of Manhattan—the very same hotel Rocky Marciano once used for training. Ali specifically picked this site to interrupt my training, but I knew this was just one of his ploys to throw me off my fight plan. It almost worked, I must admit.

I walked into a roomful of photographers and a few guys who ran the publicity for the fight. I stepped up to the scale and weighed in at a lean 217 pounds; no more than a couple of pictures were snapped. As I got off the scale, I heard a commotion coming my way, and sure enough, it was Ali.

Ali coolly strolled into Grossinger's sporting all-black attire: shirt, pants, socks, and shoes. Following in Ali's footsteps was his usual 50-man entourage, chanting various war themes and street slang to pump up the champ and grab the attention of the media at the same time. Only Elvis Presley rivaled Ali in making a grand entrance. It was no small wonder both admired each other so much.

Ali's entourage consisted of a few legitimate guys like Angelo Dundee, Luis Sarria, and Dr. Ferdie Pacheco, but most of the rest were complete bums and hangers-on who wiped the sweat off Ali's brow for a living. He even had former comedian and diet guru Dick Gregory making him fresh carrot juice in one of his special blenders. Most of the group were street characters who Ali picked up along the way in his career, chiefly one bum named Drew "Bundini" Brown, who had been aptly described by Pacheco as Ali's "camp cheerleader and spiritual witch doctor." Ali was fiercely loyal to all of the members of his entourage, but the same couldn't be said for Bundini. It's been well documented that Bundini once stole Ali's championship belt and sold it behind his back. Even when Ali found out about it, he still invited Bundini back into the fold.

Ali entered the room screaming his usual diatribes about how he was going to knock me out in the fifth round.

"I'm gonna blow Norton outta Yankee Stadium!" he blasted into the microphones. "I am the true Six-Million-Dollar Man. In money, genius, personality, and charisma. The whole world's coming to see this fight. Can't have a man being champion who walks 'round like he did in that movie." Ali was referring to a scene in *Drum* where I showed off my derriere.

"It shall not go more than five rounds," Ali predicted. "Norton got knocked out in the second round by George Foreman, and I'm Foreman's daddy."

While Ali was spouting off, Bundini rushed up behind me and grabbed my shoulder. I turned around and told the lowlife that he was about two seconds away from wearing orthopedic shirts for the rest of his life.

"Don't ever touch me, punk," I warned him through gritted teeth, "don't ever touch me."

Then Ali leaned over and whispered in my ear, "Don't make him big, man! Don't make him big!" Ali was carefully warning me not to make Bundini the focus of the fight. Bundini wasn't there to pick up a paycheck—we were.

Bundini was pulled away by other members of Ali's entourage, but not before getting in his final lick, "And I can outact you, too, Norton." He very well could have outacted me. He certainly did his fair share of acting for Ali, but his face never graced the silver screen like mine did, and he didn't get paid for it, either.

When Ali stepped up to the scales, the reporters rushed to him to record his every word and prediction for the fight. Before I left the room, Dick Sadler, who was cut loose by George Foreman and picked up by Ali, had a brown box in his hand and gave it to me.

"What is it?" I asked suspiciously.

"Open it and see," Sadler said innocently.

It was a black cat.

Knowing that I was deeply superstitious, Ali went out and bought a stuffed black cat and had Sadler give it to me. I knew that Ali was looking for some kind of negative response from me, and I certainly wasn't going to give it to him, so I faked a heartfelt thanks.

"Dick, how sweet of you. Thanks for the cat. I have a new baby girl, and she'll love it." With that, as I left the room, I smiled and winked at Ali, letting him know that he hadn't gotten to me.

"I'll see you in the ring," I said confidently to Ali as I walked out slowly past the media.

"You can count on it," replied the master showman of boxing.

When I look back now, Bob Biron was the one person who spoke right on the money about my defeating Muhammad Ali in that third fight. He looked me and said, "Kenny, you have to take the title from Ali. Nobody is going to take a title away from Muhammad Ali if the decision is anywhere close. He is boxing."

Those words would be prophetic.

GOING THE DISTANCE

Ken Norton Collection

I proudly display my new WBC world
heavyweight championship belt.

KEN NORTON

Freshman terror at Jacksonville High.

Ken Norton Collection

COING THE DISTANCE

Dating girls was easier once I received my license.

GOING THE DISTANCE

KEN NORTON

Pvt. Ken
Norton: I'd do
anything to
avoid KP!

Ken Norton Collection

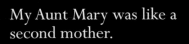

My Aunt Mary was like a
second mother.

Ken Norton Collection

KEN NORTON

Ken Jr. and I lived on a tight budget in Los Angeles. Hot dogs were a gourmet meal.

Ken Norton Collection

Ken Norton Collection

My parents, Ruth and John, with a photo of Ken Jr. in the background. They were the best parents a man could ask for.

GOING THE DISTANCE

KEN NORTON

I'm looking serious during my weigh-in with George Foreman in Caracas, Venezuela.

Ken Norton Collection

Ken Norton Collection

Getting taped during my early pro days with Master Eddie Futch.

Ken Norton Collection

Preparing for a bout with my second trainer, Bill Slayton, while Bob Biron (far left) looks on.

KEN NORTON

My manager, Bob Biron, treated me like a son.

Ken Norton Collection

WHAT'S **HE** GOT TO SMILE ABOUT?

NOBODY BREAKS MY JAW AUD GETS AWAY WITH IT!

ALI'S REVENGE? THE BATTLE OF BROKEN JAW! MONDAY SEPTEMBER 10TH.

Ken Norton Collection

A cartoon advertised my second fight with the "Greatest."

Ken Norton Collection

My Hall of Fame induction. What an honor.

GOING THE DISTANCE

KEN NORTON

GOING THE DISTANCE

Advertisement for *Mandingo,* in which I portrayed Mede.

Ken Norton Collection

Ken Norton Collection

In a fight scene from *Mandingo,* I was forced to pull my punches.

Here I am taking the fight to Ali, as I did all night long.

Ken Norton Collection

Ken Norton Collection

A ringside-seat ticket for my third Ali encounter—this one at Yankee Stadium.

KEN NORTON

The rope-a-dope, only worked on George Foreman not me.

Ken Norton Collection

Ken Norton Collection

Joking with my mentor, "Smokin'" Joe Frazier, and his son Marvis.

Welcome to Jacksonville
HOME OF **KEN NORTON**
World Heavyweight
Boxing Contender
CLOSED CIRCUIT TV JHS BOWL
LINCOLN SQUARE SHOPPING CENTER

Ken Norton Collection

Welcome-home billboard from fans in Jacksonville, Illinois

GOING THE DISTANCE

Chapter Twelve

Norton-Ali III

Yankee Stadium. The House That Ruth Built. Mecca of the boxing world. Pure history.

I'm referring to both the history of Yankee Stadium and the night of my third and final fight with Muhammad Ali.

The first fight at Yankee Stadium took place May 12, 1923, when Jess Willard knocked out Floyd Johnson in a heavyweight bout. The last time a fight took place in the stadium had been in 1959, when Ingemar Johansson knocked out Floyd Patterson, snatching Patterson's heavyweight title away from him.

My third fight with Ali also was going to make history on several levels. I had been 31 when I fought Ali in 1976. Only six heavyweights before me had ascended to the throne after reaching 30. That list included Bob Fitzsimmons, 35; Jack Johnson, 30; Jess Willard, 33; Jersey Joe Walcott, 37; Sonny Liston, 30; and Ali, 32. Years later, George Foreman miraculously won back the title in 1994 at 45.

Financially, Ali-Norton III was going down in history. The gate potential for the fight was estimated at $6 million, but that was with a capacity audience of 64,000 in attendance. The number was cut in half the night of the fight for reasons I'll explain later.

Nineteen seventy-six was our nation's bicentennial, and the Ali-Norton III fight would be boxing's contribution to the celebration. We would duke it out in a newly renovated Yankee Stadium, which had recently reopened after a $100 million face-lift. The fight was billed as the former Marine against the draft dodger. What could be more apple pie than that?

With all of the historical, symbolic, and financial significance attached to it, Ali-Norton III was a boxing promoter's dream. It turned out to be a nightmare.

The first sign of trouble that night was when the New York Police Department declared a strike, which is a nightmare in and of itself; but then it decided to use the fight as a forum to publicly air its views. The department's lack of support and supervision allowed rowdy mobs and thugs to riot and loot cars, slash tires, pickpocket innocent fight spectators, and wreak havoc on unsuspecting fight fans. I heard horror stories later that one person was stabbed, while another man trying to buy a ticket had his head bashed open and his wallet stolen. While this mayhem took place, the NYPD stood by and did nothing. Not only did they do nothing, they chose to protest by picketing at the fight. They shouted, blew whistles, banged drums, and purposely blocked traffic in front of the stadium. Even Ali's limousine was blocked, kids jumping up and down on the front fender and hood. Ali, the king of controlling a crowd, didn't risk getting out of the limo. It took quite a while before his limousine managed to inch its way into Yankee Stadium, just 45 minutes before the fight. Pandemonium reigned that night.

Mike Fitzgerald Sr. (fan in attendance): *Three of my buddies and I flew from Milwaukee to New York to see the fight. Like a bunch of dummies, we rented a limousine to take us from our hotel to Yankee Stadium. When we arrived, it was absolute bedlam. What we should have done was to take an old beat-up car or cab to the stadium because the limo was a target for street thugs. They descended on our car and rocked it back and forth. Everyone in the car was terrified. Later on, when we went to the bathroom, we had to link arms because we were so afraid of being mugged.*

The night of September 28, 1976, was breezy and clear in the Big Apple. The temperature dipped to 54 degrees at 10:30 p.m., the time of the fight.

When it was time for me to walk out of the dressing room and into the ring, we were apprised of the latest situation with potential rioters. Hundreds of youngsters were scaling the Yankee Stadium wall, and we were told to leave our wallets inside the dressing room.

"It'll be safer," we were assured.

More than 10,000 young adults, teenagers, and hoodlums scaled the wall that night and watched the fight for free. The people who paid up to $200 a seat were upset that the hooligans got to watch for free, but who could they complain to? Certainly not to the cops.

It was a strange crowd, too. Hoodlums mixed with celebrities. Among the famous faces in the crowd that night were CBS anchor Walter Cronkite; actor Jean-Paul Belmondo; singer Barry White; jazz great Pearl Bailey and her husband, Louis Bellson; former champ Joe Louis; Yankee great Joe DiMaggio; comedian Slappy White; Olympic boxing sensation Sugar Ray Leonard; tennis superstars Jimmy Connors and Ilie Nastase; movie star Donald Sutherland; and "Kojak"'s Telly Savalas.

Buford Green: *Right before the fight, I got up to use the restroom, and when I got back, Telly Savalas was in my seat. Savalas had an enormous ego and must have had about five bodyguards with him that night. Anyway, I found out who was running the publicity for the fight—a man named John X—had him come over and ask Mr. Savalas to leave. Telly wouldn't, so John X had his own private security guards escort Mr. Savalas out of my seat. When Mr. Savalas left, the press gave him a standing ovation because they didn't like him, and I got my seat back.*

Most professional athletes I know are superstitious, and each one has a unique way of getting ready for the big game or event. I also had a strange ritual that I performed in the dressing room before getting ready for a fight. Everything started from the left side. First, I put on the left sock, then the right; then my left shoe, then the right; the left hand was taped first then the right; then the left glove was put on before the right one.

Once we entered the ring, Ali stopped in each corner, motioning to the crowd to join him in chanting, "Norton must fall! Norton must fall!" The strategy worked for Ali the night he regained the heavyweight title from Foreman in Zaire. That night, Ali had the large African crowd chanting, "Ali, Bomayee, Ali, Bomayee." In English, it meant, "Ali, kill him." Surprisingly, on this night in Yankee Stadium, the apathetic crowd did not join in the battle cry.

Before the opening bell, Ali talked trash to me and wound his right hand around like a windmill in an attempt to mess with my psyche. But he forgot that this was the night I was going to take the world by storm. I was going to beat Muhammad Ali for the world's heavyweight championship.

At the bell, Ali came out of his corner with a goofy expression on his face. Then we both got down to business. We came out moving and circling, getting a feel for each other, even though we had battled two previous times. Ali attempted the first strike, missing me with a left hook but landing a soft overhand right. He was much more flat-footed than I expected, and that was good for me, because I wanted him to go toe-to-toe with me. We circled each other and then stopped to punch. Ali threw most of the punches that round, but I was more selective with mine. Near the end of the first round, Ali caught me with a decent right hand at the tail end of a combination. We clinched and then the bell rang. The first round went to Ali.

Ali decided not to sit in his corner and rest between the first and second rounds. I matched him and stood in my corner. I didn't even take a drink of water. Hell, I didn't even break a sweat because I was in such great condition. Once again, Ali tried to get the crowd to yell, "Norton must fall! Norton must fall!" Before round two, Ali looked at me and continued to taunt me, windmilling his right arm, waiting for the bell.

In the second round I applied pressure. I hunted down Ali and threw left jabs at his head and body. All the while, Ali was talking trash to me. "Come on, Norton, your mama can hit harder than that. I thought you were gonna give me a fight. Do something. This is for the title. Come on, do something."

"I am doing something," I shot back. "I'm taking your title!"

Seconds later, I scored with a looping overhand right, and we clinched. When we broke free, I measured him out with left jabs so I could connect big with a strong overhand right. Then it was Ali's turn: He caught me by faking a left jab and hit me with a strong overhand right. The tide turned when I applied pressure once more and began to go to work on his body, along with a few punches to his head. Ali countered with a few hard straight rights. I covered up while he punched at me; then after a break, we traded more punches until the bell. As I walked back to my corner, I could hear the mouth heard 'round the world jawing at me. Usually I ignored his nonsense, but I was so intense that night, I stopped, turned on my heel, and answered back to him. He was mad at me because I took round two.

Before round three, Ali was again windmilling his right hand. At the bell, he charged at me but stopped when he got near striking distance. He was about to run into my right hand, had he not stopped. Then he changed his tune and began to move and dance. I hunted him down and confused him with herky-jerky movements. I slipped or blocked most of the punches he threw. Ali was winding up to throw a big right hand when I stepped in and countered with a left jab, followed by a solid overhand right, and doubled up on a left hook to Ali's body and head. Ali answered back, landing a right hand of his own. I shook it off and threw a left jab to the body followed by a hard looping overhand right that shook Ali. Sensing his lethargy, I pursued him into the ropes, where I caught him once more with an overhand right. Ali attempted to counter but landed nothing before the bell rang. The judges gave this round to Ali because of his early activity in the ring. However, I hit him with the big shots. Many boxing writers and experts gave me the round, and so did I. According to my scorecard, I was ahead two rounds to one.

Round four started off with the two of us circling each other again, tossing out the occasional light jab. Ali countered with an overhand right and picked up the tempo, throwing a volley of punches at me. I instinctively covered up to block further punches. When we broke free, I missed him with a wild overhand right. I corrected and caught Ali with a vicious overhand right that buckled his knees. He held on to consciousness by the grace of God. Unfortunately, there wasn't much time left in the round, but I continued to stay on the offensive and pinned Ali to the ropes, landing several punches. I could see no other way than to give the round to me. Now, I had a comfortable lead at three rounds to one.

Before the fight, Ali had predicted to the media that he'd knock me out in the fifth round, so at the bell, the stakes were a bit higher and the crowd was brimming with electricity. Before the sound of the bell, Ali made a mock attempt to paw me with a glove. Keeping in mind that this was the round in which Ali was going to knock me out, I made sure to come out swinging. I came out aggressively in round five and pinned Ali to the ropes, scoring with devastating blows to the body, followed by uppercuts and hooks to the head. Ali then went into the rope-a-dope technique that tired out Foreman, but I used it to my advantage by landing an assortment of hooks, uppercuts, and crunching right hands. I was hitting him with heavy punches, scoring with hard left hooks. It was mystifying to me, because it seemed as if Ali was pissing away this round on purpose. Even though he caught me with a combination at the bell, round five was mine across the board; it wasn't even close. Once again, I scooped up another round and was clearly in the lead at four to one.

In round six, I took the fight to Ali by stalking him, landing a few stiff jabs. He had to retreat. Ali was talking to me, covering up and holding the back of my head as I stayed on the offensive. The crowd began chanting, "Ali, Ali!" in an attempt to see the legend pull out one more miracle. Ali took the time to respond to the crowd, but I bum-rushed him and backed him into the ropes, banging away with punches to the head and body. I missed him with some wild uppercuts as he attempted to stiff-arm me, trying to keep me at bay. Ali then waved me in as he lay against the ropes. I accepted his invitation and stayed busy throwing combinations. The fight then moved to the center of the ring, but it didn't matter where the fight moved: I was on Ali like ants on a picnic. I caught him again with a punishing left hand that doubled up The Champ. That punch really hurt the man, but once again, the bell was my foe and saved Ali from further damage. Round six was mine with an exclamation point. My scorecard read Norton five, Ali one.

Not only did I have a commanding lead, but I was in such great condition that I remained standing in my corner, showing Ali I came to Yankee Stadium to take his belt. Ali stood defiantly in his corner trying to match me, but it was clear to everyone that he wasn't the Muhammad Ali of old.

By now it was getting to be routine: The bell would sound and I would circle Ali like a wild animal. I started off the round with a few stiff left jabs that caught him on the chin. Ali countered with overhand rights, but didn't connect like he would have liked to because of my confusing head feints and side-to-side upper-body movement. I pinned him against the ropes and fired off a few strong left hooks to his body. Ali began jabbing and caught me with a few combinations to my head. He picked up the pace and started going toe-to-toe with me, but I was willing to do that. Ali sensed it wasn't a very smart thing to do, and he kept moving and jabbing until the bell. Not much happened in this round, and I'm willing to give it to Ali because he clearly landed more punches. My scorecard now read 5-2 in my favor.

I came out pressing the attack in round eight, and Ali answered with a counter overhand right that scored mightily. I employed jerky head and body movements to confuse Ali, and I cut off the ring to get him into the corner. Ali lay against the ropes as I let go with a repertoire of shots to the head and body. The action moved back to the center of the ring, where I scored again, this time with a vicious right hook to the body. I then trapped Ali on the ropes and scored with a combination of hooks to the head and body. Ali fired back with light punches, but they didn't have much sting. I retaliated with some punishing shots, and all Ali could do was cover up against the ropes. The best punch of the fight occurred when I got off a left hook to Ali's midsection that made him visibly wince. I knew that hurt.

At the bell, I decided to stay at the center of the ring and give Ali some of the treatment he was famous for, and I confidently began to tell him that the belt was mine. "You don't want it bad enough tonight, Ali." Round eight was all mine, and it was going to take a knockout punch or an act of God for Ali to win. The Norton scorecard was now 6-2 in my favor.

Right before the bell, Ali turned to his corner and boldly claimed, "It's time to get this sucker." My words must have infuriated Ali because in round nine he came out the aggressor, moving and dancing, popping out jabs that connected. The crowd came alive. I attempted to cut off the ring but was greeted with the Ali shuffle. For once, he was confusing me with his side-to-side movement, landing rapid jabs to my face. I stayed in pursuit but was missing him with counter jabs. Ali kept up his jabbing when, all of a sudden, I caught him with a hard looping right that sent him to the nearest corner. Ali held on to me, then resumed moving and jabbing until the bell. Although it was close, the round went to Ali, and my scorecard shifted to 6-3 in my favor.

Ali led the charge once more going into the 10th round, successfully moving and flicking out the jab. Ali raised his arm, leading the crowd in an "Ali, Ali" chant. I chased him down, attempting to cut off the ring and make him fight my fight. I was successfully slipping and blocking Ali's jab, counterpunching him in the process. I pinned him in a corner and fired away with hard body punches. Ali tried to keep me off him with jabs, but my unorthodox rhythm was throwing off his timing. With little time left in the round, I landed a volley of punches and the round was over. I was clearly the aggressor and landed a lot more hard punches; therefore, I thought I won the round. That gave me a 7-3 advantage going into the 11th round.

We came out circling each other in round 11, and then Ali fired off a couple of quick combinations. I answered back with a right and left hook that found Ali's jaw. I retreated to the ropes and waited for him to take the bait. I held my hands to my side and bobbed, slipping Ali's punches. Taunting him, I clapped and waved him in for more. I could see by how big his eyes got that he clearly didn't like to be on the other side of the teasing. It was the first bit of showboating that I had done in our entire three-bout series, and the crowd clearly loved it.

Ali took the bait and came into my lair, where we mixed it up, trading punches. He countered with a stiff jab that landed flush on my jaw. In return I landed some stinging left jabs and continued in pursuit. I managed to pin him to the ropes and landed a combination at the bell. Another close round, but I'd have to give it to Ali because he landed 14 right hands on my jaw, 10 of them clean. He inched closer to the lead, but my scorecard still had me ahead 7-4.

In round 12 I started off by connecting with a stiff left jab that snapped Ali's head back. He quickly recovered and landed a barrage of punches at ring center, but I stood my ground and fired back a left and straight right. Ali retreated back to the ropes, where I followed him, digging in with hard left hooks to his head and body, followed by hard, looping right hands. The action then returned to ring center, where Ali accidentally thumbed me in the left eye. I know it was an accident because one thing Muhammad Ali was not was a dirty fighter. He had way too much pride to intentionally do such a thing. Because my vision was blurred, I retreated to the ropes when Ali landed a combination at the bell. This round was way too close to give it to either fighter, so I considered round 12 a draw. My scorecard now read 7-4-1.

In my corner, Bill Slayton quickly applied ice to my left eye and luckily it was OK and wouldn't hinder the outcome of the fight. In round 13, I went on the offensive by peppering Ali with stiff jabs, and as he lay on the ropes, I caught him with a couple of nice, hard body shots. Ali fired back with a sharp combination. Ali continued to jab, but I stepped in to counter with a few jabs of my own. I ducked and blocked most of Ali's punches, when the action suddenly heated up. Both of us exchanged solid punches as I followed Ali into the ropes. I started banging away with hard punches to Ali's head and body. Ali then tied me up to prevent further onslaught, and the bell sounded as we continued trading punches in ring center. No question about it: Round 13 was all mine and I was inching closer to the heavyweight title 8-4-1. I would later find out, all three judges gave the round to Ali.

As I went over to my corner, I looked over at Ali. He was standing up in his corner as well, but he was leaning over, hanging on the ropes with a hangdog look on his face, trying to conserve energy. His chest was heaving up and down, and I knew I was in far better condition. The bell sounded for round 14 and I came out jabbing. Ali planted and fired off a left-and-right combination. I came back with lefts and rights to the body and head. My jabs kept connecting to his head and body, throwing the reigning champion out of rhythm. Ali attempted to pick up the tempo, firing off punches. I kept out of harm's way by using bobs and head feints to keep him off stride. Ali threw several punches, but he was greeted by a firm counter left jab. I caught him with a looping right followed by a left hook. Ali countered with a three-punch combination in ring center and stayed on the attack as I winged him with a couple of nice jabs. I missed him with a wild right hand as he kept punching away. I followed him into the ropes, throwing and landing a few shots before the bell sounded. Another close round, but I felt it was mine because I was the aggressor and landed more and harder shots. In my mind, I had already won the fight because, even if Ali won the next round, I still had the majority of the rounds. My personal scorecard read 9-4-1.

The bell sounded for round 15, and Ali and I met at the center ring and tapped gloves. When you tap gloves in boxing, it's a sign that it's nothing personal; you respect each other, but you're also going to do your damnedest to tear the other guy's head off.

As soon as our gloves touched, Ali went into his dance mode. I think he was trying to show the judges that he still had a lot of energy left and it carried a lot of weight. As he danced, I attempted to cut off the ring because Ali kept moving side to side. I stayed in pursuit, blocking most of his jabs, and attempted to counter with jabs of my own. I caught Ali with a three-punch combination on the ropes when he put a clinch on the back of my head to prevent any follow-up punching. From the break, Ali got back to doing what he did best: moving and jabbing. In an effort to score some big points, I lunged at him, trying to get off a few last punches as the bell neared. At this point, Ali was dancing away from me and I was winging punches. Finally, I managed to pin him to the ropes and flailed away with some good punches. The action slowly moved toward the center of the ring and then the bell sounded to end the fight. I stood there at the center as Ali walked by and I yelled, "You don't win! I beat you, you son of a bitch. I beat you!"

Ali held his head down, dejected. He had a forlorn look on his face that I'd never seen before. Before I knew what hit me, Bill swooped into the ring to pick me up and lift me in the air. Everyone in my corner was hamming it up, yelling and screaming at the top of their lungs. The world heavyweight championship was mine!

It is an unwritten rule in boxing that when a fight is over, you must look like you just won the fight whether you think you did or not. My corner certainly didn't need to act out that ritual, but I couldn't help but notice that Ali's corner resembled mourners at a funeral. Ali looked dejected, his head hung low, his nose slowly dripping blood. He looked old, tired, and beat up.

Total elation is how I would describe my feeling in the ring at that moment. I was smiling and crying at the same time. I had been chasing the brass ring for close to 10 years, and I had accomplished the unthinkable, beating Muhammad Ali for the heavyweight championship of the world. Hollywood couldn't have scripted a better story. Now all I needed was the official confirmation from the judges.

A calm quiet had descended over Yankee Stadium when the ring announcer read the judges' scorecards.

"Referee Arthur Mercante scored the bout 8-6-1. Judge Harold Lederman scored the bout 8-7-0, and Judge Barney Smith scored the bout 8-7-0 in favor of the world champion, Muhammad Ali."

The big television screen in center field had Ali's name on it, and the word "winner" flashed on and off. The judges' decision was greeted by a chorus of boos from the crowd. One fan at ringside yelled, "I don't believe it! Norton killed him."

I had gone from total elation to complete devastation in a matter of seconds. My emotional pendulum had swung from one end to the other. Did I hear the announcer right? Didn't I just beat Muhammad Ali by the biggest margin of all three of our fights? The fight wasn't even close.

I placed my hands over my eyes and sobbed uncontrollably. I hurt so much, I felt as if someone had ripped my heart out of my chest.

Brent Musberger of CBS tried to ask me a few questions, but I just wrapped a towel around my face and wept like a child. He never received a response to his questions. Then Musberger went over to Ali's corner, and he didn't grant an interview either. Imagine that! Ali not giving an interview.

When a fight is close, boxing officials usually award the victory to the champion. Let me say that again. When the fight is *close*, when there is doubt. Not since James J. Braddock was awarded a 15-round decision over Max Baer at the Long Island City Bowl in 1935 was a heavyweight champion dethroned on judgment day. Unfortunately for me, Ali kept that long-running tradition alive.

The crowd booed vehemently and showed its disapproval of the judges' decision by overturning the first two rows of chairs, rioting, slashing tires, and jumping on cars and trying to turn them over. Unruly youths brushed by an elderly lady in the stands, knocking her down so hard that she broke her leg.

To add insult to injury, the fight generated much less money than was predicted. A crowd of 54,000 fans had been expected, but only 30,249 ended up paying $2.4 million, added to a live gate of $12 million from closed-circuit revenues. Part of that revenue was lost because of an argument between Top Rank's Bob Arum and Teddy Brenner. Brenner wanted the fight to be blacked out in the local New York area so that the seats in Yankee Stadium would get snapped up. Arum vetoed and lost 20,000 sales in seat revenue.

Brenner was retiring from the fight game and Ali-Norton III was going to be his swan song. When the fight was over, Brenner, who had just witnessed a night of chaos and anarchy, prophetically predicted to the media, "This is the last heavyweight title fight you'll see in a New York ballpark." His words have remained true: there hasn't been one in more than 23 years.

Due to the unruly crowd, Ali needed to get to safety in a hurry. After most victories, Ali liked to dance around for the crowd and savor his win, but not on this night. He was swooped up by his entourage and taken to his dressing room as if he were a dictator of a fallen regime, and the last of the faithful were trying to protect his life at all costs.

Once in the dressing room, Ali was examined by Dr. Ferdie Pacheco, who noticed that Ali was strangely quiet that night. Ali was the first to speak what was on his mind.

"I think it's time for me to call it quits. I mean, if I can't even beat Norton . . . " Ferdie remained silent while Ali poured out his soul.

"I don't have it anymore. I was not myself out there. I see the things to do, but I can't do them," Ali lamented. "Norton will always be hard for me."

If Ali's corner after the fight resembled a funeral, my dressing room had to be as quiet as a morgue. The only sounds heard were my muffled cries for some sort of explanation as to why the judges ruled in Ali's favor.

"What do I have to do to beat him?" I asked the press who assembled in my dressing room. My eyes searched the room for an answer but there was no response.

Around 1:30 in the morning, Ferdie came into my dressing room to offer his condolences. I always liked Ferdie because he was and is a straight shooter and a sincere guy.

"It was a helluva fight, Kenny, and after three fights I still don't know who won any of them. If it's any consolation to you, I think you retired Ali," Ferdie offered.

I held back my tears and couldn't think of a future in boxing without at least another shot at Ali.

"If he retires, I retire. I don't want to fight anyone else but Ali again."

"Kenny, stay in the game," the doctor said. "You've still got a few good years in you. Pick up the big money; that's the name of the game."

"Thanks, Doc."

We shook hands and then Ferdie left. He was just as distraught as I was, but for different reasons. He had just witnessed the night Ali was no longer Ali, but that didn't take away my pain of losing a world championship fight in front of the whole world.

It's always been my belief that boxing wasn't ready to give up Muhammad Ali yet. He single-handedly brought the sport of boxing to new heights. Everybody in and out of boxing who knew him loved him. He was such a charismatic and controversial figure that once he left the fight game, who would replace him? I can't help but believe that this thought swayed the judges, who ruled in Ali's favor.

Twelve days after the fight, the *New York Times* freelance writer and former heavyweight pugilist, Randy Neumann, put it eloquently when he wrote his sardonic take on the fight in an open letter. "Ken, you have my commiseration. Ali, being a living legend, is a hometown fighter wherever he fights. The world is his backyard. Only he can score points by lying on the ropes, dancing around and auditioning for a position in a topless-bottomless lounge by shimmying his hips inside Everlast trunks.

"Beating Ali by a decision is like giving Jack Nicklaus a stroke a hole: You're beat before you start."

Even 20 years later, the January 1998 issue of *Boxing Monthly* magazine listed Ali-Norton III as the fifth-most-disputed decision in boxing history that had world title billing.

What happened to me on that September night in Yankee Stadium wasn't a simple mugging or highway robbery. No, what the three judges did to me that night was nothing short of grand larceny, and I'll never be convinced otherwise.

The first time I fought Ali, I felt it was an honor just to be in the same ring with him. The second fight was closer than the first. I thought I won by a slight margin and the judges gave it to him. About the fight in Yankee Stadium, I was very bitter. I owned him.

I wasn't bitter toward Ali, because Muhammad brought out the best in me. He was the best fighter of all time, and I've always respected him. Very few men would give up the things he gave up for his beliefs, and I admire the hell out of him. I've always liked Ali. I liked him before we fought; I liked him after we fought: Just not during.

Chapter Thirteen

The Aftermath

The judges' decision was so controversial that CBS replayed the fight the following Saturday and went round by round with the three judges and news announcers analyzing the fight. That was the first time I can recall a boxing match being questioned so openly. Referee Arthur Mercante and Judge Harold Lederman have been gracious enough to offer their reasons for voting in favor of Ali.

Arthur Mercante (referee): *I knew that Norton was real displeased with the decision. You know, it was unanimous. Presumably, we had the best officials on the fight. I had it very, very close, as a matter of fact. I had heard Ken's cornerman, Bill Slayton, tell him at the time of the fight before the final round, "Look, be careful, you have this fight. Go out there and take it easy because you have it made." Words to that effect. But anyway, that was the discerning round in my estimation because there was a great big controversy about the fight.*

All of the newspapermen in the New York area went to a restaurant called Gallagher's on 52nd Street, and they had us all on a panel and asked us to give an opinion of the fight. After much discussion, I said, "What we ought to do, gentlemen, is frame this into three parts, that is, the final round. Get the film, frame the first minute of the last round, figure out who scored the most points, frame the second minute, score that, then frame the last minute, score that."

As it had turned out, Norton hadn't thrown that many punches, and Ali was within the range of 33 to 45 punches thrown that made contact against 13-15 of Norton's. Then they printed it in the paper that they all agreed that Ali did win that last round. That last round won the fight on my card for Ali. It was close, no question about it, but I felt firmly that I made the right decision.

There's no doubt that Ken was the more aggressive fighter in that match. In boxing terminology, it's known as the "effective aggressor." You can be an aggressor, and as you're going in, you can be hit. Ali was great for that. Ali could throw lots of jabs as he was backing off and connect. You have to be a Frazier; an effective aggressor. You have to move in, make contact, do some damage. If you're the aggressor and chasing and chasing and not hitting anything, it doesn't count for anything.

You can have 10 judges judge a fight, and all 10 will have differing opinions. Every round will be scored differently. One will have it even. The other will have it another way. It happens in boxing. I hate to use the term subjective, because in boxing I believe it's objective, but all of the judges say, "Hey, it's subjective. It's my opinion." That's how they get off the hook.

Referees were actually scoring in those days. We're not now. I think it was 10 to 12 years ago that we stopped scoring fights. During the Norton-Ali fight, I was, and I scored the fight 8-6-1.

Norton had the kind of style that mystified Ali. He just couldn't figure him out. Norton had a "peek-a-boo" style that Cus D'Amato used to teach, covering up his face, etc. Ken was a tough guy, but Ken was easy for some others.

I recall being called in for an interview by Howard Cosell the following day, and I remember Norton coming into the waiting room. We saw each other there. He was not unfriendly, but he didn't say anything. He was disappointed and I can't say I blame him. It was a very close fight.

Harold Lederman (judge): *There were an awful lot of Ali supporters, and because of television, there were an awful lot of Norton supporters. I think a lot of people sitting ringside felt the way I did: that was that Ali nudged him out. But there were a lot of people out there watching television, and because of the favorable commentary on Norton's behalf, they felt he won. To tell you the truth, Ali-Norton III was terribly close.*

In scoring a fight, you have to go back to the basics. The criteria for scoring each round is based on four points: clean punching, effective aggressiveness, ring generalship, and defense.

Clean punching is obviously clean or hard shots. Effective aggressiveness is if the guy is coming forward and at the same time landing punches. Defense is when the boxer has his hands up high, he's picking off shots on his gloves, elbows, and forearms; he's ducking under and slipping the other guy's punches. Ring generalship is the guy who's controlling the fight from the ring; keeping a guy where you want him, keeping him off balance, so on and so on. A good example of ring generalship is when Sugar Ray Leonard fought Marvin Hagler and kept him from fighting his fight. But that's the textbook answer. The true answer is the rounds are scored mainly on clean punching; clean, effective punching is about 90 percent, and the other 10 percent is attributed to the other three elements. What it all comes down to at the end of the round is, "Who did more damage?" If a round is very, very close, then you look at those other three elements. If Ali's jabs did more damage in a round than one of Norton's good overhand rights, then Ali wins that round. In essence, that's what it boils down to. In Ali's case, he really did control the fight and won a lot of rounds on ring generalship, no question.

I think you had three relatively competent judges for that fight. I was relatively young—at that time I had been judging professionally for 10 years along with two years as an amateur. Then you had Bobby Smith and the legendary Arthur Mercante. If three guys saw it so close, 8-7, 8-7, 8-6-1, you have to believe that maybe Ali won the decision.

The one thing that really sticks in my mind is when you have a corner like Norton's with Bill Slayton, Bossman Jones, and Pat O'Grady— three real boxing pros—and they tell Ken to coast during the last round. I've never seen such an experienced corner in all of my profession, and their telling Ken that he had the fight was preposterous. I mean, I couldn't believe it; these three guys telling him that during a championship fight.

After the sixth round, the tide started to turn. I believe I was the only guy who gave Kenny Norton rounds two through six. Five rounds in a row. I had him with a huge early lead, and then Ali started to turn it on. Then Kenny won the eighth round, so that made him the 6-2 leader after eight rounds. Then Ali turned it on, and those three guys told him to coast in the last round and that just killed him. Had he come out and thrown punches like he did in the last 15 seconds of the fight, he probably would have won the round. He certainly would have won it on my scorecard. For 2 minutes, 45 seconds, all he did was suck up Ali's jab. He stalked him, stalked him, stalked him, and that's a case of ineffective aggressiveness.

Mercante, Smith, and I all gave the last round to Ali, and that was the deciding round. My God, Norton gave the 15th round away. I remember later, because of the controversy, CBS brought in

10 people to score the fight, and I don't think that's ever been done again. Those are the things that stayed with me all these years.

One more thing: When you watch a fight on television, you lose the velocity of the punch, especially with a guy like Ali, who jabs a lot. The only way you can tell on TV is if the opponent's head snaps back or he's knocked down. When the replay was shown on television, the audience lost the velocity of the punch. People don't realize how hard Ali's jabs were; good, solid jabs without question. Even if you go back 10 rows, you lose the velocity of the punch, and that's why I think the public was in favor of Norton for that fight.

Dan Schocket (journalist): *Muhammad Ali's third fight against Ken Norton was his one fight too many. The magic was gone; the body no longer superb. Although it was a fine performance by a skilled craftsman, there was no greatness. And greatness is the reason people pay large fortunes for Ali's services. Still, on September 28, 1976, Ken Norton was a better fighter than Muhammad Ali. Ali the fighter was not given the decision over Ken Norton. His legend was.*

Bill Slayton: *I disagree with Mercante and Lederman completely. In Ali-Norton III, Kenny just plain beat him, and I was very hurt. The reason we lost the fight was due to the politics of boxing. Whoever generates the money in the fight, and if he is with the promoter, will get the nod on the close fight. That third fight wasn't even close. The referee and the judges knew that if Norton had the title, Norton would bring in a few million dollars. But they also knew that if Ali had the title, Ali would bring in a lot more. Ali's name was more important. I told everybody that it wasn't a fixed fight, but sometimes people realize who the "house fighter" is. Nobody told 'em, "That's my fighter there in the red corner," but always notice the color of the padding in the corner. It's usually red or blue. But with Kenny, we were never the house corner, because Bob Biron was always a lone wolf. Bob never stayed with one promoter. He always went with whoever was the most lucrative contract.*

Joe Frazier: *I think Ken beat his ass in all three fights, but clearly he won that night in Yankee Stadium, I was there in person to witness it ringside. I think Ken outsmarted Ali. He was in better condition, and he handled himself like a champ. I gave him 10 rounds to five.*

Ferdie Pacheco (Ali's fight doctor): *That was the night Ali stopped being Ali. It was the night all fighters dread, the night when the body can no longer do what the mind dictates, when thoughts cannot be translated into instant action, when reflexes fail, and the body begins to feel the punishment and the exhaustion.*

Angelo Dundee (Ali's trainer): *I thought all three of their fights were close, but Kenny had a style that would give Muhammad Ali trouble every day of the week and twice on Sunday. I used to call Kenny the Hopalong Cassidy of boxing due to his unique style and rhythm. He had a style that just put Ali off-kilter and kept him off balance.*

Eddie Futch: *I thought Ken won all three fights against Muhammad Ali, but Ali had such a great name, which persuaded the judges. I personally felt the last fight of the series against Ali was Ken's best fight, but the judges gave it to Ali.*

Muhammad Ali (as told to *Ring* magazine): *Ken Norton is the toughest man I have faced. He hit me more than I've ever been hit before, and I was in great condition.*

Buford Green: *One of the New York papers read the next day, "NORTON MUGGED IN FRONT OF 30,000 PEOPLE." I also remember the scene in Ali's dressing room that night. A black journalist was asking Ali in front of all of the press, "How long do you think you can keep fooling the American public?" Ali was steamed and said something to the effect of, "I'll beat your black ass right now, and we'll see who's fooling who." I don't think I'd ever seen Ken so down. It was very traumatic, and I've thought over many times how that fight changed the history of boxing dramatically in that it would have been Ali's swan song. Ken would have been bigger for a longer time than he was and would have been able to call more shots. I think Ken would have been even more dominant in the heavyweight division than he was.*

That fight took a lot of my soul away from me. Honestly, I was exasperated because I had done all the right things, trained right, made painful sacrifices to get to the top, fought all of the top contenders, beat Muhammad Ali in front of the nation, and yet I still came out with the short end of the stick.

It wasn't quite so easy to block out this loss to Ali like I did with other defeats. This particular fight galled me. It wounded deeply. The fight was a once-in-a-lifetime opportunity, and I did everything right and it wasn't enough. Twenty-two years later I sat down to view the videotape to critique the fight for this book, and even then, it was still painful to watch.

Once again I considered retiring, because if I couldn't fight Ali again, I didn't want to fight. Finances dictated my staying in the game. I didn't know what other field would pay me more money, and I still had a good five years left in me to make top dollar. From that point on, I was in boxing strictly for the money, not for the love of the sport. Although I would eventually go on to become the heavyweight champion of the world, my heart just wasn't in it.

After that third Ali fight, I never trained the same or ran as much. Mentally, I was drained. I'd work out in the gym and do what I was told to do, but I was never the same fighter that I was for that fight.

What lessened the pain from my defeat at the hands of Ali was the birth of my first and only daughter, Kenisha Eronda Norton. Kenisha was born August 4, 1976, at Cedars Sinai in Los Angeles six weeks before my third fight with Ali. I decided after the Yankee Stadium fight I would turn my focus toward Jackie, our new daughter, and our two sons, because they had sacrificed so much during my career.

I don't know what it was about Kenisha or having a daughter, but being a parent was now different. Kenisha brought about a change in me, a different kind of love a father has for a child. She stole my heart. I tried so hard not to spoil her or give her any special treatment, but what can I say? She was daddy's little girl, and naturally, she got away with a lot more.

Kenisha Norton (Ken's daughter): *I think that being an only daughter, naturally, I was going to get away with more. I was always "Daddy's little girl," and I never feared him in any way like my brothers did. Being the only girl, I could get away with a lot, but that definitely did not work with my mom.*

Were we spoiled? Oh, we were spoiled, but not spoiled rotten. None of us kids were pampered to the point of most Hollywood kids. They are spoiled to the point of expecting things. We were never raised to think that we were better than anyone else. As a matter of fact, I always took offense when people in school assumed that I was a spoiled brat because I've always gone out of my way to not behave like that. People are always so shocked that the Norton kids are so

down-to-earth. I've had many people come up to me later and com-
ment, "I thought you were going to be a certain way but I'm pleas-
antly surprised to find out that you're so normal."

The thought of quitting now was absurd; I was still rated the
No. 1 contender in the world by two of boxing's governing bodies, the
World Boxing Council and the World Boxing Association. Big-money
offers were still rolling in, but the first legitimate offer, a tasty one indeed,
that lured me back into fighting was by boxing's latest "Great White Hope,"
Duane Bobick.

My purse guaranteed me $500,000 to Bobick's $300,000 for a
12-round fight on March 2, 1977, in Madison Square Garden, the location where I had picked apart Jerry Quarry almost two years before. The
fight had to be rescheduled for May 11, 1977. Bobick suffered torn rib
cartilage while sparring with his brother Rodney.

Bobick had defeated Larry Holmes in the 1972 Olympic Trials,
but was defeated by the legendary Teofilo Stevenson of Cuba in the
quarterfinals of the Munich Olympics.

Bobick hailed from Bowlus, Minnesota, but fought out of Philadelphia, and began mounting, on paper, a stellar 38-0 professional record,
32 of which were by knockout. That overhyped record was built up through
your typical tomato-can, bum-of-the-month-club, and journeyman fighters. Joe Frazier bought out Bobick's contract after 16 fights and took over
his career, with Eddie Futch as his hands-on trainer. Frazier had retired
from boxing the year before and could see the potential Bobick had as a
fighter.

Joe Frazier: *I was Duane Bobick's fight manager at the
time of the Norton fight, and Duane also was represented by a lawyer and a financial manager. I was his manager and sparring partner, but he listened to those two guys over me. The lawyer and manager thought Ken Norton was too old and over the hill, yet still had
name value. I asked these guys, "How in the world do you figure Ken
Norton's through? He kicked Ali's ass last September; why would you
think he's through?" I told them that Duane wasn't ready for Ken,
but they voted me down 2-1. Duane's big problem was that he didn't
listen to people.*

The fight also had another major incentive: There was a standing
offer by California promoter Ben Thompson that the winner would get a

shot at Muhammad Ali in a championship fight in Rio de Janeiro in October 1977. Once again, I would get another title shot at Ali, but I knew The Greatest would much rather face Bobick in the ring. It was almost comical that Ali was openly rooting for Bobick to win our match.

I must admit, part of the reason I took the fight was to show Eddie that I still had a lot to prove because Eddie felt that Bobick could beat me. In Eddie's own words, "Norton was just about ready to be taken."

> **Eddie Futch:** *At the time I took over Bobick's career, he was undefeated and was coming off of 16 straight wins. But like many other young, successful boxers, Bobick got to the point where he didn't want to listen.*
>
> *The night of the fight with Norton, Bobick had a lot of his Navy buddies in the locker room, and they were talking old times, and this and that, when Bobick should have been warming up. I knew Kenny was going to be gunning for Bobick and would be eager to try for an early knockout, so I wanted him to be ready and loose.*
>
> *I told Bobick, "Come on, knock off this conversation, let's get busy. I want you to come out really warm against Norton because he's gonna come out after you because you're with me. He's gonna be fighting me instead of you. So you're going to have to deal with a guy who's on a mission."*
>
> *For that fight, we had monitors in each of the dressing rooms so that we could observe what the other fighter was doing. We could see them and they could see us. I was watching the monitor in Ken's dressing room when he started out toward the ring. He was sweating like a horse, and Bobick was bone dry because every time I started him off, I'd get called away, some commissioner wanted to see me or some major reporter came in or whatever. Every time I looked around, Bobick was back talking to his friends. He went out bone dry and Norton came out steaming.*

I came into the match with Bobick a little heavier than usual, around 222 pounds, five pounds more than the third fight with Ali. This fight was Bobick's debut as a ranked contender, coming in at No. 5. More than 10,000 people showed up at Madison Square Garden to watch, and 42 million viewers were predicted to watch the fight on NBC.

In trying to drum up publicity for the fight, the boxing critics were quick to point out to Eddie that Bobick's record was not that impressive and they asked, "Who has Bobick fought?" Bobick's fight before his and mine had been a lackluster 10-round decision over Fred "Young Sanford" Houpe.

Eddie could get cantankerous when his judgment was called into play and he countered, "You ask about who Duane has fought before Norton. Well, who had Norton fought before I took him into the ring against Muhammad Ali for the first time? Duane Bobick knows all he needs to know. I think we're making a good move now with Duane."

When asked for a comment, I angrily retorted, "I'm going to make a liar out of him. He doesn't know as much as he thinks he knows." This fight was becoming a battle between Eddie Futch and Ken Norton. I had nothing personally against Bobick, but I was going to make sure Eddie was going to eat his words through his overhyped boxer.

Once again, Eddie was asked to reply to my comment, and his words were biting and scornful. "Norton's not as quick as he thinks he is. Outside of Ali and Foreman, Norton hasn't fought anybody better than Duane fought. Jerry Quarry had come out of retirement to fight Ken and had only 10 days to get ready. I made most of the other fights, so I know. I think Norton's chin is more suspect than Duane's. I've had to pick Norton up off the floor a couple of times. And that's not easy.

"I like this fight for Duane very much," Eddie continued. "There was no one fight where he could gain more and lose less. There are other fighters around whose styles might be more difficult for Duane, but why take them when Norton is the road to a sure title shot?"

OK, my man, we'll see, I thought to myself. We'll see come fight night who's a sure thing.

Bobick even played off of Eddie and mouthed off to the *Minneapolis Star,* "I've never felt so good, trained so hard or felt so prepared for a fight as I have this one. I feel a lot quicker. My left jab is better. He fights flat-footed and can't move back. He proved that in the George Foreman fight. So I'm willing to go toe to toe and slug it out with him.

"Norton is a different type of fighter. He's a fighter—if you give him room, he's going to beat you. I'm not going to give him any room. I'm going to be in on him. We have to wait and see if he can stand up to the pressure and make him work hard. Once the bell rings, everything will be great," Bobick said.

He bragged that his best weapon was his aggressive body attack that wears down the body. I made sure he wouldn't get that opportunity.

Our fight had a feeling of Hollywood as show-biz introductions were made. The Garden was darkened as Bobick and I entered the ring under spotlights. In the dark, I accidentally walked into the microphone suspended from above, which produced many laughs. The announcer introduced me as "the man they call the uncrowned heavyweight champion," in reference to my disputed loss to Ali.

Bobick, the 2-1 underdog, was clearly the crowd favorite. He entered the ring wearing a floral wreath, but I was going to make damned sure it was a funeral wreath for his professional career.

At the opening bell, both of us came immediately to the center of the ring and exchanged jabs and tried rights, looking for an opening. I found the first opening in Bobick's leaky defense. When he didn't come to me, I went to him. I threw a right to the body because I wanted to see where Bobick's eyes would go. His eyes went down, and I pounded home a blistering overhand right that caught Bobick's chin. Many experts felt that I hit Bobick's Adam's apple. Even Bobick thought so; but what actually happened was that Bobick's chin was knocked downward, and it was his chin that hit his throat, not my punch.

While Bobick clutched for air, I lashed out four more smashing right hands to the head. The final blow that derailed Bobick was a roundhouse swing that caught him on the side of the head and sent him downward as the crowd of 10,000 Garden fans came to their feet.

Bobick rolled over on his right shoulder and struggled to his feet, and referee Petey Della motioned for him to continue. When it became apparent to Della that Bobick was out on his feet, he signaled that the fight was over. A first-round victory! The fight was comparable to a tornado striking a Kansas farm house.

Bill Slayton: *Kenny had a vendetta going with Eddie Futch because Eddie had left him to work with Joe Frazier, who had retired by now. Kenny kept saying, "Eddie think's he's smart. Eddie thinks Bobick can beat me. I'm going to show Eddie, I'm going to show him." Kenny showed him all right. First-round knockout.*

When Bobick got back to his dressing room, his sense of humor was still intact as he playfully told the press, "Brush that resin dust off my knees. I'm always a slow starter. I guess I started even slower than usual." When the NBC announcers showed up for a post-fight interview, he asked, "Guess you guys had a lot of time to fill, huh?"

In all, it took just 58 seconds to finish off Bobick, a Madison Square Garden record at the time. It was the easiest payday of my career.

Duane Bobick: *Joe Frazier was my manager then, and a couple of days before the fight an article appeared in the local paper that Frazier had actually picked Norton to beat me! Mentally, that really threw me off. I still have a hard time believing that Frazier actually said it—he may have been taken out of context—nonetheless, it still threw me for a loop.*

I do remember my body showed up that day in Madison Square Garden, but my head was just not there. I take nothing away from Norton; the same result could have happened, but my head was just not there.

The shot that took me out was a right uppercut that hit me in the throat. Ken could throw a mean uppercut. All I can remember about that fight is going out and jabbing a couple of tentative jabs and then waking up on the canvas and hearing the referee count four.

As far as being punched in the throat, I was real raspy and hoarse and I couldn't talk much after the fight. The punch in the throat didn't have anything to do with the outcome of the fight because Kenny defeated me fair and square. I always did and I always will have the utmost respect for Ken Norton.

Bobick's career continued, but the large hype and promises of huge paydays vanished. The media made him a prime target after our brief encounter. The next day, the *New York Times* labeled Bobick "the Great White Elephant." Johnny Carson, the host of "The Tonight Show," made Bobick the butt of many jokes in his monologue for weeks.

"Hey, did you hear about the Duane Bobick doll? Wind it up and it falls down!"

"Hey, did you hear about the one-minute commercial Duane Bobick did? It lasts 58 seconds!"

Poor Duane. I found out through the newspapers that the circus took over Madison Square Garden the day after the Bobick fight. I have to shake my head and laugh at the irony. When you think about it, is there really much difference between professional boxing and the circus?

Chapter Fourteen

A Hollow Victory

Muhammad Ali's last fight also was going to be his biggest. A proposed fight in Rio de Janeiro, Brazil, in October 1977 was to be his swan song, and the grandest exit that boxing had ever witnessed. At 35, Ali was going to retire from the boxing world, defending his title against the winner of Duane Bobick vs. Ken Norton.

Ali proposed to hold a "box-off," a tournament of top contenders for the privilege of fighting him in his last boxing match. Ali was guaranteed a $12 million payday and the challenger $2 million. Another $1 million was set aside for promoting the extravaganza, including $250,000 in training expenses for each fighter.

Ben Thompson was attempting to overthrow Don King as boxing's biggest promoter with the proposed Rio de Janeiro fight, and he claimed to have the exclusive rights to Ali's "last fight" against the Norton-Bobick survivor. Thompson also had an oral agreement with the winner of the George Foreman-Jimmy Young fight to box the winner of the Bobick fight.

Thompson was a 36-year-old Californian who made his fortune selling air-conditioning units and new cars. Like most people who followed boxing, Thompson assumed Foreman would easily dispose of Young in their San Juan, Puerto Rico, bout March 17; but Young, a Philadelphia native, shocked the boxing world when he beat Foreman in a unanimous 12-round decision. Plans for a second Ali-Foreman fight evaporated, much to Ali's relief.

Young's manager, Jack Levin, made an oral agreement with Thompson before the Foreman fight, so the deal was set. Even after the fight, Levin was happy to keep the proposed agreement. But when Thompson arrived in Philadelphia to sign the contract, Levin pulled out of the deal without any explanation.

Being a relative newcomer to the sport, Thompson was left scratching his head as to why Young would walk away from a $2 million payday.

"I can't understand this," Thompson said to his business advisor, Bill Caplan. "People in business just don't do this."

"This isn't business," Bill replied. "This is boxing. Sometimes people in boxing do things that don't make sense."

Amen to that.

What became clear later on was that Don owned Young's promotional contract, and in an effort to thwart Thompson's foray into the world of fighting, Don sandbagged Thompson and threw a monkey wrench into the works. Thompson contended that Ali, under the terms of the $12 million deal, could not defend his title against anyone except Alfredo Evangelista, in Landover, Maryland, on May 16, 1977. Then Thompson came to my camp and Bobick's camp, making the same offer.

Despite all the confusion, I needed to keep my skills sharp. The top promoters could not duck me forever, and in the meantime I tuned up against former Italian heavyweight champion Lorenzo Zanon. Zanon was a hard-looking 26 and weighed in at 206 pounds, almost 15 pounds lighter than I was. Zanon had a respectable 20-2-1 record, but only seven of those victories included a knockout. He was a finesse fighter with not much steam in his punches. I predicted to the press that I would knock him out early.

Our fight was the second bill of a five-fight series called "Night with the Heavyweights," which was aired nationally on NBC from Caesars Palace in Las Vegas August 14, 1977. The first fight aired was Young vs. Jody Ballard. NBC wanted to capitalize on the upcoming box-off between Young and me that was scheduled seven weeks later on November 5, 1977.

I watched the first fight in the dressing room on a closed-circuit monitor. Young won a unanimous decision over Ballard, but the fight went the full distance in a 10-round yawner that produced little action by either boxer. That didn't stop Young from mouthing off to the media.

"I was ready for Norton tonight," Young boasted after his victory. "I could've gone 15 rounds easily. By the 10th round I was just getting started. Norton can't fight; he's nothing but an experienced amateur. Look at all that jewelry he wears. Who does he think he is, Sammy Davis Jr.?"

When asked for a response later, I didn't mince words.

"Young could have gone 500 rounds out there tonight, but he didn't do anything, just a lot of holding and a lot of crying. Young can't hurt me; he hit Ballard with 1,000 punches tonight and none of them stunned him." You could say I made things a little more personal than I should have, but what the heck, this was boxing, and prefight banter is the key ingredient to promoting any good fight.

Zanon and I entered the ring. At the opening bell, I pressed him, moving in and out, throwing out the occasional light combination. Zanon easily took the first round on points.

Round two was more of the same, with Zanon racking up points, but midway into the round I pinned him to the ropes, catching him with a good combination. He suddenly spun me around and caught me off guard, and I picked him up in the air out of frustration. The referee warned me, rightly so, and it was one of the few times in my career that I lost my cool. Zanon continued to throw soft pitter-patter punches, and then I blasted him with a strong right hand that connected to his jaw and backed him into the ropes.

Zanon kept moving and boxing, piling up points in the process. By now, I was well behind on points. Zanon had outscored me with his awkward and perplexing movement and style. However, Bill Slayton wasn't concerned, because he knew I had the ability to take my opponent out at any given time. The only advice Bill gave me was to become more aggressive in the fifth round.

Midway through the fifth, I found an opening and battered Zanon with a good combination, but he managed to escape and started moving in on me, jabbing, getting within my reach. Now I had him where I wanted him. When he moved in, I shifted and turned him into the ropes and blistered him with a powerful overhand right that sent the former Italian champion to the canvas. After an eight-count, Zanon got up, and I swarmed all over him with a flurry of rights to the head and body. One last booming right made him see stars, and he went down for the 10-count at the bell. Under Nevada State Boxing Commission rules, the count continued after the bell, and referee Joey Giambra, a former middleweight contender, declared the fight over.

I approached that fight in a businesslike manner. I needed the workout to help get me in shape for the upcoming Young match, and Zanon offered up a game fight.

After the Zanon fight, I rested only two days before starting to train for Young. The only way to get to Ali was through Young, and I wanted Ali badly, but a new scenario was beginning to play out. The World Boxing Council told Ali that he must defend his title against the winner of my fight with Young. He was to sign a contract before December 31, 1977, or he would be stripped of his title and forfeit his championship belt. Ali would be forced to fight me for a fourth time, providing that I beat Young. The rumor mill had it that Ali was anxious to fight Young, but not so anxious to fight me again.

My fight with Young was the talk of Las Vegas betting parlors for weeks. The oddsmakers had me a 9-5 favorite, but if the fight went the full 15 rounds, the same oddsmakers, based on track record and performance, gave the nod to Young.

At the time, Young's record was a more-than-decent 22-5-2, and he had beaten some impressive opponents: Jose Luis Garcia, Earnie Shavers, Ron Lyle (twice), and, most notably, Foreman. Many of those who were present at the Ali-Young fight believed that Young deserved the decision against Ali in a close fight, but the judges were once again swayed by Ali's hypnotic charm.

Young was considered the best counterpuncher in boxing and had a reputation for suckering opponents into awkward situations. He was proclaimed a "garbage-style" fighter because he came at you with all kinds of junk.

The World Boxing Council declared the bout a heavyweight-title-elimination championship fight, and it was nationally televised by NBC. My purse was $1.75 million to Young's $1 million. More than 4,700 fans packed Caesars Palace Pavilion to watch us go to war.

Ali had suggested to the press that he would gladly meet the winner of the fight for the right price, but his price was out of this world. He had the figure of $12 million in his head and couldn't get it out ever since the proposed fight in Rio de Janeiro that never got off the ground. He was lucky to get $6 million for our fight the year before when his performance was dismal. Now he wanted promoters to double his price, which he knew no promoter would match because there was simply no way for a promoter to make money even after the ticket and closed circuit and television rights were sold. Ali was stalling.

An indignant Bob Biron bluntly told the Associated Press, "Now he (Ali) says he will fight the winner for the proper price. Now his proper price ($12 million) is something no promoter will meet." And Bob was correct. No one ever did meet that price. Bob also stated for the record, "Ali has gotten by for years with conning the public, and we feel it's time this was stopped. We don't even care how much money Ali gets for fighting Ken again. All we care about is that he gets in the damn ring."

Don King was trying to get together $8 million for a proposed Ali-Norton IV fight, and Bob gave Don 30 days to make the fight happen. Don said that Ali's manager, Herbert Muhammad, and his attorney, Charles Lomax, were taking the offer under serious consideration. Ali was just stalling for time and considering his other options.

The WBC was starting to get the picture and its president, Jose Suliaman, said to the media, "I don't care who Ali fights for or how much he fights for, just that he commit himself within 60 days to fight the winner of Norton-Young within six months or be stripped of title recognition.

When asked for my reply to that possible scenario, I responded, "I would rather win it than have it given to me. Naturally, I would accept it." Later, I would receive a lot of grief for accepting the heavyweight championship belt without winning the actual fight, but Ali knew what was coming down the pike if he did defend his title against me: a big fat loss.

It had been more than 2 1/2 years since Ali had made a mandatory defense against the WBC's top contender. It was obvious to me that there was a special rule book for Ali. The WBC's rules on mandatory defenses call for the champion to defend against the No. 1 contender at least once a year.

Every fighter wants his shot at the champ; that's what this business is all about. What's the sense of climbing to the top of the ladder if you can't get the shot? The rules should be enforced.

Champions in other divisions were forced to defend their titles. John Conteh was stripped of his light heavyweight title for not adhering to the mandatory defense rule, and if the WBC didn't enforce it with Ali, how could it be taken seriously? Why was the WBC making a different set of rules for Ali?

As for me, I lived up to every rule. I beat three contenders in 1977. I didn't care about the purse; Ali could have the lion's share of it for all I cared. His stating that he'd fight me if he got $12 million was actually his way of saying that he wanted no part of me.

I was getting the sinking feeling that Ali would never fight me again. As long as there were promoters willing to pay him millions of dollars for taking easy fights, he'd take the path of least resistance.

Ali knew that his chances of beating me a third time in a row were slim to none. Every fight we had had was grueling, both physically and mentally. I knew he didn't want to put himself through that ordeal again. It wasn't just the fight itself, but the rigorous training period he would have to go through to get ready for that kind of sustained pressure. I still considered myself near my prime, whereas Ali's skills had shown serious signs of erosion.

Ali first said that he'd meet the winner of my fight with Bobick. When I knocked out Bobick in 58 seconds, Herbert Muhammad, Ali's manager, walked out of the Garden shaking his head in disgust. The wrong man won and so they went to Plan B.

Ali ordered WBC president Jose Suliaman—I repeat, ordered—Suliaman, to have Young and me fight each other for the right to fight him. Ali told Suliaman that he was too old and couldn't fight us both, but that he would meet the winner of such an elimination bout.

Suliaman and the WBC complied with Ali's wishes, but if I won the fight and Ali reneged on the deal, the WBC would look foolish. That's why I had to fight Young. I squared off with him November 5, 1977, for the right to a No. 1 ranking and a mandatory shot at the WBC heavyweight title.

The first round of the battle was uneventful. The two of us spent the round studying each other's battle plans. I threw out a few ineffectual jabs and Young countered by throwing a three-punch combination coming off the ropes. I was a little shaken, but I continued an all-out offensive assault and missed Young with a wild overhand right. Young retreated with me in pursuit. Although it was close, the Judges scored the round for Young.

Round two saw me coming out bobbing and weaving, shooting straight lefts at my opponent. Young attempted to clinch me while I continued firing left hooks to his head and body. He backpedaled, flicking out soft jabs, and landed an occasional left hook. Then Young caught me with a left-right combination that hurt me. He was using all of the tricks in his boxing repertoire to confuse me and it worked. Young was the victor of the second round.

By round three we had established a pattern: I would come out in pursuit and he would always retreat. I took advantage of my upper-body movement to slip his jabs as I pressed forward. When we got too close, Young clinched me. As the referee broke us apart, we traded jabs, and then Young scored with a lead right, left-hook combination. His tricky defensive style confused me, but I kept plucking forward. Young greeted me with right-hand leads and combinations as I countered with a few nice body shots; then he slipped away. Young took advantage of my defense when I carried my left too low and got off an occasional right lead to my face. I pressured Young near the end of the round but still had difficulty getting a clean shot at him. However, the round went to me for my aggressive pursuit.

I came out of my corner in round four the aggressor, stalking Young, but at the same time having difficulty landing clean shots on the elusive fighter. I finally caught him with a straight right, but he managed to spin off the ropes, and out of danger. He surprised me with a lead right that forced me to take a step backward. Once I caught my footing, I chased him back to the ropes where he clinched me to prevent anymore offensive blows. While Young attempted to counterjab, I effectively used my head movement to throw him off. I worked my way into range of throwing body blows and caught him with a few shots, but his effective jabs kept me out of rhythm and from further exploiting him. Young even managed to sneak in a right uppercut and left hook. As the end of the round neared, I hunted him down, attempting to land a left hook to his head and body. Once again, I was the effective aggressor, and the round was scored in my favor, tying us at two rounds apiece.

It wasn't much of a contest, taking the fight to the always on-the-run Jimmy Young, and early in round six I caught him with a solid double left jab that sent him retreating. I kept pouring it on, attempting to catch him with more punches, but his defensive style caused me to miss wildly. I was looking to catch Young with a powerful leaping left hook to end the fight with one home run punch. His patient defensive style was frustrating the hell out of me.

What angered me even more was the fact that he could sneak in a punch anytime he desired, and this time he snuck in an overhand right. Then he picked up the pace by throwing lefts followed by solid right-hand crosses. The only thing I could do was pin him to the ropes, where I caught him with a powerful left hook that hurt him badly. Young held on to me until the final bell. Round five was all mine, and for the first time in the fight, I was in the lead.

When I came out in round six, I was much more confident than I had been in the previous round because I felt I had him. I shifted into high gear early and pinned Young to the ropes, attempting to land a potent left hook. The game plan in this round was to switch the attack from Young's body to his head. As I got him within my sights, Young illegally shoved me off, and he was warned by the referee, Carlos Padilla, for holding. I kept up the assault, but Young successfully fought me off with counterpunches, specifically left jabs and straight right hands. One of his punches knocked me off balance, causing me to miss with a wild left hook and leaving me open for a straight right-hand counter. Young was effectively hitting me with counter shots, and anytime I got close, he'd clinch me before I could return any punches. No doubt about it, Jimmy Young was a clever fighter.

We managed to break, and I came at Young with right hands to the body followed by left hooks to the head. I wanted to hit him with one more punch in an attempt to steal the round, but once again Young grabbed onto me for a breather. However, I managed to squeak out the round in the eyes of the judges.

In between rounds six and seven, Young appeared to be tiring from the accumulative body punches I threw. While he was gasping for breath in his corner, I was standing in mine, smiling at him.

I came out punching with my left jab in round seven, hoping to stop Young with a killer shot. He countered with an overhand right to the head, but I picked up the pace once more with a lead right to his stomach, then followed up with a few more shots to the head and body. Every time I got close to polishing him off, Young grabbed me to prevent further follow-up. We traded jabs for the remainder of the round, with me landing infrequent body punches. In a surprise, the judges scored in favor of Young. The scorecard now read 4-3, with me hanging onto the lead.

I came out a little more timid in round eight. Both Young and I met in the center ring, trading light jabs. I picked up the attack and pressured him, firing off shots to his head and body. Young managed to pick off most of the punches, but I clearly was the aggressor. Young came alive, landing several jabs, and backed me into the corner, firing off several shots. I started pressuring him again, but was having difficulty finding the mark. Young was awarded the round and tied the fight once more.

I came out in fine form in round nine, chasing Young down, feeling quite confident that his punches, no matter how hard, could not effectively hurt me. I scored with a few jabs to Young's head and body, and then traded punches at ring center with me digging shots to his midsection. Young caught me with a solid right hand counter in an attempt to pick up his offense. We clinched several times, then I landed a beautiful overhand right lead. I followed up and trapped him on the ropes and fired off a volley of punches. Young managed to answer back with a few punches as the bell sounded, but it was clearly my round.

We met at ring center for the first part of the 10th round, trading ineffective jabs. Young scored first with a solid right-hand counter and followed up with a left hook and a pair of chopping straight right hands to my jaw and mouth. I was shaken for the first time in the fight, and Young was in the driver's seat. He quickly turned into the aggressor and landed another right hand over my carelessly low-hanging left hand that found its way to my jaw. I quickly returned to the role of the aggressor, stinging Young with left jabs and occasional right-hand shots to the belly. Even though it was Young's round, I appeared to be the fresher of the two fighters as he limped off to his corner and I stood in mine. The fight was even at five rounds apiece.

I came out confidently in the 11th round, sticking left-hand jabs in Young's face. Young became aggressive as we both tangoed at ring center. I managed to dig a combination into Young's body and pushed him into the ropes, where I flailed away with a barrage of body punches. I scored heavily with several stiff left hands and blocked Young's counter-attempts. Round 11 was all mine.

The beginning of round 12 was no different from most of the other rounds, with me hunting down Young, working my way in with body punches, trying to tire him out. I was waiting for some action from Young, picking off his jabs with my open right hand, and slipping his punches with slick head movements. We traded punches and were ring center when Young picked up the tempo, scoring a combination to my stomach.

It appeared as if Young had caught his second wind as he moved and scored, dousing me with punches. For the remainder of the round, we traded punches, and anytime I got within striking distance, Young clenched me. This was clearly his round. As always, I stood up between rounds to show him I was just getting started.

The fight was slowing down a tad in round 13 as we came out pawing and circling. I vainly attempted to land punches to his body, but I got tied up. When we were separated, I started landing a few stiff left jabs. Both of us were wearying as Young threw a few combinations that I clearly blocked off. We were tired warriors circling each other, feeling each other out for an opening, hoping to land the occasional punch. I was awarded the 13th round in this closely contested affair, making the score 7-6 in my favor.

When the bell rang for the 14th round, Muhammad Ali shouted from his ringside seat: "I'm tired of fighting Norton. Win, Jimmy!"

I had Young on the retreat from the bell, but he scored first with a left hook. I pursued him until we traded punches, both lobbing out harmless jabs. He managed to dig in a combination to my midsection while I caught him with a solid shot to the body. Once more, Young tied me up. He scored again with a right- hand, left-hook combination on the inside as I missed him with a wild left hook. The round ended with the two of us trading punches at ring center, Young getting the best of the exchange. Going into the 15th and final round of the fight, Young had evened up the tally 7-7.

Bill Slayton made sure he hit home the point that I had to be the effective aggressor going into round 15. It was do-or-die, and at the sound of the bell, I unleashed an arsenal of jabs and combinations. Young answered back with his best offensive attack of the fight, but it was a little too late. I pinned him to the ropes and battered away at him with strong hooks to the midsection. Young held on as the fight moved to ring center. I pushed onward but was getting tired. Young greeted me with a tremendous eight-punch combination, but I kept pursuing him.

He kept up the counterattack and returned back to me any punches I threw at him. In the last minute of the round, I pinned him to the ropes and flailed away at him, scoring heavily on the judges' three cards. Young vainly tried to fight back, but it was clear that I was dealing out most of the damage. I kept up the attack until the sound of the final bell as Young held on to me. I did what I wanted to do, and that was to end the fight as the aggressor. Round 15 belonged to me, giving me the edge in victory.

Young later admitted that he hadn't thrown enough punches, something he would correct in a rematch if I gave him a shot, but my thoughts were on snatching the title away from Ali.

Our fight was a 2-1 split decision in my favor. Jimmy Rondeau of Seattle, who had officiated my fight with George Foreman in Caracas, Venezuela, scored in my favor for the fight 147-143. Raymond Baldeyrou of France also scored it at 147-143 in my favor, but called 11 rounds even. Only Art Lurie of Las Vegas favored Young at 144-142, and saw only one round as being even. After the decision was announced, even the Associated Press favored me by 143-142.

At the postfight press conference, a dejected but sportsmanlike Jimmy Young said: "Do I think I won the fight? Of course I do. I disagree with the whole scoring, but what can I do about it?"

Young's wife, Barbara, was in tears. For years she sat at ringside, hoping one day her husband would be the champ. She boldly stood by her man and said to the press, "This is just a temporary setback. Jimmy will still win the title one day. You watch."

Sadly, Young never got the chance again.

At times, it was a close fight, and at other times, it was uneventful. A lot of rounds were extremely close and difficult to judge, but there wasn't too much action in this fight, as Young's style would never allow an all-out brawl. Young was defined as a "cute" fighter, boring and defensive-minded. He rarely had any entertaining fights, but that didn't take away from his brilliance.

The Young fight wasn't tough physically; however, it was my toughest fight mentally. He was the hurdle before Ali, the man I wanted to meet in the ring as soon as possible.

My victory over Young cemented my No. 1 ranking by the WBC and the WBA, forcing Ali to either commit to a fight with me or forfeit his title. At no time did I ever want to become known as a "Paper Champion." In boxing terms, that meant that I didn't earn or win the championship, but that I was simply awarded the title. Ali signed a contract with the WBC stating that if he didn't defend his title against me by January 5,

1978, it would vacate the title, and the winner of the Norton-Young fight would be declared the heavyweight champion of the world.

When the time came to enforce this ruling, Bob Biron and I went to Madrid, Spain, for the WBC Convention to see if they were going to live up to this commitment to me. The WBC cowardly chose to compromise its position in an effort to land Ali another interim title fight with Leon Spinks, who was viewed by many in the boxing world as an easy payday for Ali.

Working behind the scenes was Don King, who by now was boxing's most powerful promoter. During his reign, Don controlled eight of the top 10 fighters in the heavyweight division, but he did not have a contract with Ali. In effect, Don would work closely with the WBC president to oust Ali, easily the biggest draw in all of boxing. That gives you some sort of indication how powerful and influential Don King was, and still is, I might add.

The WBA sanctioned its version of a title fight in February 1978 when it offered Ali an easy $3.5 million to fight Spinks, a former Olympic gold medalist who had only seven professional fights to his credit. Spinks was 6-0-1 and was unproven as a professional. This would certainly be his biggest test to date. Ali lost to Spinks in a surprising 15-round decision in Las Vegas. Leon Spinks was now the WBA heavyweight champion. What a mess.

So the WBC and the WBA came up with a simple solution: Spinks and I would meet for the unified world-title championship. Easier said than done. Like Ali, Spinks wanted no part of me. He was offered a handsome sum to fight Ali again seven months later in September. In taking the rematch with Ali, he would pick up a nice payday in addition to avoiding me for the championship; in effect, killing two birds with one stone. Why wouldn't he try to avoid me like the plague?

The WBC had finally had enough. On March 29, 1978, in Mexico City, Spinks was stripped of his title, and I was declared the heavyweight champion of the world.

It was a moment I had been waiting for all of my life, but I wanted to defeat my opponent in the ring, hear the announcement of my victory over the P.A. system, have my arm raised in victory by the referee. I wanted to be declared the heavyweight champion of the world from inside the ring, not in some formal office in another country. Winning the title this way was a hollow victory.

Chapter Fifteen

On the Downside

I didn't have much time to savor my WBC championship belt.
My first title defense title was just 84 days away, when I had to face Larry
Holmes on June 9, 1978.

Holmes was the WBC's No. 1 contender, and our fight was a
highly anticipated nationally televised heavyweight championship between
the respected new champion and an unbeaten contender that featured
ranked heavyweights Jimmy Young and Alfredo Evangelista in separate
undercard bouts. Promoter Don King wanted to showcase both Young
and Evangelista as future opponents for the Holmes-Norton fight. Don
was always two steps ahead of the next guy.

Young came in overweight, pudgy, and ill-prepared at 220 pounds,
losing in a shocking split decision to Osvaldo Ocasio. The fight was a
snoozer. Evangelista barely squeaked by Jody Ballard. So much for great
matchmaking.

Holmes lost to Duane Bobick in the Olympic Trials in 1972 and
had difficulty finding financial backers to launch his professional career.
Holmes' journey to a title shot had been a long, undistinguished climb
that started on the lightly regarded Pennsylvania club fight circuit where
he earned just over $60 for his professional debut. Most of Holmes' early
bouts took place in Scranton, Pennsylvania, for small money. Holmes
only had his loyal amateur coach Ernie Butler behind his cause.

Fortunately for Holmes, Muhammad Ali recognized his potential. He soon became one of Ali's chief sparring partners and saw action
on several of Ali's undercards. Holmes scored a revenge victory once removed by stopping Duane Bobick's brother, Rodney, in the sixth round
beneath the "Thrilla in Manila" in the Philippines.

Holmes felt like an overlooked pawn in Don's vast heavyweight
stable, and at 29, after going unbeaten in his 27-fight career, Holmes

would never be more ready for his first shot at heavyweight glory. Those years with Ali gave Holmes a taste for the good life and the spoils of what being a champ was all about. Holmes desperately wanted to break free from the stranglehold of Don's vise-like grip. Don not only promoted Holmes, he managed him as well. On paper, Don's son, Carl, managed Holmes, but what that ultimately meant was that every time Holmes fought, the Kings took a chunk out of Holmes that only Uncle Sam could fully appreciate. Holmes equated winning the title with freedom, but mostly what he wanted was respect.

"I'm not fighting for a title," Holmes told the media at our press conference announcing the fight. "I'm fighting for respect. Once you have respect, everything else just falls into place: titles, money, everything else I need." Then Holmes started getting personal.

"Norton thinks he's God's gift to the world. He thinks he's so pretty," he continued. "I won't win any beauty contests, but I'll win this fight."

At the time, I couldn't understand Holmes' rage against me. Usually, this type of display was for the press and the public to generate interest in the fight, so I took it with a grain of salt. But hearing his words, I could tell there was venom behind them. When reporters asked me about Holmes, I tried to remain a gentleman.

"I don't like Holmes, but the man can box. He showed that against Earnie Shavers." Holmes outclassed Shavers in a 12-round fight to get his shot at the belt.

Right before I left the room, I noticed an ugly sneer from Holmes, who was leering at me. He was bidding a fond farewell to me, and it mystified me as to why he was behaving like a common street thug. Only with the passing of time did I realize that I was a roadblock to the title for Holmes. I represented all the pain and heartache and humiliation that he had suffered at the hands of Don King, and now I was the focus of that anger and rage. It was definitely what you would call "bad blood."

One boxing scribe keenly observed, "Norton is introspective. Holmes wears his emotion like a badge. Norton, the only child of middle-class parents, is well educated. Holmes left school at the age of 13 to help support a family of 12 children. Norton has parlayed his ring career into acting roles while Holmes, until recently, toiled away in obscurity.

"The two men are as diverse in their beliefs and lifestyles as one can imagine. The one thing they have in common is a desire to be the heavyweight champion of the world. The one thing they cannot tolerate is each other." Well put; couldn't have said it any better myself.

A few days before the fight at Caesars Palace Sports Pavilion, Holmes decided to put his ill will to the test and tried to intimidate me while working out. His session was supposed to end at 4 p.m., and mine was to start at the same time. Holmes purposely lingered around the gym, shadow boxing, pounding the training bag, and entertaining 15 reporters covering the fight with a crowd of 2,000 spectators on hand. His real intention was to cut into my training time and irk me in one fell swoop, but it didn't work.

I came out of my dressing room with disco music blaring from the loudspeakers, and Larry was no longer the focus of attention. I stole his thunder with my movie star entrance.

I took off my robe and began jumping rope to the rhythm of the music. Holmes sat nearby with a group of sparring partners, corner men and fans.

"Look at that pretty boy jumping rope," Holmes said loud enough so that I could hear.

"Larry," I said while the sound of the rope was whizzing, "the reason why you're so jealous of me is that you're so damn ugly and skinny. Anything next to you looks pretty." The sound of the guffaws coming from the reporters and fans inspired Holmes to take action. He slowly walked over to where I was jumping rope and got right in my face.

"What did you just say to me, pussy?" Holmes asked, looking me square in the eye.

Before I could mutter a comeback, he thrust both of his palms into my chest and pushed me in front of everyone.

I knew it was a stupid little intimidation tactic on his part to upset me, but he did piss me off. I was furious. Bill Slayton got in between us and kept the peace as both camps were ready to go into an all-out war.

I found out later that Holmes and his friend, Eddie Sutton, went back to their suite, where they played a piano duet as other members of his entourage clapped and sang along. It was all a charade, but it could have been a costly charade. I stood to make $3.7 million while Holmes was pulling down $500,000, by far his best payday, but it could have vanished if a fight had broken out, a punch had been thrown, or a finger or hand had been broken. It was childish on Holmes' part, but in the end, it increased my motivation.

Bill Slayton: *It was all bull. It was stupid for Holmes to do something like that. One punch and the fight might have been called off. I've never seen a fighter act in such a low-class, cheap, lousy*

*manner, especially given the fact that both fighters were going to see a
nice paycheck and that could easily have been blown all to hell.*

In addition to wanting to kick Holmes' ass more than ever, the
scuffle made me train harder than I had originally planned. I sparred 200
rounds and abstained from sex for about five weeks.

There is an age-old myth that a boxer should abstain from sex
before a fight. Each boxer has a different opinion on the subject. For
example, former light-heavyweight champion and notorious playboy Harry
Greb claimed that a fighter must abstain from sex at least prior to the
second glove being laced on! I can't say that I agree with that philosophy.
I compared sex more to a marathon. I realized lovemaking could sap
strength and energy needed during an exhausting battle. However, if I
had a sprinter's mentality toward sex, then I wouldn't have been so concerned. I also feared that sex might tire my legs, as well as take away my
aggression that built up through the long training process. More than
anything, sex was a mental thing with me, but I wanted to get the edge in
this fight, so I abstained.

After our bout, rumors circulated that Holmes fought with torn
tissue in his biceps. Six days before the contest, Holmes supposedly injured his left arm connecting with the elbow of a sparring partner. If Holmes
was hurt, he never let on or let it affect his gutsy performance.

All the hype had come to an end, and it was time to fight. I
wanted my initial title defense to be memorable, and I was ready to get
down to business. Holmes was the challenger and had to enter the ring
first. I made my way through the ring ropes and focused my mind on the
challenge ahead.

Before the bell for round one, we met for referee Mills Lane's
instructions. Holmes stood at ring center, glaring at me. I ignored his
glare. After Lane finished his instructions, Holmes slammed his face into
me in an amateurish attempt to psyche me out. Some bad blood was
about to spill.

"Let's get it on!" the referee yelled, and the fight was on.

Holmes came out dancing, moving side to side, but I threw out
the first left jab. Holmes countered and flicked out quick piston-like left
jabs that connected to my face. He was fast, no doubt about it, but I used
crafty head movement to slip his rapid jabs, even defensively catching his
powerful jabs with my open right glove. As I stalked him, throwing out
infrequent punches as he circled me, I scored with an unorthodox lead
left hook. I jabbed my way within firing range, but then Holmes countered me with a four-punch combination. Undaunted, I charged forward

and threw a volley of punches, but Holmes picked them off. He was good defensively, no doubt about that. I managed to connect on a few jabs in the latter part of the round, and the first round clearly belonged to me.

In the next round, Holmes continued to fire off jabs that made their way past my cross-handed defense. As I had done with Ali, I tried to cut off the ring and make Holmes go toe-to-toe, but he eluded me with his silky-smooth quickness and managed to stay in the center of the ring. While I attempted to jab my way into punching range, Holmes scored while doubling up with the jab and followed with a straight right hand. Without warning, he spun me around and blasted me with a hard right to the head, followed by a left jab that snapped my head back. Instantly, my left eye was reddened and began to swell up. I stayed in pursuit, attempting to land jabs to Holmes' body while using jerky upper-body movement to confuse him. I scored one last time with a jab, but Holmes caught me with three more punches as the bell rang. Round two went to Holmes.

At the start of round three, I came out stalking rather than punching, and Holmes fired off three quick jabs in succession, making me visibly blink. He was good at using the entire ring, popping out fast left jabs, scoring to the head and body. Getting a little cocky, Holmes held his arms dangerously low at his sides with his head and chin sticking out at me, daring me to hit him.

At first I tried to use some shifty upper-body movement to work my way to the inside because I wanted to fight in close quarters. I threw a few jabs to keep him honest and then landed the first hard punch of the fight, a looping hard overhand right. I was starting to reach him, stepping in with stiff counter jabs. We traded jabs at ring center for the remainder of the round. Easily, the round belonged to me, but for reasons I still can't figure out, the judges scored it evenly.

While I was sitting on my stool, Bill suggested that I give up the idea of trying to offset Holmes' lightning quick jab.

"Start counterpunching," Bill told me. "Let him make the first move, then make him pay for it."

Holmes continued to use the whole ring and jab at me in round four. I threw a left jab followed by a right cross, but Holmes blocked both punches, and the fight returned to ring center. I stepped in and landed a vicious lead left hook, but then Holmes started scoring with hammerlike left jabs, attempting to land with follow-up rights. I attempted a right to Holmes' body, but I was greeted with a solid four-punch counter combination. Due to carelessness, I was carrying my left hand a little lower than usual and Holmes caught me with two lefts followed by a right at the end of the round. Holmes racked up a lot of points and easily outscored me to win round four.

The action heated up a few frames in round five. Holmes was dancing up a storm, which perplexed me, but I managed to pin him to the ropes and connected with a stunning overhand right that stopped him in his tracks and shook him up. I attempted to follow up, but Holmes fired back two jabs, and then we stood flat-footed and went toe-to-toe in the middle of the ring. I welcomed the invitation.

The exchange of fire was even, but my jab was becoming a factor, and I began reaching Holmes with solid stiff jabs. He danced his way out of this tête-a-tête and began hopping around with his hands at his sides and snuck in a right lead to the head. This round could have gone to either one of us, but the judges gave it to Holmes. With five rounds expired, I began to realize that Holmes was pitching a shutout, winning every round so far. I was giving the title away.

There was little action for the first half of round six as Holmes danced around the ring, tossing out the occasional left jab. I followed him, attempting to score with lefts of my own. I chased him near the ropes and scored with two left hooks. Then he feinted, causing me to step back cautiously, leaving an opening for him to score with a series of jabs. Then he dropped his hands to his sides again and I stunned him with a beautiful right to the chin. Then I trapped him on the ropes, going to work on his body with a left hook and another right hand to the liver.

Amazingly, Holmes' hands were still down to his side as he danced away, throwing lefts for the remainder of the round while I racked up points with jabs of my own. Round six was all mine.

I took a seat on my stool in between rounds. My left eye was almost swollen shut, so Bill applied an ice pack and it helped my vision. I came out in round seven firing the best jabs so far in the fight, but Holmes used shrewd foot movement to keep the action at ring center as he scored with sharp left jabs. He tried to strike with a right but was off balance because he was bouncing on his toes. He missed me with another right, and I caught him with a devastating overhand right to the head. Holmes continued to peck away at me with jabs, but my body attack began to take a toll, limiting his movements. I tried to pick up the tempo and scored with hard body shots as I got him up against the ropes. To my dismay, the judges scored in favor of Holmes.

Then, the momentum of the fight swung sharply in my favor. Holmes hit me with three right leads at the outset of round eight, startling me a bit. The punches cut my left eye, but I stayed in pursuit, and I caught him with two thunderous left jabs. Holmes began bleeding profusely from the lip. (The next day, Holmes would need 11 stitches to sew it up). I continued winging fierce overhand rights at him, some of them hitting the bull's-eye, and I began to come alive. Now Holmes' movements were strictly in retreat, and he stopped throwing punches. I backed him into the ropes and landed another overhand right that snapped his head back. My confidence continued to soar while Holmes seemed to be tiring. At the end of the bell, I jarred him with another right hand and won the round handily.

Round nine opened with Holmes tossing out a few tentative jabs, and he motioned for me to join him and fight. I obliged and caught him with a right that crashed into his face like a ton of bricks. Just out of earshot, I heard his corner tell him to stay loose. That told me he wasn't following with his game plan. Worse than that, the sting was gone from his punches, meaning he was going to pay a heavy price for any punch he tossed out at me.

Holmes continued shooting out the left jab while moving at a slower pace. I was blocking most of his punches and countered with a few choice shots of my own. I caught him with a wild left and then missed him with a jab while he countered beautifully with a combination. I hurt him with a stunning lead right, and grazed him with a second overhand right that could have done some serious damage if it had found its way to his chin. I caught him one last time with another crushing right to the skull, taking advantage of his lower-hanging left hand. Holmes closed the round by scoring two solid jabs and a short right, which gave him the edge in winning the round.

When Holmes took a drink from a water bottle in between rounds, referee Mills Lane noticed that his water had a much different consistency than regular drinking water. The boxing rules specifically state that water and orange peels are the only things a fighter is allowed in the corner.

The referee told Dick Young, "It looked thicker and darker than water to me, so I took the bottle and handed it to the commissioner at ringside."

Later, it was discovered that Rich Giachetti, Holmes' trainer, had put honey in the water. Even though it was a clear violation of the rules, nothing came of it after the fight. Good thing, too. I didn't want to win or lose a fight on a stupid violation for such a trivial matter.

At the start of round 10, I backed up Holmes with a solid left jab that snapped his head back, but before I could move in for the kill, he danced his way out of trouble by moving and jabbing. I stayed in pursuit, but every time I closed the gap, Holmes grabbed me. He snuck in a lead right but I kept chugging forward. I kept chasing an ever-moving Holmes in an attempt to land a shot whenever I could. He tried to go to the body, but I fended off three blows to the face. He moved back and forth, looking for some kind of opening, and finally got off two jabs at the close of the round. Holmes' round.

The crowd at Caesars was getting its money's worth and was divided in its applause. The din increased at the start of the 11th round as I kept moving forward, catching Holmes with a left hook in close quarters. Holmes then scored with a right cross, but I answered him with an overhand right. He kept moving, bringing the action to ring center, popping out jabs. I leapt forward, catching him with a left hook, and forced him to the ropes, where I delivered a hard, solid left hook to the body and an uppercut to the chin, ending with a right to the rib cage. I could tell I hurt him, because his hands were at his sides again and he was moving and dancing to keep away. I got Holmes against the ropes one last time and whaled away with both hands, finishing off an eight-punch combination with a devastating looping overhand right. I followed up with a heavy left-hook, right-hand combination. The round was mine, big-time!

"Stick and move," Holmes' trainer yelled aloud to him in round 12. "You've got to stick and move!"

Holmes flicked out the occasional jab while circling around the ring, but he was tiring. The sweat was pouring off of us as we desperately lunged at each other. I picked up the attack, shooting left jabs to his head and body, following up with right crosses. Holmes kept jabbing, but I was landing successful overhand rights. We traded right hands, Holmes catching me more often, but my blows were doing more damage. By this point, Holmes' movement had slowed and he played into my punching range. I scored with a left hook and right hand before the bell. I had rallied back to win five of the last six rounds.

Holmes caught me with five crisp jabs at the start of round 13, and for the first time since early in the fight, he was in control. I was reeling after taking three straight rights to the head, and my knees buckled. I staggered back, and Holmes jolted me with a right uppercut. It was almost lights out for me. In desperation I tried to punch back.

Miraculously I recovered and came back at Holmes with a left-right to the ribs, but he had me in trouble once more by landing three consecutive left-right combinations. I winged several left hooks as he punched back, hitting me at the end of the round with four rights to the head that left me stunned. I stood in the center of the ring at the bell, gasping for breath, but I was still standing. The crowd went nuts. I retreated to my corner.

Amazingly, I came out strong on my feet to meet Holmes for round 14. I was tired but clear-eyed, and I showed no effects from the pounding of the previous round. Holmes came out jabbing, I missed him with a wild hook, and he countered with a right hand. I wouldn't give in, and I lowered my head and drove home a series of blows to Holmes' midsection, driving him back into the ropes. I had him in the corner and scored with a right. Holmes fought back valiantly with lefts and rights, but he couldn't get off the ropes. I scored again with a quick short combination on the inside. The round ended with me digging into Holmes with left hooks and finishing with a right uppercut and left hook.

Now the fight was even. It all boiled down to the 15th round. Who could have known that the last round would be such a barn burner that fight fans would watch it time and time again through the years?

As we came out for round 15, both Holmes and I knew that the fight was up for grabs. It all came down to this final round. Whoever won round 15 locked up the championship.

We tapped gloves at ring center and a classic round of boxing began. I got in a solid right hand that left Holmes with blood pouring out of his mouth, but he gamely fired back. I caught him with an overhand right, but he fired back. I scored with a left hook on the inside and kept pushing forward, trying to deliver a fight-ending knockout punch.

One more time, we went toe-to-toe and traded nonstop punches at ring center, both of us displaying an amazing amount of courage and heart. Holmes stood his ground and kept punching back. In the middle of this heated exchange, a powerful right uppercut sent his mouthpiece flying out of the ring. By now, the standing-room-only crowd at Caesars Palace was on its feet, shouting its approval for the nonstop action. I scored once more with a heavy left hook followed by a powerful right hand.

Now it was Holmes' turn. He raged at me, whipping a left and a right to my head, staggering me with the last shot. I punched back, and we traded some of the biggest bombs that boxing had ever seen. It was an extremely violent round, to say the least. Holmes connected with a brutal right uppercut. I retaliated with a double hook to the body and head. Holmes found the strength for a final rally in the last 60 seconds. In that final minute, Holmes snapped my head back and my knees buckled. Before the final gong, I got in one last big lick—a right to the head. The bell sounded, and the crowd roared for our efforts, giving a standing ovation to Holmes and me for one of the most awesome rounds of boxing it had ever witnessed.

We ambled our way back to our corners, physically and emotionally spent.

"That last round was the greatest I have ever seen or been a part of," referee Mills Lane later told me.

"It was a John Wayne movie," wrote Dick Young. "Both men stood in center ring, legs spread apart for balance, and took turns at pot-shotting the other's chin. It was as though they were playing a game called you hit me and I'll hit you."

I knew the fight was going to be close, but I believed that I had won because of the punishment I gave to Holmes. Then came the decision.

"Judge Harold Buck: 143-142 for Holmes. Judge Lou Tabot: 143-142 for Norton. Judge Joe Swessel: 143-142 for Holmes. For the winner and new heavyweight champion of the world, Larry Holmes!"

> **Bill Slayton:** *Going into the 15th round, I told Kenny, "It's close. You've got to go out there and give me three good minutes." He went out there and went as long as he could. He trained for 15 rounds, and he gave it his all. It wasn't that he saved something.*
>
> *I thought that Kenny was winning that round for 2 minutes and 30 seconds, but he punched himself out. In the last 30 seconds, Larry really scored, but if it went another 30 seconds, Larry might have dropped. Every time I see a tape of that round, Kenny threw more punches and landed more punches. But the last 30 seconds Larry came on at the end to steal the judges' eye.*

I walked to my dressing room, completely deflated. Boxing had been good to me, but it also had given me my share of heartaches. This was a close second in terms of disappointment; the third fight with Ali ranked at the top.

I lay on my stomach in the dressing room on the massage table, already spouting plans to regain my title. The door flew open. It was my dad.

"Well, I tried, pop," were the only words I could find.

My father put his hand on my shoulder and said stoically, "You fought a hell of a fight, son."

Holmes was so high from the adrenaline that he bolted from his dressing room with his new green-and-gold championship belt around his waist and sprinted across the tennis courts of Caesars Palace and leaped into the pool.

Some in the boxing world have questioned Holmes' heart because of the fight against Bobick in the 1972 Olympic Trials, but on this night, he showed a tremendous amount of guts against me.

Larry Holmes: *Of my 70 fights, the toughest guy I ever fought, I gotta go back to the guy I won the title from back in 1978. I fought Kenny Norton for 15 rounds. Hell, he didn't want to give, and I didn't want to give, and that's what made me what I am today. Kenny Norton, in my book, was one of the greatest fighters of all time. He didn't get his just due, but he was a great fighter, a great human being. I thank him for the opportunity he gave me to become heavyweight champion of the world. That was the best fight I ever had; that was the hardest fight I ever had.*

Ruth Norton (Ken's mother): *After the fight with Larry Holmes, I think Ken lost interest in the sport. That fight took some of his soul away from him.*

Holmes remained the WBC heavyweight champion of the world for another seven years.

As for my career, well, it was on the downside. I was never quite the same after that fight. I was a wounded bird and stayed in boxing solely for the money; it was something that almost cost me my life.

Chapter Sixteen

The Crucial Confrontation

The bitterness from the Larry Holmes defeat left a bad taste in my mouth and I contemplated retiring from boxing while looking into more movie roles. However, my bitterness wore off and my competitive juices began to flow again, when I realized that I still had the potential to reach the top. I returned to what was the quickest route to a fast and easy payday: boxing. I also realized that my name still meant something at the box office and returned six months later against a young and relatively unknown boxer.

My return to the ring was the featured undercard bout of Holmes' first defense against Alfredo Evangelista televised live on ABC in Las Vegas at the Caesars Palace Sports Pavilion. I was taking on a young upstart from Dallas by the name of Randy Stephens. Actually, it was more of a boxing lesson. Holmes toyed with Evangelista for seven rounds and then with 2:14 left to go in round seven, he put the kibosh on him real good. If I won the fight against Stephens, it still left me in a good position to get another rematch with Holmes.

On paper, this fight had the makings of a total mismatch. Stephens was considered a virtual novice, with only 14 professional bouts to his credit. But this was far from the truth. Stephens had been the 1974 All-Service Champion and looked impressive in a three-round exhibition with Muhammad Ali in front of his hometown fans in Dallas.

In his previous contest, Stephens had traveled to his opponent Gerrie Coetzee's homeland of Johannesburg, South Africa, and dropped a highly disputed decision to Coetzee that was booed loudly by the partisan South African crowd.

Although he was unheralded at the time of our bout, Stephens proved he could fight, and with an opportunity to shine in front of a national audience, he would be in shape for his one shot at boxing glory. Boxing insiders such as Howard Cosell openly called for an upset, assuming I would have difficulty mentally preparing myself for an unknown like Stephens. Then again, Howard claimed that my first match with Ali was the mismatch of the century. I always took what Howard said with a grain of salt.

At the sound of the bell, Stephens came out moving and jabbing. He was much faster than I had expected. I immediately cut off the ring and aimed my attack at his body in hopes of slowing his progress. Stephens kept circling, firing jabs and holding onto me when I got close. I plodded forward and slipped most of his punches. Stephens used good side-to-side movement to stay out of danger. He caught me with a solid left on the inside and confidently was willing to stand and trade punches. I dug in a pulverizing left hook that made Stephens grunt in pain. Every time he got close, I fired to the body. I caught him flush on the jaw with a well-aimed left hook near the end of the round. He obviously felt it and held on for the rest of the round. That first round, I just felt him out. I wanted to see if he was going to box me, and I was lucky that I had a chance to hurt him early. I was awarded the first round.

I stayed in pursuit in the second round. I began reaching Stephens with jabs and backed him into the ropes. I opened up with my full arsenal, pasting Stephens with a barrage of hooks, uppercuts and looping overhand rights. Stephens was hurt and clung to me for dear life. He definitely was game as he stood and traded punches with me at ring center. The action slowed a bit as we circled each other, then I fired a left hook followed by an uppercut that caught Stephens flush, standing him straight up in the process. Stephens and I continued to slug it out, while I dug in with several left hooks in an attempt to slow him down. Near the end of the round I battered him with stiff jabs and solid left hooks, but the young warrior fired back each time I landed a punch. The action continued at ring center until the bell. I was now ahead on the judges' scorecards 2-0.

I wasted no time in letting punches fly at the start of the third round. I snapped Stephens' head back with a stiff left jab. He attempted to counter, but I slipped the punch and returned a left hook. He played into my hands by continuing to trade punches with me at ring center. Although he was extremely courageous, I managed to outpunch Stephens in virtually every exchange.

Stephens then landed a left hook that I felt from head to toe, but I instinctively answered back with a jarring left hook that momentarily stopped him in his tracks. For the most part, his punches lacked power; he wasn't much of a banger, and I was willing to trade punch for punch. It was a game plan that would have made my old partner, Smokin' Joe Frazier, proud. I hit Stephens with a left hook followed by a looping right hand and a pulverizing left hook that caught him right on the button. He wobbled forward, then backward, obviously unconscious and out on his feet. I had plenty of time to load up with another haymaker, but I knew it was over. Seconds later, Stephens made an attempt to grab the ropes but missed them and plummeted to the mat, collapsing on his back.

After the fight, Stephens' manager came over to me and thanked me for not hurting his boxer when he was reeling on his feet. I could see the kid was out.

The lesson I learned in this fight was that I lacked the killer instinct that so many other champions have: the ability to beat an opponent into the ground.

Although I had displayed mercy in the ring against Stephens, I soon found out that I had a monopoly on such kind acts. My next fight was against boxing's most murderous puncher, Earnie Shavers. Fatality is potentially only a punch away when squaring off against the likes of a bomber like Shavers.

He entered our contest with 57 victories to his credit, 55 of those coming via knockout. In his one lone bid for the title, Shavers lost a close, disputed decision to Ali September 29, 1977, in New York. Misery loves company, and I knew the bitterness Shavers felt, being outpointed by Ali, but I also knew he needed to win our fight to resurrect his career. Without a doubt, "The Acorn" (a nickname given to Shavers by Ali because of his black bald head) would be in top condition for our shootout.

Training camp was set up in the small Southern California town of Hemet. I got up each morning at 5:30 for roadwork. During the grueling run, I concentrated on the Shavers fight. I prepared for a fast battle, realizing a knockout either way was imminent.

I entered the contest with Shavers as the WBC's No. 1 contender. As soon as the bell rang, our fight moved to ring center. We shot out tentative jabs. All the while I kept in mind Shavers' tremendous punching power. He told me once that the secret to his extraordinary punching power was hours of chopping wood. I was hoping he wasn't eyeing me as some sort of firewood for his cold cabin in the woods!

I bobbed up and down, slipping most of Shavers' bombs, and countered with hard left hooks to the head and body. My confidence soared with each landed punch. Suddenly, Shavers caught me with a thunderous left hook, and the tide of the bout immediately turned. His powerful left hook rendered me semiconscious as I attempted to grab him to buy some time. Unfortunately, I had no such luck.

He continued to swing away, eventually depositing me on the seat of my pants. I somehow wobbled to my feet before referee Mills Lane's count reached 10.

I managed to get back to my feet, but my head was still cloudy as Shavers came right back firing. I tried to fire back with punches, but they lacked steam. The next thing I remember is attempting to once again gain my footing. Another one of Shavers' potent punches had sent me back to the canvas. I made it to my feet and wanted to continue, but the referee called a halt to the battle. Good thing, too. I was too out of it to even protest. Mills had done his job and protected me from myself and Shavers.

Bill Slayton: *Kenny's heart wasn't in this fight. He had a real bad rib and he didn't like heavy punchers. He didn't even like to train with heavy punchers. He was leery of 'em. Before the Shavers fight, Kenny said, "This is going to be it for me." But afterward, he decided to buy a new home that cost about $850,000. I told him, "You got the money. You got all your marbles. Why do you wanna fight anymore?" He said, "Two fights, I'll make a million dollars." Then he asked, "Ain't you gonna work with me?" I said, "Kenny, you know I'll be with you, man, whatever you decide to do, because if it's not right, I'll protect you. I'll throw the goddam towel in." That's when he came out of retirement for Scott LeDoux, Tex Cobb, and Gerry Cooney.*

The first bout of "Operation Comeback" was set to take place on enemy turf November 10, 1978, in Bloomington, Minnesota, against courageous local sentimental favorite, Scott LeDoux.

LeDoux was a tough, brawling fringe contender who had fought most of his battles in the Minnesota area. LeDoux and I shared many of the same opponents. LeDoux also had defeated Ron Stander and Larry Middleton, but had suffered knockout defeats from George Foreman and Duane Bobick. LeDoux's best effort had been when he held then-undefeated Olympic gold medalist Leon Spinks to a draw October 2, 1977, in a bout many felt LeDoux deserved.

In his previous fight, LeDoux had lost in a disputed decision to Johnny Boudreaux in Annapolis. LeDoux dropped Boudreaux early in the second round, cutting him twice, and yet still lost the fight. What stung the most was that Boudreaux had the bad sense to call LeDoux a chump in an interview with Howard Cosell inside of the ring. Once LeDoux heard the word chump, he went ballistic in front of a national audience. LeDoux tore across the ring, attacking Boudreaux with a vicious kick to the face and dislodged the toupee off of Howard's head in the process. Two for the price of one! For that kick, LeDoux won a lot of notoriety and the hearts of a lot of boxing fans, not for kicking Boudreaux, but for making Howard look like an idiot.

My match with LeDoux August 19, 1979, was dubbed by the Minnesota promoters as "The Crucial Confrontation." It was a crossroads of sorts for both LeDoux and me. I was going to receive a purse of $150,000 compared to LeDoux's $50,000.

The bout was originally scheduled in San Diego a month earlier, but was postponed and moved to Bloomington when I injured my ribs during a training session. Actually, the move was a boon for ticket sales because Bloomington was the hometown of LeDoux, and it was the first time the city got a chance to host a world-class heavyweight fight. The gate at the Met Sports Center still holds the Minnesota fight record, exceeding sales of $106,000 at the gate with 8,100 people in attendance. We even held three press conferences to accommodate the local media. It was the biggest battle in Minnesota since the Sioux uprising.

At one of those press conferences, LeDoux threw the first verbal blow.

"It's frustrating to see a guy like Norton get so much admiration when the only thing he's ever done is beat Muhammad Ali once," said the native Minnesotan.

Is that all?

"The thing about Norton is that he can't take a big punch," LeDoux continued.

"They say Norton never backs up. He'll have to back up this time. I hope he won't talk about another rib injury or break a leg or have any other alibi before I knock him out." Then LeDoux turned to me and asked, "By the way, Kenny, how are your ribs?"

His reference to my ribs was a cheap shot, but my only response to LeDoux's stinging accusations was, "Let him make a fool of himself with silly talk. When the bells rings, he'll have to show whether he can fight as well as he talks. I plan to fight like I always do, and see what he does." Not exactly fighting words, but then again, I preferred to let my fists do the talking.

LeDoux preferred to fight his fight in the media: "Four times I tried to get this guy in the ring, and I'm actually surprised to see him here today." He was starting to get under my skin.

LeDoux trained for our fight in the loft of a barn on his father's farm in Crosby, Minnesota, and I often wondered if he hit slabs of beef like Sylvester Stallone did in *Rocky*. LeDoux also possessed the mythical courage of the Italian Stallone, and I knew a difficult day at the office was in order. I planned to take the action to LeDoux from the beginning.

From the first-round bell, I continuously nailed LeDoux with stiff left jabs and solid left hooks that he managed to block with his face. I noticed LeDoux carried his hands very low and punched much too slowly. Another trait LeDoux had was to back up most of the time, which made me the natural aggressor in this fight. That surprised me, considering the trash he had talked in the press conference. Luckily for me, that awarded me lots of points from the judges. This fight looked like it was going to be a cakewalk.

The next six rounds were so boring that it's not even worth writing about, other than to say I won five of those six rounds with LeDoux, possibly winning round three.

The tide changed around round eight, as LeDoux rallied back and scored heavily with solid flurries, pinning me up against the ropes. As I tired, it appeared as if LeDoux grew stronger, scoring with powerful rights. The crowd was worked into a frenzy by the action.

In the ninth round, LeDoux again delivered more of the damaging blows, cashing in on his renewed vigor. While I attempted to fight back, my punches lacked zip, and I was tiring quickly. By the end of the round, the LeDoux crowd was on its feet showing its approval.

In round 10, I knew LeDoux was going to come out swinging, going for the knockout punch. In an attempt to get my juices flowing one last time, Bill put ice cubes down the front of my trunks and most of the cubes splattered out all over the canvas. Good idea, bad execution. Referee Wally Holmes halted the fight for 30 seconds to clear the ring of ice. When the action resumed, LeDoux tagged me against the ropes and let fly a blistering flurry of lefts and rights, battering me into the canvas for an eight-count.

I managed to get up, but rather unsteadily. I then made a staggering attempt to dance, which only proved my fatigued condition. The crowd was once again on its feet, cheering the hometown boy on, and LeDoux unleashed a solid right that caught me on the side of the head. I went limp. LeDoux nailed me with another right to the head, draping me over the top strand of the ropes, leaving me in the precarious position of being half in and half out of the ring.

Once again, I got up on unsteady legs. For all intents and purposes, I was out on my feet, staggering around the ring. The bell sounded before the referee could start a count on me. With so much noise, many in the Met Sports Center felt as if LeDoux had been given a technical knockout, but they soon found out the judges' decision.

Legendary announcer Jimmy Lennon Sr., who was specially flown in for the fight, announced that there was a split decision, and the crowd voiced its disappointment. Lennon gave the scores: referee Wally Holmes, 95-94, LeDoux; judge Denny Nelson, 95-94, Norton; and judge Leroy Benson 95-95, a draw. The official verdict: a draw.

Although many in the crowd felt LeDoux got a raw deal, they forgot that I had built up an impressive lead up into the eighth round. I'll admit that LeDoux had me on the ropes, but he didn't finish me off. Early in the fight he slapped me good and popped my eardrum, but other than that I did all the punching. The judges were correct to call the fight a draw.

I was hoping this fight was the first step back on the ladder that would lead to another shot at Holmes, but it was obvious that I should retire from boxing. A few years earlier in my career, I would have manhandled LeDoux.

I know LeDoux felt he had won the fight and was cheated out of a victory.

Scott LeDoux: *I have a lot of respect for Ken Norton. He's a nice man and has a lot of courage. I knocked Ken down twice and we had a pretty good fight. Kenny won the early rounds, and I won the later rounds. He got tired later on and he was hanging onto the ropes when the bell sounded to end the fight. When it was announced a draw, the fans went nuts, booing, throwing stuff in the ring. It was in my hometown, and everybody was emotionally charged up. I had done real well with him, and the crowd certainly felt that I deserved the decision. I haven't changed my mind at all about that day. I still believe I won that fight.*

The LeDoux battle had turned out to be tougher than everyone originally expected, and I knew I should have put more effort into training. After that struggle, I once again announced my retirement, and for the next several months, I pursued my announcing and acting careers.

But during the time off, I kept thinking about how I didn't like the way my career had ended. Slowly, my motivation to continue boxing returned.

Everyone, especially my wife, Jackie, was against my returning to the ring. But when the offer came to fight Randall "Tex" Cobb, I had to go back to the gym to prove to Bill and Jackie that I could train hard.

Cobb was a charismatic and entertaining prospect who had built up a record of 18-0, with 17 wins coming via knockout. His lone decision victory came against Cookie Wallace, who I had knocked out a few years before. Cobb's most impressive victory had been his last fight August 2, 1980, when he impressively stopped Earnie Shavers in the eighth round. Cobb proved he had a granite jaw by swallowing Shavers' best shots early in the fight. Eventually Shavers tired and Cobb knocked him out, breaking his jaw in the process.

Despite Cobb's success as a pro fighter, he didn't experience much success in the amateur ranks. As Cobb tells it, "I had only two fights as an amateur and lost both of then. Heck, I figured I didn't have much of a future there, so I turned pro."

Our fight took place November 7, 1981, in San Antonio. Cobb was rated No. 8 by the WBC, and being from Texas, he received a loud ovation from the crowd. I also received a warm welcome during the introductions.

In round one I came out moving, catching Cobb with the first solid jab I threw. I planned to move and box in the opening round, hoping to shed some ring rust from my "retirement." He had obvious physical advantages in size and reach. Cobb kept lumbering forward behind a strong left jab, and he was more than willing to stand and trade punches with me. Hell, I think he even liked it! He'd get a crazy look in his eye as if he relished the pain. This was one crazy white boy.

I slipped most of Cobb's jabs and countered with left hooks while working off the ropes. I bobbed and weaved, making him miss me with most of his punches. I connected with every jab I threw plus a few counter left hooks. Cobb landed a straight right hand, then dug a left hook, which I definitely felt, into my side. We traded punches for the rest of the round. The judges gave this round to Cobb.

In the second round I found myself fighting with my back to the ropes. I stood my ground, landing a succession of left jabs to halt Cobb's offensive attack. I managed to land a sneaky right-hand lead. At 35, my legs weren't what they used to be, so I kept stationary while battling it out with Cobb. My slick upper-body movement helped me avoid most of Cobb's punches. I caught him with a looping overhand right and a heavy left hook, but Cobb never flinched and kept firing back. However, I was landing a higher volume of punches while still slipping most of his bombs. I snapped Cobb's head back with a solid straight right hand. Cobb never attempted to avoid a punch. I've punched heavy bags that were more difficult to hit. Cobb picked up his attack and started to land heavily to my body. I caught Cobb with a big left hook near the end of the round and tied it up, one round apiece.

I decided to move the fight to ring center at the start of round three. We circled and jabbed. The kid was tough, and I realized early on that I was going to have major problems trying to put this big Texan away. I needed to win this fight to salvage my career. I kept pumping my jab and shooting the occasional overhand right to Cobb's head. He kept pushing forward, but he was far less reckless and slowed his punch rate. Once again, the action moved to the ropes, where Cobb and I exchanged our best shots. I moved off the ropes, snapping out stinging lefts. Cobb and I traded punches until the bell in this grueling affair. The round was even.

At the start of the fourth round we continued to trade jabs at ring center. Cobb kept in pursuit and moved me to the ropes, where we traded punches nonstop. He was landing solid body punches, but I managed to avoid most of his head shots. Then I spun Cobb around and landed a right to the body followed by another right to the head. Cobb kept loading up on his right hand, but I gamely fired back each time he connected. Cobb rallied near the end of the round in this exhausting battle—he wasn't going to give me anything. This round went to Cobb.

In round five, the fight moved to the ropes quickly as Cobb attempted to turn the battle into a street brawl. I stuck to my boxing skills as I fought off the ropes, attempting to keep the action at ring center where I could move freely if I got in trouble. Cobb's jab was more effective than before, and he followed through with solid rights. I landed a punishing right on Cobb's granite chin, followed by a stinging left hook. A five-punch combination near the end of the round made round five all mine.

The action didn't slow down in the sixth. Sensing that the fight was close, I picked up the attack against Cobb, opening up with both hands and catching him with a barrage of hooks, uppercuts, and right hands. I retreated to the ropes, where Cobb followed, throwing shots as he pursued me. I fought off the ropes, catching Cobb with jarring uppercuts. But Cobb stood his ground and fired back. I was caught with a powerful left. This was one tough young buck. Most fighters would have quit under these circumstances, but Cobb didn't know how to quit. We went toe-to-toe right to the end of the bell. My round.

In round seven, I started strong, greeting the Texan with a series of left hooks and uppercuts. He stood his ground and fired back. It had been a long time since I had engaged in such an exhausting contest. Maybe retirement was not so bad after all. I started popping Cobb with left jabs and connected on a brutal right uppercut. I knew he felt that one. I also unloaded some heavy leather on Cobb, hitting him with everything but the kitchen sink. A beautiful right cross landed on Cobb's chin but didn't even faze the guy. It appeared as if his game plan was to absorb as many punches as possible until I tired of throwing them. His chin seemed to defy damage. I worked off the ropes again, landing punches on Cobb continuously. Cobb took my best shots and fired back. At the conclusion of the round, we received a standing ovation from the appreciative crowd. Round seven was all mine.

Round eight saw us right back to slugging from the very start. I connected first with a powerful right cross that didn't even shake Cobb. The strong-chinned brawler fired right back. Cobb appeared tired and kept his mouth open most of the round, sucking some serious wind. I dug deep within myself and kept punching back. Cobb tried to rally back, but I met him punch for punch. I went back to the ropes, and Cobb followed in pursuit, connecting with a series of blows to my head and body. I fired back, but my long layoff from the ring and the furious pace were starting to take their toll. At the bell, I wearily strolled back to my corner. This round was Cobb's.

Our close-quarters shootout continued in round nine, and Cobb hurt me with a combination off the ropes, but I stood my ground and fought back. I caught Cobb with a brutal right uppercut that snapped his head back. I spent the last 30 seconds of the round laying against the ropes as Cobb threw everything in his repertoire at me. I ate more leather in the end of that round than I ever wanted. I tried to fire back, but the long battle had left me fatigued. Cobb took another round from me.

The action for the 10th and final round started right away when I landed a well-timed right uppercut that snapped Cobb's head back. We both knew it was a close fight, and I wanted to finish strong. Cobb fired back, but I was busier. I sucked it up and fired a six-punch combination at ring center that Cobb must have felt. The crowd was on its feet as we stood and traded punches. I had my back to the ropes, but fired back at Cobb. Finally, thank God, the bell rang and the fight was over.

Soon, the fans threw coins in the ring as a sign of appreciation, telling us that they had gotten their money's worth. I had never felt so sore following a fight, and I vowed to retire once more.

My late-round surge made the difference in the scoring. It was a split decision. I couldn't spare a hometown decision loss at this stage in my career. I gave a big sigh of relief when it was announced that referee Tony Perez and judge Chuck Hassett had it 97-94 and 96-95, respectively, for me. Judge A.D. Bynum penciled in Cobb 97-95.

I thought the judges' decision had ended my fight with Cobb. But I had one final encounter with him. That night at the hotel, Cobb wanted to settle things in the lobby "mano a mano" and frankly, he scared the piss out of me. I wanted no part of him, and the only thing I could do was to call the cops, which I did.

I later discovered that the reason why Cobb was so disgruntled over my victory was that because he had bet his entire purse of $200,000 on himself. He walked away from our bout without a penny.

Like many former boxers, Cobb hasn't fared too well in life after the ring. Despite a successful movie career, far more successful than my own, Cobb owed the IRS $260,000 in back taxes. That alone can break a man down, but add to that gambling debts from him, two ex-wives, and a few hucksters who called themselves managers who weaseled whatever he had left. Cobb ended up without a dime to his name and is now broke and living in a rundown apartment in Philadelphia. But he still has a heart of gold.

"I was never about the money," said Cobb recently. "I was about the fight—anywhere, anytime you want to don silk and leather, sunshine. I come to war. That's what I did."

I hear that loud and clear, sunshine. I remember the Alamo!

Boxing was no longer in my blood. I had surpassed my goals in regard to boxing, but huge paydays were flaunted before me. The Cobb payoff had been sizeable, but the offer I was given to fight media darling Cooney seemed larger than Fort Knox. If I defeated Cooney, millions more awaited in a rematch with Larry Holmes.

The fight with Cooney was scheduled for February 23, 1981, as the main event to one of boxing's biggest scheduled extravaganzas. The undercard, billed as "This Is It!" featured three main-event-worthy clashes: Thomas Hearns vs. Wilfredo Benitez, Hilmer Kenty vs. Alexis Arguello, and Matthew Saad Muhammad vs. Eddie Mustafa Muhammad. What was billed as "The Greatest Boxing Card in History" never materialized. Instead, we were involved with one of boxing's major scandals.

The fights were promoted by Muhammad Ali Professional Sports Inc., which was headed by Harold Smith, a former rock concert promoter. Ali had been given a large sum of money to use his name for the organization but had nothing to do with the management or control of it. Each boxer was promised inflated purses for signing his name on the dotted line. It was Harold Smith's purpose in life to wipe out the competition, chiefly Don King.

Just three weeks later, before the scheduled February date, Harold disappeared after he was linked to $21 million missing from a Beverly

Hills Wells Fargo bank. Within days of the scandal, the undercard fights were scrapped, but my main-event bout with Cooney was saved by Madison Square Garden and rescheduled for later in the spring.

Even though my heart wasn't in boxing anymore, I couldn't walk away. My surrogate father and manager, Bob Biron, had passed on. He had been hospitalized for quite some time and eventually had to have brain surgery. I was devastated to hear that he hadn't come out of surgery alive. He was 66. His death left a terrible void in my life.

Bob never had a son but always wanted one, so he treated me as his own. My longtime trainer Bill Slayton was all I had left from the glory years.

Despite my current disposition, I went through the motions of training camp in preparation for my upcoming fight with Cooney. For all intents and purposes, I thought I had at least one good fight left in me.

Cooney was one of the most heavily hyped prospects to come upon boxing in many moons. He was being carefully groomed for a shot at the heavyweight title against Holmes and was the No. 1 heavyweight contender in both the WBA and the WBC. Cooney had an impressive undefeated record in 24 contests, with 20 of those victories registered inside the distance. However, the only big-name opponents on his record, Jimmy Young and Ron Lyle, were "golden oldies," well past their fighting prime when they faced Cooney.

The scouting report on the Irish giant was that he had an awesome left hand featuring a devastating left hook. However, it also was reported that he couldn't crack an egg with his right. Cooney had fought only 86 professional rounds before our bout, with his fights averaging just over three rounds. I planned to box Cooney from the opening bell and use my experience to take him out in the later rounds.

The bout with Cooney represented a substantial payday ($850,000), and if I got past him, I would be in the hunt for larger paydays and a rematch with Holmes. At my age I felt I was in a must-win situation if I was to keep my career alive. Although our bout would be staged at Madison Square Garden in front of Cooney's hometown fans, two of my greatest fights had been in the Big Apple, when I shellacked Duane Bobick in one and the highly disputed loss in my final bout with Ali. I felt confident of victory, despite the 4-1 odds in Cooney's favor.

A partisan crowd of 9,436 filed into Madison Square Garden May 11, 1981, to witness what turned out to be my final bout. I entered the ring first and paced in anticipation of Cooney's entrance. I received a lukewarm response at my introduction, but the place exploded when the announcer said Cooney's name. Although I had been in this game too long to get psyched out, I had trained for a long battle and came out circling at the bell.

Cooney snapped a long double jab, and I slipped it with crafty head movement. I stepped in with a straight left that landed. I kept moving, pawing out jabs to Cooney's head and body, attempting to figure out his style. Cooney connected with a right hand that buckled my knees. So much for the rumor that Cooney didn't have a decent right hand. Cooney also dug a solid left hook into my midsection that sent me retreating to the ropes. I stood my ground and traded bombs with the local favorite.

I was holding my own, punch for punch, when all of a sudden Cooney connected with a left hook that rocked my world and sent me spinning in the corner. I covered up as Cooney opened up with both hands. Another left hook landed and sent me slumping towards the canvas; however, the bottom rope caught me on my way down, and I was in a sitting position as Cooney fired away. The referee was out of position and thought I was in a defensive crouch instead of semiconscious and held up only by the ropes. Cooney landed more devastating right uppercuts followed by lethal left hooks that landed against my already swirling head. Finally, the referee, Tony Perez, jumped in to halt the one-sided affair.

I had erred by trading punches with a puncher, but I felt fortunate just to be alive. The referee's bad judgment almost cost me my life. The fight doctor said that I was four seconds away from death.

Gerry Cooney: *I got a little bit frightened because I kept hitting him and he was unconscious.*

Three New York State Athletic Commission doctors, Frank Guarino, Earl Shaw, and Frank Folk, were quickly in my corner to make sure that I was all right. After giving me the once-over, I was pronounced neurologically OK and was able to attend the postfight conference.

Exactly four years before, to the night, I had knocked out Bobick in Madison Square Garden, I was knocked out in 54 seconds, which ironically, broke my record for the fastest knockout ever recorded in the Garden.

What can I say? Payback's a bitch!

Bill Slayton: *Kenny got caught in the first round. Cooney came out and jumped right on him, and that's something we didn't plan on. Cooney caught him cold. If he had beaten Cooney, he prob-*

ably would have had another fight, because it's hard to turn down a couple of million bucks.

Buford Green: *The thing I remember about that fight was that Ken was out of it for a long time. When he finally came to, the ref asked Ken where he was, and he answered, "Madison Square Garden." Then the ref asked what round and Ken answered, "First round." Then the ref asked, "Count backwards starting from a hundred," and Ken complied. Jackie was on the phone hysterical because she was at the hotel and someone told her that Ken had died, so I had to go into the room and assure her that he was fine. I think Ken had stayed in the fight game a little too long, and I think Ken will agree with me.*

Chapter Seventeen

Game Over

The game was up and I knew it. I had pushed my abilities to the limit, and I nearly paid for it with my life. I was still a relatively young man, only 37, but old for boxing, and I had other opportunities I wanted to pursue.

My total purse for my career was $16 million, second only to Muhammad Ali during his reign. Today, I would probably be earning somewhere in the neighborhood of $10 million a fight, but Ali definitely set the standard. Purses for boxing are out in the stratosphere today.

I have always felt that it takes a different kind of man, or athlete, to get in the ring and go one-on-one. It's different from basketball, football or anything else. I had been involved in team sports, but I took to boxing because it let me be my own man. In boxing I had to depend only on myself.

I was very lucky both in and out of the ring. I met a lot of nice people and made friends who helped open other doors of opportunity. I don't think anyone can say that I ever intentionally injured someone, or that I didn't treat everyone with respect. Many times my opponents were helpless, and I didn't take advantage of them. I think a lot of that has to do with my upbringing. I got some static for not hurting others when I did have them helpless, but I won't apologize for that. I had some regrets along the way, chiefly, that I didn't train hard for certain fights at the end of my career. I got into cutting corners and took things for granted. I was not as devoted as I once had been, and, in the end, I was the one who suffered.

All in all, I think I had a very successful career. Boxing changed my life in many ways. I have often wondered what I would have done if I had not gotten into boxing.

Once out of the limelight, I stayed out, although I still received plenty of offers to fight. I was offered $500,000 to fight Ron Lyle, big money for a rematch with Scott LeDoux, and a huge sum to fight Big John Tate.

My sole focus became my family, because I had put them on the back burner for eight years while my professional career was in high gear. One of my proudest achievements, and one of the least known, is that I was twice voted "Father of the Year" by the *Los Angeles Sentinel* and the *Los Angeles Times*.

After my first retirement following the LeDoux fight, NBC television offered me a broadcasting contract as a boxing analyst for the 1980 Olympics held in the Soviet Union. I had some previous experience in 1975 when Ali fought Joe Frazier for the third time. Boxing fans remember this classic as the "Thrilla in Manila." I was ringside at the fight with legendary broadcaster Don Dunphy, and I studiously watched his every move. He made me comfortable, and I enjoyed our banter while I gave my own perspective on the fight.

In 1983 I became a sports agent and formed the Ken Norton Personal Management Co. In the early 1980s, as the stakes and money grew higher for professional sports, there were many athletes who were being taken advantage of or not getting their full due. I felt that athletes, specifically black athletes, could benefit from my knowledge and years of experience working with Bob Biron. One thing I learned from Bob was to treat your clients as human beings, not as potential meal tickets or dollar signs. I wanted my clients to realize that they only have a few good years physically and to invest their money wisely so that they can live well after they leave the game.

The first pro client I signed was Southern Methodist University running back Eric Dickerson, the most exciting rusher to come along in 10 years. Dickerson was not only a big back, but he had speed, quickness, and agility. In his first year in the National Football League, Dickerson was named both Rookie of the Year and National Football Conference Player of the Year. The next year, 1984, Dickerson shattered O.J. Simpson's 11-year-old title for the single-season rushing record by gaining 2,105 yards. At the end of his career in 1993, Dickerson became the third-leading rushing of all time, having amassed 13,259 yards.

With Dickerson as a client, I added many more clients to my roster, and many opportunities arose that added to my company's stock.

When the Olympics came to Los Angeles in 1984, my company became an official licensee for the '84 Olympic Games, and the company sold such items as gold pins and key chains.

In the meantime, various movie offers rolled in, but I wanted to make sure that Ken Norton Personal Management was on its feet and running. Only when I knew that things were running smoothly did I accept an offer in 1985 to star in *Oceans of Fire*, an ensemble action thriller starring Gregory Harrison of TV's "Trapper John," football star Lyle Alzado, and boxing great Ray "Boom Boom" Mancini. With that kind of inspired casting, how could you not have a good time? And best of all, the filming would take place in beautiful Cancun, Mexico. It was better than a paid vacation.

In the movie, we played a group of oil riggers who fight a fiery, out-of-control blaze. The filming went smoothly enough, but a black cloud seemed to follow the cast. Not unlike what happened to the casts of *Rebel Without A Cause* and *Poltergeist*, the cast of *Oceans of Fire* found itself eerily following the same course of untimely death. A few months after the movie was shot, a major executive from the film died in a freak car accident. Things went from bad to worse when my good buddy Lyle told the press he was dying from years of steroid abuse. It was only a matter of time before my number was up.

Up to this point in my life, everything had been perfect. I had had a great boxing career; became a millionaire; had a wonderful wife, great kids, and a loving family; ran a successful sports agency; and got plum movie roles. Life was good, no doubt about it.

When I retired, I became friends with a gentleman named Bobby Moore and started drinking liquor, smoking cigarettes and going to bars with Bobby. Every Saturday night, Bobby and I would faithfully go out drinking, but I also made sure that Bobby and I were in church Sunday morning no matter how bad our hangovers were. I'm sure there were a few parishioners who gave us the once-over when we stumbled into church looking a little bleary-eyed and reeking of the previous night's booze. Looking back, for the life of me, I can't understand why we always made it a point to be in church on Sundays, no matter how bad we felt.

The alcohol made me bloat up, and I tipped the scales at 250 pounds, the heaviest I had ever been in my life. I wasn't an alcoholic, but I was definitely in the same ZIP code. I drank vodka and orange juice almost every night, but I didn't need to drink. I considered myself more of a social drinker; I liked to drink, but my body didn't crave alcohol.

I believe everything happens for a reason, and I can say with certainty today that this was a time in my life where I wasn't giving God my fullest attention. I was paying him my respects by giving him a nod every now and then when I appeared in church on Sundays, but I didn't have a personal relationship with him. I was out drinking every night, living too fast, and the big guy upstairs soon was going to give me His full attention.

On the evening of February 23, 1986, I lent my name and time to a fund-raiser for Los Angeles mayor Tom Bradley at the Biltmore Hotel. Ironically, on this night I had just one drink: a glass of wine. Other than that, I drank water that night. When I left around 11 p.m., I took the Santa Monica freeway home and the Vermont Avenue exit. That's when my world turned upside down.

From the accounts I've heard, my 1978 Clenet Excalibur most likely hit a curb on the ramp and ricocheted and hit another curb before going over the edge of the roadway. The car crashed into a tree near an abandoned house.

Ken Norton Jr.: *There are many theories about my father's accident. The one that makes the most sense to me is that at the off-ramp where the accident occurred there isn't much of a lane to merge for oncoming traffic. I think there must have been another car merging into the lane and that driver must have been stubborn, and I know how stubborn my father can be, so the two of them must have not wanted to give up or slow down behind the other. To avoid an accident, my father must have swerved to the side, hit the curb, and flipped over.*

It was a miracle that I was found at all. A 10-year-old boy heard the crash from his house, and he left his bedroom to seek out my car. When he spotted me strapped upside down in the car, he woke up his parents, and they called 911. Many witnesses, including my business partner, Jack Rodri, vouched for me in the *Los Angeles Times*: "Norton didn't drink, and he was in good spirits when I left him. He was totally alert." Eventually the accident investigators determined that neither drugs nor alcohol were involved, but that certainly didn't stop the speculation.

Paramedics came from the Los Angeles Fire Department, and the crew had to use the Jaws of Life to pull me out of my car, which was a twisted heap of metal and glass.

I lay there in that position for three and a half hours, until a helicopter transported me to Cedars-Sinai Hospital at 3:30 a.m., where my condition was listed as serious and unstable. I went from being a healthy, virile, sculpted athlete, an actor and nationally renowned broadcaster, to a man barely hanging on to life by a thread with brain seeping out of his skull.

I was wheeled into the emergency room for a three-hour life-or-death operation in which skull fragments were removed from my brain. The top of my head looked like it had caved in, my jaw was broken in three different places, and the right side of my face was partially paralyzed. My face was a mess. When I got out of the operating room, I was listed in serious but stable condition. I was wheeled back into my private room, where my family had a chance to see me for the first time, but I was still under heavy sedation. It was a miracle that I wasn't a vegetable at this point.

When I awoke from my accident, I had no clue where I was or what had happened to me, but worst of all, I couldn't speak. Words wouldn't come out of my mouth because my jaw was wired shut. I only knew that when I awoke, I was in a strange place and was strapped down to a bed. My wife, Jackie, told the hospital staff to strap me down because I would probably take off when I woke up. For a second, I could have sworn that I was in the nuthouse.

Ken Norton Jr.: *I was a junior at UCLA when I got the phone call about my father being in the hospital. Jackie was already at Cedars-Sinai when I arrived. I was devastated. The man who had been like Superman to me was in a tremendous amount of pain. I had to help the hospital staff hold him down so X rays could be taken. Here was Superman screaming in pain, in pure agony, and I felt so horrible for him. Suddenly, I was the man of the family at 20 and I had to keep it all together and be strong for everyone. The doctors told me that he might not make it, that he probably would never walk again, and that he might be a vegetable. After I walked in and saw him fighting everyone, I said to myself, "No, he isn't going to die." I didn't know how he would fare mentally or if he would mend physically, but I knew from that point on that he definitely wasn't going to die.*

Kenisha Norton (Ken's daughter): *I remember being dropped off at school that day and three people came up to me and asked, "Is your father OK? I heard on the radio coming to school that he was in an accident." I said to them, "As far as I know, he's doing fine." I thought this whole thing might have been a big, elaborate joke. Finally, a teacher came up and asked me about my dad, and that's when I started to worry. After that, I decided to go to the front* *office, and I asked the school secretary if she had heard anything about my father, and she said she hadn't but would let me know if she did. I went through the day without hearing anything more, but when I got out of school, a friend's mother came to pick me up. Usually, my dad picked me up, so when I saw this lady, I knew there was something terribly wrong. From there, I was taken to the hospital, where the rest of the family was in my father's hospital room.*

When I entered the room, he was bandaged from head to toe. His jaw was wired and he had to eat and drink everything through a straw. I remember a doctor telling him that he might never walk again. His leg was broken, his jaw was broken, his skull was fractured. My father later called himself the "human bowling ball" because he had these three indentations in his head. He later had another surgery where a bone was taken from behind his ear to fill the three holes.

Ruth Norton: *John and I were asleep when Jackie called us, and I don't think she wanted to tell me how serious it was because Ken had had accidents before. I asked her if she thought I should come out and she said, "Yes." John had just gotten out of the hospital from a stroke, so I called and made arrangements to go out to California, and John stayed with his sister.*

When I first saw Ken, I wondered if he was going to live. To me, it was that serious. His skull had all sorts of metal and debris in it from the accident, which would have had to affect his personality. He was humbled by it, that's for sure.

Muhammad Ali stopped and paid me a visit. I was unconscious for I don't know how long, but when it counted most, Ali was there for me. I couldn't recall who he was at that moment, but I remember thinking, Who's this crazy man standing by my bed? Ali was performing magic tricks, making handkerchiefs disappear, and he levitated. I said to myself, If he does one more awful trick, I'm gonna get well just so that I can kill him. Ali proved to me just what kind of man he is with his show of support, that he was more than a professional competitor of mine; he was a friend in my time of need.

After four weeks of hospitalization, with stitches in my head from one ear to another and 52 pounds lighter, I was released from the hospital. But I was years away from a full recovery. My vocal cords were shattered, the right of my body was paralyzed, and my jaw was wired shut. My body was healthy from years of training, so I was able to survive the accident, but I wanted to do more than just survive. I wanted to walk and talk and do all of the things I was able to do before.

The hardest adjustment I had to make when I got home was to learn to be subservient. I was bound to a wheelchair. I couldn't feed myself. I couldn't go to the bathroom alone. Ken Jr. had to carry me from room to room or to the shower to get cleaned. He pushed me in my wheelchair for long walks and kept me alive mentally. He'd dress me in the morning and undress me at night. My son, at 20, became my caretaker.

Worst of all, my memory was almost completely wiped out. I remembered nothing of the accident, or for that matter, anything that happened three years before the accident and three years after the accident. It was like a tape had been erased. I figure now I'll live six years longer!

It upset me that I couldn't communicate with anyone because of my injured vocal cords. When I talked, it sounded clear to me, but not to anyone else. I remember sitting at home and staring at a chair. I'd say, "Chair" to myself, and it was my goal to someday be able to get up and walk to the chair. But I couldn't tell anyone about it, because I couldn't speak. It was horrible not to be able to have a normal conversation with anybody, especially my kids. I went several months with my demands being misunderstood, even by my wife.

Once, when I went to my son's football game at UCLA and I was being helped down a corridor, Keith Jackson, the ABC commentator, came toward me. Keith said some kind words about Ken Jr., and I tried to reply. The words were in my head but they never came out of my mouth. I wanted to answer but I was physically and mentally unable to do it.

I would also have periods of blindness. I went to the Rose Bowl to watch Ken Jr. play, and after I'd sat in the sun for a quarter, the sun's rays blinded me. I mean, I couldn't see a thing. I had to sit in the car and listen to the rest of the game on the radio.

I felt as if I was emerging from a dream. Each month it became more real, but I had a long way to go. I was aware of my surroundings, but I didn't believe it sometimes. Everything was surreal, as if I were watching my life through a television set.

Ken Norton Jr.: *During those first six months after he got home from the hospital, the one thing my dad kept asking me over and over was, "What happened to me? What happened?" And I'd have to tell him. There were certain things he couldn't do any longer,*

*like drive a car. He could be so damn stubborn sometimes, because
he'd want to drive and I'd have to say, "Pop, you can't." Then he'd get
mad and ask why. There were times where I'd have to park my car
behind his van and stay in it for hours at a time to make sure he
wouldn't drive. And yet it was that same stubbornness and refusal to
quit that made him get up out of that wheelchair and walk again.*

My ultimate goal when I got out of the hospital was to walk
again, but before I could do that, I faced years of physical and mental
therapy. When you're in the situation that I was in, something has to
rattle deep within your core. Your soul has to be so stirred up that it finally
makes you angry enough to do something about it and go for it. I think
what had galled me the most was the handicapped placard that hung on
to my van's rearview mirror. I didn't want to be known as crippled. Hell, I
had a perfect physique, but now I was reduced to handicapped status.

For two years I was wheelchair-bound, but I worked my way up
to a walker. At the Saddleback Chiropractic Rehabilitation Center in Laguna Niguel, California, I began lifting weights and went through a rigorous program that included treatments with a helium-neon-laser acupunc-
ture process.

Dr. Janice Kowalski (Ken's therapist): *We balanced the
right side of Ken's body, which had suffered the most trauma, with
the left side. He had a significant loss of coordination on his right
side. The trouble was that he couldn't get the signals from his brain to
his leg to tell him where it was. The helium-neon-laser treatments
stimulated certain pressure points to balance the flow of energy in his
body. He had some numbness in his leg, but it had been completely
numb before. The man is dedicated, that's for sure. The doctors didn't
think he'd walk again.*

The regimen for rehabilitation was not quite the same as it was
for training for a fight, but the discipline was the same, and not giving up
was the key to walking again. Ninety percent of the battle was uphill. I set
my goals high, and when I surpassed what I thought I would do, I went a
lot farther than I thought I ever would. For two years I couldn't walk;
then I moved to a walker. Then the cane. I couldn't use crutches because
my balance was so bad.

At first the doctors thought I might die, and if I didn't die, I
wouldn't be coherent. Then they thought, even if I could talk, I'd be a
cripple. Now I was talking and walking; hell, I could even chew bubble
gum and walk at the same time.

Kenisha Norton: *I don't think it's right of doctors to tell a patient, in this case my father, that he'd never walk again. In life, you never know what may happen. I think they're welcome to their medical opinion, but patients need reassurance and optimism. My dad has very strong willpower. Dad used to tell us kids that if you want something in life, you have to go and get it. I remember him telling me a story about how he used to push himself when he was training. A part of his training was to psyche himself into running up and down this great big hill, and he would accomplish this by buying something that was a little bit above and beyond what he could afford, like a brand-new Lincoln Mark III. He had to win that next fight to pay for the Lincoln or to pay the next month's bills, but that's how he'd get himself to run that hill. He controlled his destiny, and that's how he looked at his rehabilitation.*

The accident definitely gave me a reason to reevaluate my life. The brush with death changed my outlook on a number of matters. I had a better appreciation for my wife and children. When you come as close as I did to meeting The Maker, it makes you realize how close you were to losing your family. I used to take my family for granted, but not anymore. I no longer fear death and have learned to enjoy life more.

My faith also took a turn for the better after the accident. God had always played a factor in my life, but my belief is much deeper now. I truly believe this was God's way of getting my attention. I had ignored Him while things were going well, and I felt this was His way of letting me know who was in charge. But God wasn't ready to take me. I'm in no hurry to visit His kingdom, and I think that I was left on earth to fulfill a purpose.

My accident made me see how lucky I am. Every time I see an individual who has been paralyzed, bedridden, or is homeless, it's a reality check for me. Now I understand that no matter how bad my life might get, there are others who have it much worse. For example, during my recovery, I had to disband Ken Norton Sports Management Co. There was no way I could handle the necessary tasks, and I wouldn't have trusted anybody who was in the current shape that I was in. My past efforts with Eric Dickerson and the 1984 Olympics had returned a nice windfall, and it hurt to let go of the business. Now I look back and tell myself that life definitely could have been a whole lot worse.

Physical therapy became the highlight of my day. I never missed a session. It was the one place I could work off life's frustrations. The noticeable results of my efforts also helped guarantee my daily return. Life, with my positive outlook and determination, was starting to show some signs of normalcy. However, I had no idea that a tragedy in the form of a bitter family dispute was in my near future.

Chapter Eighteen

Back on My Feet

Life was slowly returning to normal. I continued to improve from my near-fatal auto accident, but I had a pronounced limp, and my voice was deep and gravelly. Sometimes I slurred my words, and many in the media and the boxing world thought I was punchy.

Throughout my recovery, my son Ken's successful college football career at UCLA provided an extra incentive for me to regain my health. Ken would visit me daily at the hospital. He would help bathe me by undressing me, then pushing me into the shower, wheelchair and all. He was always there for me during this critical period of my life. I just wanted to regain my health as soon as possible so I could watch him play football again and lead a normal life.

My memory improved with time, but I still had difficulty recalling certain events or people. Usually a long conversation with an old friend would jar my brain, and I'd remember past events. At other times, I could have a conversation with a stranger, have them leave the room and return five minutes later, only to introduce myself to them again.

Ken finished his promising career at UCLA by making the All-American team his senior year. Not bad for a kid who never touched a football until the 11th grade. Boxing was not the only sport I steered Ken away from. I didn't give my consent to Ken's playing football until his high school coach promised me that Westchester High no longer taught head-first tackles. I remembered my days on the gridiron and recalled too many paralyzing injuries. Ken was a big kid, but I had no idea that he would turn into such a terror on the football field.

One of my most exciting moments as a father came in April 1988, when Ken was drafted in the second round by the Dallas Cowboys. I was a little shocked at first, because teams like the Cleveland Browns and San Francisco 49ers had shown more interest initially. However, I couldn't have been happier. The Cowboys had been Ken's favorite team as a kid. He grew up worshiping the likes of Tony Dorsett, Roger Staubach, and Ed "Too Tall" Jones. Besides, Dallas was only a short flight away. Also, a part of me was having a difficult time letting go. Ken had attended UCLA because it was close to home. He wanted to be near me throughout my ongoing recovery. Apart from my wife, Jackie, he was the only person I felt totally comfortable around. Now he was moving on to the National Football League in Dallas.

Ken invited me on his first visit of the Cowboys' training facility, where we were given an informal tour of the Cowboys' Valley Ranch by linebacker coach Jerry Tubbs. I hit it off with Jerry right away. Jerry said he felt comfortable standing between a guy who could run a 4.5 40 and a man who could knock anybody out. I liked his sense of humor. During the tour, Jerry discussed the Cowboys' plans to move Ken from his natural position of inside linebacker to outside linebacker. I had complete confidence that Ken would have little difficulty adjusting to a position change. He originally had been recruited by UCLA as a running back before switching to linebacker.

From the first time he laced up his shoulder pads, Ken became dedicated to football. I never had the same desire to excel in football as Ken had. I was so fanatical about his football career that Jackie claimed I was reliving my second childhood through Ken.

Ken had hoped he could sign without any contract disputes or holdouts. We agreed that I would in no way attempt to act as his agent. Even though I had successfully represented running back Eric Dickerson a few years back, Ken could probably do much better with me out of the picture.

I went to Dallas several times in the fall of 1988. I was the proudest father in the stadium, but felt for Ken at the same time. He had a long and disappointing rookie season. To accompany the pressures of professional football, he had been plagued by injuries for most of the year. He had seen action in only three games, and his only highlights all year were a fumble recovery and one knocked-down pass. Ken was not much of a complainer, but I knew him and intuitively felt his frustration.

His rookie season had been doomed from the beginning. He fractured his thumb in preseason training camp and spent most of the year on the injured list. Ken was not allowed to even work up a sweat for fear the metal pins in his thumb would rust. He couldn't even jog or pump iron to release his pent-up tension. To make matters worse, he had difficulty grasping Dallas' flex defense. Ken initially failed to live up to his considerable promise, and no one was more troubled about it than he was. He planned to return to Los Angeles immediately after the season ended. I anxiously awaited his return and joked that I would give him free membership at a Gold's Gym I owned in Laguna Hills as an added incentive to return home.

Ken returned home with a steely determination to be an NFL starter in his second season. He started an off-season training program that rivaled in intensity my preparation for the third Ali fight. He ran six miles every day and followed it with a strenuous weight-lifting session. Ken was not going to bow out without a fight. He trained like a champion boxer to prove his lackluster rookie season had been a fluke.

My son had spent most of his early life watching me run five miles a day at 4 a.m., followed by long days laboring in a car factory. Then, after work, it was off to the boxing gym for a grueling workout. Ken had witnessed firsthand the sacrifice it takes to make it to the top. In the off-season after his rookie year, Ken proved to me that he had learned the value of hard work. I was proud and amazed at his prowess to make himself a productive player in the NFL. Fortunately, everything started to come together for Ken upon his return to Dallas.

Ken Norton Jr.: *My father did such a tremendous job of raising me, letting me know he loved me without spoiling me. Even though he was making more money as I grew older, he made me earn any money I received. He may have been more strict with me because he did not want to indulge me and, in hindsight, I thank him for that because I grew up with a hunger and a desire. I was not fat and catered to like many rich kids.*

In a bold move, the Dallas Cowboys replaced the legendary Tom Landry with one of college football's finest coaches, former University of Miami head coach Jimmy Johnson. The Cowboys' new defensive coordinator, Dave Wannstedt, eliminated as much pressure on Ken as possible by promising to treat his next season as if it were his rookie season. Dave had confidence in Ken right from the beginning and predicted he would be a future starter. The new, less complicated, but more aggressive defense also benefited Ken. As training camp ended, Ken earned a spot as a starter at outside linebacker or middle linebacker, depending on the defensive situation.

Ken proved his worth as a starter in the first game of the 1989 season. Although the Cowboys got hammered 28-0 in the opener against the New Orleans Saints, Ken recovered a fumble and registered eight tackles. He played consistently and improved as the years passed. For the next few seasons, I went to great lengths to attend as many Cowboy games as possible.

Ken's career with the Cowboys continued to be productive until a knee injury prematurely ended his season in December 1990. He was having a fantastic season up until the injury, registering 119 tackles.

It is difficult to explain, but I really got a rush when Ken played football. I never had any concerns for him on the field; I knew he could take care of himself. I realized I had made the right choice by shielding him from my boxing career. I know I would have been overprotective, and I probably would have been quick to stop one of his bouts if he was taking any kind of punishment. That would not have been fair to him. It was different on the football field. Ken was confident and knew how to play the game. The only fear I had was when I saw him injured on the field. As a parent, it was difficult to stomach.

While Ken's football career gained momentum after a full recovery from his knee injury, my movie career was evaporating. My last feature movie, *Kiss and Be Killed*, was released in 1991. Hollywood can be a finicky town, and I blame the accident for cutting short my career on the silver screen. My voice was still slurred and gravelly, and no matter how hard I worked at my rehabilitation, I could not get rid of my limp. Most of my roles had been as a strongman. There wasn't a lot of work for a muscle-bound actor with slurred speech and a limp.

My final appearance on the big screen to date was a small cameo appearance in a 1998 flick starring comedian Norm McDonald and titled *Dirty Work*. The three years I had spent in acting school seemed like a waste. I would miss many of the wonderful people I had met in the movie industry: guys like Lyle Alzado and Ray "Boom Boom" Mancini, and Mr. T, whom I befriended on the set of the "The A-Team." I had had a small part in the third episode of the popular TV show, where I played a character named Jackhammer, who battled BA's (Mr. T's) friend in a fight-to-the-death boxing match for freedom.

Even though I worked for hours on end, my vocal cords never completely healed, and my voice would never regain its former tone. So, my days at the microphone calling fights also were over. I had had some good times working as a radio color commentator for the 1984 Olympics. And I will never forget calling the live closed-circuit telecast of the "Thrilla in Manilla" with Don Dunphy and actor Flip Wilson. I can only laugh when I recall how we were short one seat for the announcing team that evening. At times I played a comical game of musical chairs with Don and Flip while we attempted to keep our composure calling the fight.

Not all of my radio broadcasts had ended on such a high note. Art Aragon, a former top contender in the early '50s, hosted a radio talk show in Southern California and invited me on as a guest. Art was quite the villain during his heyday as a boxer, and as he continued with the interview, he kept referring to all the guys of my era as "bums." After the fifth time, I got irritated. I took it personally, even though he only meant it as a figure of speech. When the radio show broke for a commercial, I stood and asked if anybody in the audience had a baseball bat. I was attempting to make light of the situation, but at the same time, I was ticked off. Fortunately for Art, no one had a baseball bat. I had met Art a few times before, and on this occasion the man would just not shut up. He tried to come off as a boxing insider, but he really came off as a guy who may have taken too many punches to the head.

Although I was officially out of the entertainment industry, life still went on. I attended numerous charity functions whenever possible a as way of giving back to society. I will never forget one such reality check.

The Miami Project, founded by former Miami Dolphin Nick Buoniconti, hosted its annual Great Sports Legends dinner as a fundraiser for paralysis research. I was invited to receive an award for my rapid recovery from temporary paralysis. I was honored by the loud ovation I received as I walked across the stage to accept my award. I grabbed the microphone and announced, "I just wanted to show everyone I could do it."

Earlier that evening, I pushed Nick's son, Marc, in his wheelchair to his table. Marc had become paralyzed in a college football game. It was quite an eye opener. It made me realize how lucky I was to be alive and reasonably healthy. My current condition was light years away from paralysis. That evening made me realize how lucky I was to be back on my feet.

One of the highlights during my rehabilitation was the release of *Champions Forever*, a video documentary produced in 1989 that featured highlights and interviews of the championship bouts between Muhammad Ali, Joe Frazier, Larry Holmes, George Foreman, and me.

Parts of the video were shot at Johnny Tocco's Ringside Gym in Las Vegas. The gym had been a Las Vegas boxing institution since Johnny abandoned St. Louis and opened the place in the late 1950s. Tocco's Gym hosted workouts by top contenders throughout the years. Iron Mike Tyson trained there for all of his Vegas bouts. He preferred the spartan surroundings of Tocco's in lieu of the populated casino atmosphere. Johnny once had trained heavyweight champion Sonny Liston, and now he was playing host to five former world champions.

The five of us sat in the middle of the ring on chairs and fielded questions from former baseball slugger Reggie Jackson. Topics ranged from Ali's three-year exile to thoughts on battles with each other. Rarely had all of us been in the same room together, and it was good to see old warriors again. One noticeable change was the personality transformation of George Foreman. He had changed from the scowling hard-ass bully of his early title days to one of the warmest, most gregarious people I have ever known. Some things hadn't changed, and Ali and Frazier continued to trade verbal barbs. Ali was playful as always, but I got the distinct feeling that Frazier was still a little bitter from all of the harassing he had taken over the years from Ali. All in all, we had a great time reminiscing and telling old war stories. We share a special camaraderie; we're always in good company when the five of us get together.

I hooked up with Ken whenever our schedules would allow. Ken had been in Dallas for a few years and had completely taken to the city and life in the NFL. He had also fallen in love with a charming and beautiful young woman named Angela Fike. I had met Angela several times during the two years that she and Ken dated. We hit it off from the very beginning. As time went on, Ken confided to me that he wanted to marry her.

After getting to know Angela, it was easy to understand why Ken had fallen for her. But, as his father, I took it upon myself to inform Ken of my thoughts on his marriage. I didn't want him to rush into anything. After all, I had married young and it had failed. Since approximately half of all marriages end in divorce, I suggested to Ken that Angela sign a prenuptial agreement. He was a young buck, making excellent money, and I wanted him to protect himself.

What I got was a pain worse than any punch ever landed by George Foreman or Gerry Cooney. Ken became extremely angered as a result of our father-to-son discussion. We did not speak to each other for over two and a half years!

Ken Norton Jr.: *I think it had a lot to do with the fact that I was no longer living at home and resided in Dallas. I had told my father how I thought this was the girl I was going to marry. I was 24 and my own man, an adult. Then all of a sudden, my dad and Jackie are telling me, "Wait a minute. We don't know this girl. Don't rush into anything."*

Two and a half years is a long time to stop communicating with someone you love. Looking back on it now, it all seems so pointless. Ken had many traits I admired, such as determination and integrity, and I would like to think I passed those traits on to him. Unfortunately, I may have passed on one of my less-positive traits, too: stubbornness. I felt that Ken owed me a call to clean up the problem. It was a call that I never received. The silent war had started. Internally, it ate me alive, but externally, I did not want anyone to know it. I think that's what they refer to as foolish pride.

The first year was the toughest. I was a basket case in the beginning. We had a large picture of Ken hanging in the living room, but it hurt too much to look at it, and I took it off the wall. I could feel the loss of my friend right from the beginning. The guy I raised alone as an infant was no longer a part of my life, and it killed me. We had always been the best of friends. After I was injured in the accident, it was Ken who became my chief caretaker. I had never been more proud of my son than at that time.

My mind drifted back to a few disagreements we had had during my rehabilitation. I remember one time I demanded to drive our van home, even though it was strictly against doctor's orders. Ken refused to allow me to drive and I was angry with him, but he would not give any ground. After he dropped me off at home, he waited in his parked car several hours just to make sure I didn't attempt to drive. After disagreements like that, we always managed to make up. This time it was different.

Kenisha Norton: *I remember the beginning stages of their rift. Dad was always deep in thought instead of being the happy-go-lucky prankster that defines his personality. He would just sit there quietly, with his mind in another world. You could tell he was in a lot of pain. It was really hard for all of us.*

Once I decided to focus my energy on my three children at home—Brandon, Kenisha, and Kene Jon—the problem with Ken became more manageable. The year 1992 definitely was the most difficult period of my life in regard to our family feud. However, one bright moment lifted my spirits: I received notice that I would be inducted into the International Boxing Hall of Fame. Approximately one in a thousand boxers ever receives such an honor. It ranked right up there with my victory over Muhammad Ali as my greatest sports accomplishments.

Ed Brophy, director of the International Boxing Hall of Fame, gave me the news. Inductions would be held in the small town of Canastota, New York, in early June 1992. To be honored on the same level as guys like Muhammad Ali, Joe Louis, Archie Moore, and Joe Frazier meant a great deal to me. This would be only the third year of inductions, and to be voted in so quickly was an honor in itself.

The International Boxing Hall of Fame opened its doors in 1989, and boxing was long overdue for this type of facility. Ironically, Cooperstown, New York, home of the internationally known Baseball Hall of Fame, is only an hour's drive away. Canastota, a small town with a population of 5,000, had produced two homegrown world champions in Carmen Basilio and his nephew, Billy Backus. Ed felt this was the ideal location to recognize great boxers from around the world. My induction class was composed of 29 boxers or ring personalities. In all, only 108 people in boxing had been inducted. I felt special, to say the least.

The three-day Hall of Fame weekend was one of the most memorable of my life. Fellow inductee, trainer Angelo Dundee, put it this way: "I feel like a pig in slop." More than 10,000 boxing fans jammed Canastota for the event. The weekend played host to such boxing greats as Kid Gavilan, Ike Williams, Archie Moore, and Willie Pep, to name a few.

The weekend featured plenty of opportunities to mingle with boxing fans and former fighters. I had always had a blast pulling one of my numerous pranks on an unsuspecting fan. One of my favorite God-given talents was the ability to clench my fist in a way that released a momentary slight breeze. I would squeeze my hand real quick and release a blast of air. I had the best time sneaking behind someone and shooting a gust of wind behind their car. Then, I would quickly turn away and act as though I had no idea what had just taken place. People would often blame the person next to them as I admired my work from a distance.

Dinner each night was spent at Graziano's restaurant, located across the street from the Hall of Fame. After dinner, I always made sure the waitress placed my tab on the table of some unsuspecting fan whom I had never met. It was always good fun to watch the reaction of the surprised individual.

Despite threatening weather and rain on the day of the inductions, boxing's die-hard fans turned out by the thousands for the ceremonies and the Parade of Champions that followed. It was a memorable day, and I could not have shared the podium with a classier bunch of individuals. Unfortunately, due to health reasons, Germany's former world heavyweight champion, Max Schmeling, couldn't attend. One international boxer who did take the podium was Eder Jofre of Brazil. Jofre was a former two-time champion, but his uniqueness centered on the fact that he won his two world championships almost 13 years apart! Jofre's entire introduction speech was translated by Angelo.

Angelo developed 12 world champions, and he was still active in the sport at the time of the induction. Howard Cosell put it best when he said, "If I had a son who wanted to be a boxer, the only man I would entrust him to would be Angelo Dundee." I couldn't have said it better myself.

Finally, it was my turn to take the podium. My brief speech focused on Angelo.

I remember looking out into the audience. Carmen Basilio and Gene Fullmer were seated in the front row. Thirty years earlier they twice waged war in savage encounters. Now they appeared to be best friends. I told the crowd that I had become known because of a guy named Ali. I then looked over at Angelo, who had been seated next to me, and remarked, "My bank account grew out of my association with Ali. Thank you, Angelo." Everyone in the place broke out in laughter.

One fellow inductee who cannot go without mention is the classy former three-time champion Alexis Arguello. During my entire speech, Arguello pretended to be asleep. Then I playfully mentioned the time Aaron Pryor whupped his butt pretty good in Miami. As you can imagine, that woke up Arguello pretty fast. Arguello had the dubious distinction of being the first inducted Hall of Famer to return to the ring. He had originally retired in 1986, which satisfied the five-year retirement eligibility before being elected to the Hall of Fame in 1992. Two years later, Arguello returned to the ring for an ill-advised two-bout series. Fortunately for all of us, he soon retired again in perfect health.

Because I enjoyed the weekend so much, each June I attempt to make the trek back to boxing's shrine in Canastota. The annual weekend gives me a chance to catch up with prominent boxers from my era. Fighters such as the granite-jawed George Chuvalo and the bar-brawling Chuck Wepner made it a point to attend my induction.

Wepner is a boxing original. He once had more than 70 stitches sewn into his face after a bloody match with Sonny Liston. Wepner's skin tore like wet tissue, but the man had no shortage of guts. One of my favorite Wepner stories is the time he had been rocked hard in a fight and was given a standing eight-count. The referee checked Wepner's mental condition by questioning the dazed boxer on how many fingers he was holding up. "How many chances do I get?" was Wepner's first response!

Boxing is a special fraternity, and the weekend brings out many of its top stars. Each inductee receives a gold ring at the induction ceremony and a plaque of each member also is placed in the Hall of Fame.

Although my induction was a source of great pride, I would never find true happiness until my family life was back in order.

Chapter Nineteen

Burying the Hatchet

I can remember on more than one occasion picking up the phone and dialing Ken's residence. I would have almost all of his numbers punched in and then I would hang up the phone. Several thoughts raced through my confused mind. What if he didn't want to talk to me? That would have been too painful to handle. Then, eventually my mood would switch, and I would get angry and bull-headed. If this mess was ever going to be patched up, he would have to call me. I know it sounds silly now, but at the time it was extremely painful. For the first several months of our dispute, no one but our family knew there was a rift. When I did not attend his wedding, word of our disagreement started to spread. Ken and I did share one common thought: we both wanted to keep our personal business to ourselves. The world did not need to know about the Nortons' dirty laundry, but the media would eventually make sure that would not be possible.

Kenisha Norton: *We know what the media is capable of and that you cannot always believe what you read. I think the media took a statement and used only a portion of it to satisfy themselves. And you hear only a piece of a statement and only hear that being taken out of context, then you misinterpret what's been said. Though that was only part of it, these two men were grown adults and should have been man enough to call each other up on the telephone. The media did play a role, but they should have been strong enough in their relationship not to believe what they were hearing.*

The media spilled the story right before the Super Bowl. However, I had been living the nightmare for several months. I no longer attended any games in Dallas. In the past I had always been allowed on the field to attend pregame warm-ups for all Cowboy games. But I had been conspicuously absent the entire 1992 season. In October, the Cowboys came to Los Angeles to play the Raiders at the Coliseum. I didn't attend the game because I hadn't been invited. Looking back on it, sometimes our misunderstanding bordered on the absurd.

A separate telephone line had been installed so Ken could contact Kenisha and Kene Jon without interruption. Ken called on Christmas Eve and the day after Christmas. He sent Kenisha and Kene Jon presents, but I did not come to the phone. Maybe I should have just grabbed the phone and said, "Merry Christmas," but we had not spoken since our argument, and when he called, it was always on the private line. I knew it would take a lot of internal fortitude to call him, but I didn't want to give the wrong message to my family. At that time, I felt giving in would show weakness, and I did not want my children at home to lose respect for me. Looking back, it was all a lack of communication. The wounds were still fresh, and in no way was I going to grovel to my son. If he was angry with me, I knew at the very least he still respected me. I never wanted to jeopardize that. If he ever called, I would tell him to come home and straighten out this mess. It was a call I hoped for every day, but never received.

If he was troubled by our disagreement, at least it did not affect him professionally. On the football field, Ken was having another superb season in 1992. He rarely left the field on a defensive play. While his teammates shuffled in and out of second and third down, Ken always remained in the game, only shifting to a new defensive position. Ken covered for the injured Billy Bates in the nickel defense and continued playing weakside linebacker in the standard defense. Ken did not seem to mind being consistently on the field. When he started his career with the Cowboys, the defense was on the field over 30 minutes a game. The defense had drastically improved over the last two years and was now ranked first in the NFL. Ken's first two seasons in the league constituted playing on a 3-13 team his rookie year and even got worse the second year when the Cowboys went a dismal 1-15. Now Ken was playing on a squad that would be headed for the Super Bowl. I never spoke a word to Ken through the entire season, but I caught all the Cowboys games on television and closely monitored my son's career through the news. Even though we did not speak, I still loved him and rooted for him quietly from a distance.

Our rift became public on January 16, 1993, when the *Los Angeles Times* splashed our story on the headlines of the sports page in an article titled "A Broken Bond." The Cowboys were set to play the San Francisco 49ers at Candlestick Park for the NFC championship. I had not planned to attend, and unfortunately, the newspaper took it upon itself to make it the world's business. Ken was extremely angry about the news going public. He had always been a very private person. The only comment I had ever read in the paper from Ken concerning our rift was basically "No comment." I also did my best not to add any fuel to the fire. Unfortunately, they had found a story line they became quite fond of.

Ken Norton Jr.: *It was horrible! The thing is, what the press does not know, they will just fill in the spots wherever and whenever they feel like it. I think the media kept the rift going longer than it should have because they had no idea what was going on and they would just make things up.*

A reporter from a local news station popped by the house to confirm that I would not be attending the 1993 Super Bowl, which would be taking place at the Rose Bowl in Pasadena, a 90-minute drive from my home in Laguna Niguel. The cameras were rolling as soon as the interview began. I felt fine early in the meeting with the reporter as I confirmed my status as a no-show for the Super Bowl. However, the more I talked about Ken, the sadder I became. I could feel tears running down my face. When I looked up, the camera was still rolling. Instinctively, I grabbed the camera and promised the reporter that if that particular part of the interview were aired on television, he would have to personally face my wrath. The interview aired shortly after, but the reporter kept his word and cut the interview off during mid-sentence just before I got choked up. Many friends approached me about what happened as to the conclusion of that conversation. Fortunately, the newscaster kept his word— fortunately for him—or else an unsanctioned knockout victory would have been added to my record.

Super Bowl XXVII was one of the best games of Ken's career. I'm sure Ken was angered by being left off the Pro Bowl team, and his determination showed through during the game. My parents flew out from Jacksonville to catch the game, but without an official invitation, there was no way I was going to go. I caught every moment, even Michael Jackson's crotch-grabbing halftime show, from the comfort of my own home.

The Cowboys stomped on Jim Kelly and the Buffalo Bills 52-17 to record the third Super Bowl victory in franchise victory and Dallas' first in 15 years. The Cowboys' defense had never been better, tallying four interceptions and five fumble recoveries. My son was right in the middle of the action. Ken recovered a fumble that he returned for a touchdown and became the eighth player ever to score a defensive touchdown in the Super Bowl. He recorded 10 tackles and even knocked quarterback Jim Kelly out of the game with a fierce hit.

Kene Jon and Kenisha were sad about missing the game, and I promised them that if Ken ever returned to this extravaganza, regardless of our situation, they would get to see their brother play, even if it meant buying my own tickets. I tried to put it all behind me and concentrate on my fatherly duties. I had certain responsibilities to attend to, such as making sure the rest of my family was OK. My daughter Kenisha would be attending her first prom, and it was up to me that she came home at a decent hour. I was hip to what went on at proms, and especially a prom night.

Kenisha's senior prom affected me in several different ways. First, I was a little worried because I did not want my baby girl out all night. I remember firsthand the potential activities that can take place on prom night. Since it was my daughter attending this late-night affair, I was very protective. On the other hand, the occasion gave me an opportunity to get my point across in a joking manner.

Kenisha Norton: *As soon as my date arrived, Dad pulled him into the library for a heart-to-heart discussion. I was in the kitchen helping Mom prepare a wonderful candlelight dinner for me and my prom guests. Later on, I was told by one of my friends that my dad had given my date the third degree. By the time I got there, Dad had already pulled his prank.*

The young man who picked Kenisha up was a polite fellow, and I decided to converse with him in an adult manner. I looked into his eyes and stated my feelings: "Now let's get something straight. If you lay a hand on my daughter, I'll kick your butt! And if you don't like that and you want to tell your father what I just said, I'll kick his butt, too!"

I definitely wanted to get my point across. I then slapped the young man on the back in a playful manner and said, "If you plan on any funny stuff with my daughter, you had better make sure your life insurance is paid off." When the youngster's eyes nearly popped out of his head, I could no longer keep a straight face. I fixed my eyes on the floor, fearing that he might have had an accident in his fancy tuxedo. He just looked at me and replied, "Yes, Mr. Norton."

My psychological ploy worked to a tee. The dance was scheduled to be finished at 12:30 a.m. My daughter was home 15 minutes early!

Kenisha Norton: *I would always warn anyone I took home that my dad was going to mess with their head. I'd tell them, "He's just playing around." Sometimes he would grab a kid and push him against the wall and ask, "What's up?" Then he would bust up laughing. He was always pulling some kind of antic. I'd beg him, "Daddy, stop fooling around! Nobody wants to play with you today!" He'd practically scare all of my dates to the point where they didn't want a second date with me.*

In order to be a productive parent, I even had to learn how to drive again. I had completely forgotten how to drive a vehicle. Unbelievably, I came close to having another tragic accident! An elderly lady ran a red light and plowed into my pickup. The crash sent my vehicle spinning, and I saw my whole life flash before me. Eventually I skidded into a chain-link fence, barely missing a huge tree. I was fortunate to only have suffered a few minor scrapes and bruises, escaping serious injury. However, I still suffer from backaches and have to get a weekly rubdown because of that particular accident.

After several weeks of practicing behind the wheel, I was able to drive without trepidation. My only uneasiness occurred when I drove by the large amount of construction being done on the Los Angeles freeway. I would feel real apprehensive when I drove near a construction divider, they were located so near the edge of the freeway. With time, my fear passed.

Once again I spent the fall football season watching Cowboys games in my living room instead of in Dallas. An article in the December 12, 1993, issue of *Sports Illustrated* gave me hope. Ken was quoted as saying, "Sometimes I sit back and think about it, I think about what a great feeling it was to do all the things I did in the Super Bowl. But I think how it would have benefited my father had he been at the game." Although we had not talked in over a year and a half, I knew he still cared.

The Cowboys once again were headed to the Super Bowl. Ken had finally received his long-overdue selection to the Pro Bowl. I planned to honor my promise to Kenisha and Kene Jon and booked three flights to Atlanta. Kenisha and Kene Jon were just innocent victims in this mess. Ken had no idea we were coming. We came to see him play, disregarding what had transpired in the past. We all still loved him and came to support him. It was his second Super Bowl, and we wanted to be a part of it this time around. I had no tickets or hotel room but I felt confident everything would fall into place. When it comes to family, sometimes people act on instinct and that was exactly what I was doing. I did not know what else to do. Even our respective ministers had talked. Hopefully this journey would break the ice.

We arrived in Atlanta with no real game plan. The only activity I had planned was a lunch date with Muhammad Ali. My personal assistant had been searching for tickets since the Cowboys' victory over San Francisco in the NFC championship game. Kenisha and Kene Jon wanted to support their brother whether he wanted them there or not. I had even planned to hit Ali up for tickets, but soon everything fell into place. We managed to find a vacant hotel room in a respectable place where, as luck would have it, the Buffalo Bills were staying. It was purely coincidence, and I planned to switch places if the opportunity presented itself. A friend came up with two tickets for my kids. I planned to catch the game in my hotel room, but courtesy of NBC-TV, I scored three tickets on the 50-yard line. At first I thought it was an act of pure kindness, but as the game progressed, I kept seeing my face on the big-screen monitor next to the scoreboard. Then it dawned on me: Ken Jr. and I had become a sideshow subplot for NBC. What can I say? I got sucker punched!

Ken Norton Jr.: *The media definitely blew the whole thing out of proportion. It was news, and when we finally made up, it was no longer newsworthy. But yes, there were times when I would pick up the paper and say, "Did he really say that about me?" I think that's just human nature, but I also knew what was true and what was false. But I do not think you can help but question it sometimes.*

Ken was once again a terror on the football field despite a season-ending biceps injury. In the ninth game of the season against the Philadelphia Eagles, Ken made a tackle, and his arm was twisted badly. The results were much worse. Ken's biceps in his right arm was torn from the bone. Newspaper reports declared it felt like a muscle cramp. The muscle had ripped away and formed a big bulging knot located high on his arm. Ken had the option of an immediate operation or he could play injured through the season. He elected to finish out the year in hopes of adding another Super Bowl ring to his hand. Ken could not make a complete fist or put his hands above his head, but he played through the pain. Tremendous heart is a trait I admired in any human being. Ken finished the regular season with a career-best 159 tackles, including 10 of which caused loss of yardage.

Even after the Cowboys were once again victorious, we still did not speak. I realized Ken was probably tied up with postgame victory functions. We quietly left town hoping to catch up with him later. During the off-season, Ken opted to go the free-agency route, accepting a lucrative five-year contract with the San Francisco 49ers, a contender in their own right.

At first, the move had been tough on his family. Ken's stepdaughter, Brittany, was only eight years old and didn't want to leave her friends behind. Angela was originally from Dallas and also did not want to leave her family. Eventually, only Ken would stay in San Francisco and visit his family in Dallas whenever possible. Ken and Angela had also given birth to a daughter named Sabrina. I did not get the opportunity to meet my granddaughter until she was over a year old. It was extremely painful. Angela soon became pregnant again. From all reports, Ken was thrilled to be a family man. No matter what macho act I displayed externally, inside I yearned for nothing short of a full reconciliation.

> **Kenisha Norton:** *In the early stages of the rift, I used to call Ken on the phone and ask him to call Dad and talk it out. He knew it hurt Dad, and the whole family, for that matter. I asked him, "Why can't you guys sit down and talk?" He told me, "There is so much more to it than you can comprehend." When he left to play college ball and in the NFL, I was quite young, but now I was 18. He thought I was still a little girl and he would then change the subject to something else. I'd tell him, "What if something ever happened to one of you guys? You would never be able to forgive yourselves." I used to talk to Angela, his wife, and plot how we could get them to sit down together and talk.*

Ken's first season with the 49ers meant a difficult adjustment. He was learning a new defense, living in a new city away from his family for a majority of the time. He was openly criticized in the sports papers as a "big free-agent bust." The media hardly gave him a chance to get acclimated to his new surroundings before heavily blasting him in print.

Ken was signed by the 49ers to help defend the run, but after the first five games, the 49ers' defense was ranked 12th in the NFL. The media looked upon Ken as the scapegoat. They jumped on his case way too early, and by the end of the season, Ken was making them eat every one of their words.

Eventually, Ken returned to his old form and led the team in tackles right into the playoffs. Now, I jumped on the 49ers bandwagon and rooted for Ken in his quest to be the first person to ever play for three consecutive Super Bowls champions. The only major obstacle standing in the way was the Dallas Cowboys, who they squared off against in the NFC championship game.

Ken was not the only one attempting to reach an unprecedented three-peat in the Super Bowl. However, everyone else attempting to reach that plateau played for Ken's old team, the Cowboys. It was a very emotional game for Ken when Dallas came to butt heads with San Francisco. Once again, the media was all over Ken about our relationship. Can you believe the same story line was recycled for the third consecutive year? Ken was quoted in the *San Francisco Examiner* as saying for the record, "I'm just hoping the whole thing is old news now. It's my life and my family's. Let's get on to something else."

The 49ers looked spectacular that day as they discarded the Cowboys for a 38-28 victory and a trip to the Super Bowl. Each time Ken made a key tackle, he fired a punch in the air.

Ken entered the record books as the first player in NFL history to play on three consecutive Super Bowl champions. The 49ers dismantled the San Diego Chargers, posting a decisive 49-26 victory. The 49ers' defense looked fantastic, limiting the Chargers' rushing attack to a meager 67 yards.

I was proud of Ken entering the record books and playing for another championship team, but another part of me ached because I had not been a part of his recent success. It hurt like hell, but fortunately the ice in our long-running disagreement would soon be melting.

Ken and I had officially hooked up a few times before making amends, but I left each encounter feeling unfulfilled. During the off-season, Ken held a charity auction at the Planet Hollywood in Dallas. I attended the function to help support my son. We spoke, but unfortunately, not at any great length. We arrived together for the charity benefit, and at the very least, it was a start. The next time we saw each other was in Los Angeles when the 49ers were in town to play the Rams. I took Kenisha and Kene Jon and we all sat in Ken's complimentary seats, and the day was doubly sweet when the 'Niners were victorious. Ken and I embraced, but we still had not buried the hatchet as far as our differences were concerned.

Eventually, Ken and I would close the book on our dispute, and if it had not been for Kenisha, Jackie, and Angela, who knows how long the rift would have lasted. They secretly planned for all of us to get together for Ken's birthday. I was both excited and apprehensive about this encounter. I hoped things would work out, but at the same time, I feared how I would feel if they didn't. It was definitely a chance worth taking.

It was a small get-together staged in a hotel suite. The only people present were Jackie, Kene Jon, Kenisha, Angela, my granddaughter Brittany, and me. Even though it was Ken's birthday party, I left the gathering with the best present: I got my son back. We had a conversation at the party. It set the groundwork for resuming our relationship.

> **Kenisha Norton:** *It was Ken Jr.'s birthday. My sister-in-law, Jackie, and I had been plotting it, trying to get them in the same hotel room and get the two together. We arranged to have the birthday party at a suite in the hotel. Kenneth went over and greeted my dad. Dad had been real quiet beforehand, so none of us really knew how it was going to turn out. It turned out better than we ever could have hoped. Finally, they were on speaking terms again, ready to resume their relationship.*

> **Ken Norton Jr.:** *My wife was chiefly responsible for the two of us patching things up. She saw how miserable I was the first year of our rift. After the first year, I realized I had a life I had to get on with. It was tearing the whole family apart. My dad had called once in between the whole time, but what had led to our eventual making up was a party for me. My wife invited my father, and that night we made a vow never to stop the communication, no matter how bad things may get. From that day on, we have been in touch. We are making up for lost time.*

Ken and I had a nice conversation. We did not dig up the past and rehash the gory details. Instead, we both apologized for our parts in the silent war and agreed to never let it happen again. We knew we might disagree again in the future, but we promised each other never to stop communicating. That was the key: an open line of communication.

> **Ken Norton Jr.:** *At first it took a while to get as close as we used to be. It took some work. He knows I love him, and I know that he loves me, and that's why we made up for lost time. It's a terrible thing to know that you have lost two or three years of your life and you cannot get it back. I learned a lot as a result of our split. It is extremely important to keep the lines of communication open no matter what. To be able to say to each other, "I disagree with you, but*

I still love you." Also, I was 24 and stubborn and immature. I think I have grown since then and would have acted differently today. I did not like having an ultimatum given to me. My dad was also stubborn and didn't want to let his little boy go, but in reality, it was time to let me go. That's why I don't hold a grudge toward my father, because it was done out of concern for me.

I was relieved to have the family crisis behind me. I could go on to being a full-time 49ers fan. Ken and I were in frequent touch with each other. Ken's large portrait was back on the living room wall. Finally, what seemed like an eternity was in the past.

Ken Norton Jr.: *My dad is everything to me. He is my Superman. He is a wonderful father, a fantastic role model, and has passed on to me all of his good traits. I know it was never easy on him as a single parent to have me around, but he never gave me up. He gave me an extraordinary sense of family that I have passed on to my family. There are so many dysfunctional families out there, and my father passed on his wisdom and his sense of family to me. I cannot imagine being without my family, and of course, my father is a vital part of the whole picture.*

I flew to San Francisco just days after our reunion to witness Ken and the 49ers taking on the New York Giants. Ken was quoted in the local paper as saying, "You only get one daddy in life. My father has been an extremely important part of my success as a person and a player. I think you will be seeing a lot more of him." Ken's productivity on the field increased dramatically in the weeks that followed our reunion. Those words were music to my ears.

A few weeks after the family reunion, Ken played his best game as a 49er and even took a page out of his old man's book. Ken was voted Miller Lite Player of the Week. He intercepted two passes and returned both for touchdowns. After each touchdown, Ken ran over to the goalpost and started punching away as if he were on the heavy bag in a tribute to me. Even the fans in St. Louis seemed amused. Ken's power punching exhibition was shown on sports highlights for the next week. I laughed every time each announcer had to throw in his two cents worth of opinion and compared his boxing form to mine. The 49ers coach, George Seifert, claimed Ken's punching was a tribute to his father's success.

You never know what you miss until it's gone. It was awesome having Ken back in my life.

Chapter Twenty

Going the Distance

Now that the hatchet was buried between Ken and me, I had to laugh when I read about it in the daily paper. First, I needed the aid of a magnifying glass to view the small print that covered our reconciliation. The article was lost in the back pages of the sports section near the women's field-hockey results. Our reunion obviously was less newsworthy than our squabble. Nonetheless, the difficult part of my life was now in the past.

Ken has continued to play a prominent role in the 49ers' defense. He emerged as the team leader, anchoring the defense to many victories. He continued to be an iron man on the field, not missing a football game since an injury in the last game of 1990 with the Cowboys. Despite all of his success on the football field, in 1997, Ken attempted to follow my footsteps in the ring.

Surprising everyone, Ken signed up to participate in the super-heavyweight division of the Dallas Golden Gloves tournament. Outside of his punching combinations against a football goalpost, he had never shown much interest in the sport, if ever. Personally, I think he just wanted to see what it was like. Despite all the media coverage, USA Boxing, the sport's national governing body, denied Ken admission to the tournament, citing that the rules of amateur boxing prohibit pros from other sports from fighting. They felt it would set a bad precedent to sanction a professional football player to compete on the amateur level. Ken hoped an exception would be made, but USA Boxing stuck to its guns and disallowed him from entry in the tournament. If Ken wants to box, that is his personal choice, but as a father, I was much more excited to hear of Ken's return to UCLA to complete his degree.

My son has been in the NFL for 10 years, and with a little luck, he has several competitive years remaining on the gridiron, but during the off-season, he decided to get his degree. The last time he had set foot in a classroom had been almost a decade ago, but that did not deter him in any way. The day after the 49ers lost to Green Bay in the playoffs, Ken found himself in a classroom. He never ceases to amaze me.

I had to laugh, picturing Ken on his first day back to school. I'm sure that even Rodney Dangerfield looked less inconspicuous on his film-role inspired return to campus. Ken wore a pulled-down UCLA hat his first day back. Still, his vain attempt at staying anonymous did not last long after the first roll call. He was getting hit up for autographs right in the class. He studied extremely hard and pulled a B+ average for the semester—much better than his initial trip to UCLA where he had barely stayed afloat just above the C level.

Ken only had one real obstacle to overcome when it came to his studies—me! After 10 long years, my son was back in town. We managed to get together at least three times a week. I really missed him when he headed back to San Francisco for the football season. He deserves a lot of credit for showing the discipline to come back and get the job done. I know he used to get quite involved in his 12-year-old daughter Sabrina's academics. He also used to speak at school functions on the benefits of an education. Maybe he felt guilty over a period of time, which prompted him to finish his sociology degree.

Ken Norton Jr.: *I'm really pushy when it comes to education with my children. And I thought, "How can I be preaching all this mess when I haven't done it myself?" I felt like the biggest hypocrite in the world.*

There is an old saying that once boxing gets in your bloodstream, it's impossible to remove. Although I had not been involved in boxing in any way since 1986, I was now entering my mid-fifties and was itching to get back in the sport. Not as a fighter, but as a trainer. An old Marine Corps buddy of mine, Lou Lake, was training a promising young heavyweight, King Ipitan, and requested my assistance.

I wake up each morning and tell myself how lucky I am to be alive. I know that I was left on this earth for a reason. Maybe it was to train fighters. Lord knows I learned from the best, Eddie Futch. Somewhere down the line, hopefully I will find out, but in the meantime, I enjoyed being back in the boxing business. Three times a week I met with King Ipitan at Ultimate University in Mission Viejo, California. Basically,

I studied Ipitan's style to see what he did best and just worked off that. The first thing we did was work on his defense. By the time Ipitan was ready for his first fight with me in the corner, he was looking like a contender in the gym.

My near-fatal accident now only affects me in a minor way. My voice is still hoarse, and outside of occasional stiffness, I can function just fine. In order to benefit Ipitan, I had to remember how I once fought. I still have completely forgotten the four years before my accident and the three years that followed. Sometimes certain discussions can jar my memory, and I can recollect the person or the event. On more than one occasion, I have run into an old friend whom I have not seen in years and have lost all memory of him. He'll think I'm joking when I cannot remember where he fits in my life. Often after listening to him describe our previous relationship, my memory kick in, and then it all comes back to me.

On June 12, 1998, I made my official debut as chief cornerman. Ipitan already had an impressive record of 16-1 going into this contest against veteran James Wilder. Wilder was a club fighter out of the Midwest who once had defeated Leon Spinks. Ipitan looked like a future world champion as he dismantled Wilder, stopping him in the second round. Unfortunately, Ipitan did not look as impressive in his next outing, being held to a technical draw a month later. We immediately went back to the gym and worked on Ipitan's punches coming off the jab, as well as improving the fluidity of his ring movement. It was a thrill being involved directly with the sport again, but I was also busy with other aspects of the sport as well.

Through a mutual friend, I was introduced to Jerry Haack of Newport Marketing. Jerry and I hit it off right from the beginning, and he has since become my booking agent and good friend. He's one of the few guys in this racket whom I completely trust.

Jerry Haack (Ken's event booking agent): *Since Ken and I became acquainted in 1993, I have kept him on the go. Ken does several autograph signings a year and has also done work for the Showtime Network, doing prefight analysis work. He also found time to appear on the Arsenio Hall show. One of Ken's favorite gigs is the public relations work he does for the MGM Grand Hotel in Las Vegas.*

It always brings me great pleasure to run into Muhammad Ali at sports collector shows all over the country. I have always had great admiration for the man, and when fans at these shows see us together, they're amazed by the mutual love and respect we have for each other. But Ali is also one of my favorite targets to pester. At these autograph shows, people are always lined up around the block to get Ali's signature. I take great pleasure sneaking up behind him and putting him in a chokehold. As everyone knows, Ali's motor skills have diminished greatly due to his Parkinson's disease, but his mind is still sharp as a tack. Ali just focuses his eyes on me, staring me down before breaking out in laughter to everyone's amusement. They really do get their money's worth when the two of us work the crowd!

I will go to my grave convinced that I won my third fight with Ali, but I don't hold it against him. He wasn't one of the judges. To tell you the truth, I rarely even think about it anymore, only when someone else brings it up. When I think of Muhammad Ali, I think of a man who is my good friend and nothing less. I am not a medical doctor, but I feel the accumulative effect of the punches Ali received did not necessarily cause his disease. I honestly feel that he is just suffering from a disease. Parkinson's disease symptoms are also found in many men and women who have never taken a punch.

When I retired in 1981, I had all of my faculties. After the automobile accident, there are minor differences in my speech and movement that some people feel, upon meeting me for the first time, came from boxing. I can now proudly boast that I am almost fully recovered.

Before the accident, I used to feel invincible. Now, I only feel slightly vulnerable in only a few instances. For example, if a physical encounter ever took place, I still feel very confident in my abilities. If somebody ambushed me in a small room or area, they would be history in a heartbeat. If I ever got mugged on the street corner, I now have little difficulty turning as sharply as I once could. The accident affected the section of my brain that controls my balance. But if confronted, I can still defend myself. I still keep in excellent physical condition, although I'm about 20 pounds over my fighting weight, but that's due to some added muscle from weight lifting. I like to maintain a strict low-fat diet consisting of no red meat and mostly chicken. I adhere to a rigorous weight-lifting regime. During my career, I never touched a weight, but now I can only wonder what a difference it may have made.

Many of today's champions use weights in their training program. Look at Evander Holyfield—he fought as a light-heavyweight in the 1984 Olympics. Upon joining the paid ranks, he slowly built himself into a heavyweight. With victories over Mike Tyson, George Foreman, Riddick Bowe, and James "Buster" Douglas, Holyfield will surely go down as one of history's greatest fighters. When I fought, we were told that lifting weights would make you tighten up and become muscle-bound. But today in every sport—basketball, baseball, distance running, swimming, etc.—everyone is pumping iron. Sports specialists have found that weight lifting enhances strength and speed. If I would have added weight lifting to my overall conditioning program, who knows how far I would have gone?

The generation of fighters in my day was a unique group. George Foreman reinvented himself to compete on a championship level with the next generation of fighters. Back when I fought Foreman, he relied heavily on intimidation. He was cantankerous, arrogant, and frigid at press conferences. Today, he is now one of the funniest and most gregarious people I have ever met. Today we are friends, and overall, he is a much better person to be around.

Larry Holmes has also maintained a certain degree of competitiveness, fighting late into his forties. He soundly defeated then-unbeaten Olympic gold medalist Ray Mercer in 1992 and went the distance in a losing decision to Evander Holyfield later that year. Although Holyfield deserved the decision, Holmes gave a respectable effort, frustrating the champion on several occasions. One of my defining career moments will always be the final round of my bout with Larry Holmes.

In an article titled "The 12 Greatest Finishes of All Time" in the September 1998 edition of *Ring* magazine, it lists the final round of my contest with Larry Holmes among its selections. The article describes it as possibly the best single round ever in a heavyweight title fight. Although the scoring of the round had not been in my favor, I still considered it an honor to be listed among such dramatic finishes as Joe Louis' come-from-behind victory over Billy Conn.

> **Larry Holmes:** *Kenny is a good guy and was a sensational fighter—always a force to be reckoned with. To be honest, he's a part of what I have today. Kenny will mostly be remembered as the guy who broke Ali's jaw, but people in boxing will always respect Kenny for what he has accomplished.*

Throughout my career, I have had the privilege, if you want to call it that, of facing some of history's most fearsome sluggers. Guys like Foreman, Cooney, or Shavers were capable of taking out an opponent with a single shot. I will give Shavers credit for hitting the hardest. When Foreman hit me, I got up. When Shavers dropped me, I never came close to beating the count.

Gerry Cooney: *I was aware of Kenny since I was a kid. I saw him in* Mandingo, *and I thought he was a monster after that movie. Kenny will always be remembered as a guy with tremendous heart who would fight anybody. He was a tremendous athlete who got a late start in boxing but did very well. I still see him from time to time, and I think the world of him. We even filmed a couple of commercials together. Kenny always did well against boxers; it was the punchers who gave him the most difficulty.*

Throughout my career, I have always taken criticism for my losses to Foreman, Shavers, and Cooney. The word on the street was that I could not beat a puncher. Tex Cobb landed more powerful bombs on my chin than I care to remember. I also traded some heavy artillery with "Smokin'" Joe Frazier during numerous sparring sessions. Jose Luis Garcia also scored with thunderous blows in both of our encounters. Plain and simple, any man hit cleanly by Foreman, Shavers, or Cooney is going to go down.

The 1998 holiday issue of *Ring* ran an article I am extremely proud to be mentioned in: "The 50 Greatest Heavyweights of All Time." It is a difficult task to compare so many fighters from different eras, and I could not agree more with *Ring's* selection of Muhammad Ali as the all-time greatest heavyweight. It credited Ali with the fastest feet and hands ever to grace the heavyweight ranks. The magazine also noted that he was the master of psychological warfare. After squaring off with The Greatest three times, I had lived through a slew of his head games. Foreman and Holmes also were included in the top five slots. All told, six of my one-time opponents were listed in the top 50, which gives you an indication of how tough the heavyweight division was in the '70s. I came in at No. 22 on the list and rated above former world champions like Bowe and Jack Sharkey.

Occasionally I still bump into some of my former adversaries. Jack O'Halloran, a man I swapped leather with early in my career, also tried his luck on the silver screen. He landed parts in such flicks as *King Kong, Farewell My Lovely* and *Superman III.*

I'm also happy to report that Scott LeDoux will be remembered as more than just the guy who kicked the rug off Howard Cosell's head. LeDoux is one of the most revered athletes in his home state of Minnesota and even has a sandwich named in his honor; a local restaurant in the Twin Cities has a French dip on its menu called the "LeDoux Dip." LeDoux always has been a colorful character, and for a brief time following his retirement, he tried his hand as a referee in professional wrestling. When a heel like Baron Von Rascke pulled an illegal maneuver, LeDoux would restore order by delivering a knockout punch and saving the day!

Scott LeDoux: *I have a lot of respect for Ken Norton. He's a nice man, and I'm glad he has made a full recovery after the car accident. Kenny had a lot of courage and a unique style that drove Ali nuts. Style makes fights.*

Duane Bobick also suffered a terrible injury years after his career had finished. He was working at a paper mill in his hometown of Little Falls, Minnesota, when the utility knife he was working with got caught in a roll of paper he was cutting on a collating machine. The machine pulled Bobick's right hand into the grinder, along with the utility knife. As Bobick pulled with his free left hand, it also got dragged into the machine. Both of Bobick's arms were pulled through past his elbows. His arms were badly skinned and he tore several muscles and tendons. He almost bled to death.

Bobick spent a month in the hospital following a 14-hour surgery. The latest report I received was that Bobick had regained full use of his left arm and was showing constant improvement with his right. I wish him a complete recovery.

Credit for any honor I receive must be shared with two men who guided me through my career: my two trainers Eddie Futch and Bill Slayton. Eddie trained over 20 world champions before calling it quits in 1996. Personally, I feel Eddie is the greatest boxing strategist of all time. It was Eddie who masterminded the first two defeats of Ali's career. The first time was with Frazier and the second time was with me. Eddie taught me more about boxing than anyone. Riddick Bowe was the last heavyweight champion Eddie ever worked with. Bowe's lethargic training habits and penchant for ballooning between fights frustrated Eddie and eventually led to his premature retirement from boxing at the ripe old age of 86!

Eddie Futch: *History will have to remember Ken Norton as the second man to defeat Muhammad Ali. Only four other fighters have done so, with Joe Frazier being the first. But more than that, Ken Norton is a good man. I've always maintained the attitude that if the person I'm training isn't a good person, I don't have time to fool with him. Ken Norton is as good a man as I've ever worked with.*

Bill Slayton is another man I will always hold dear to my heart. The 76-year-old trainer is still working with amateur and professional boxers at the Broadway Gym in South Central Los Angeles. Bill bought the gym with his earnings from his work with me. Even in some of the no-hope amateurs he trained, Bill always was concerned with the best interests of his fighters: Bill was concerned with getting kids away from gangs and the nearby ghetto and teaching them something valuable. Many people outside of boxing feel that boxing is just teaching a kid how to fight, but that's not the case. Boxing instills discipline, self-reliance, and a winning attitude. For many people in the ghetto, boxing is their only way out. Even today when I run into Bill, we always share a good laugh. Bill earned close to one million dollars while working with me, and he invested it wisely. He owns at least three homes, and to this day he always tells me I can have one of them if I need it. It sounds like a wonderful gesture, but I know if I ever called Bill out on it, he would sign over the papers in a heartbeat. He is one of the nicest guys I have ever met.

Bill Slayton: *Ken Norton should be remembered as a credit to boxing. He had a style that was pleasing, and in certain fights, he could really rise to the occasion. He did nothing to hurt the sport and never made any enemies, and let me tell you that's saying something. If Kenny's your friend, you've got a friend for life.*

I only harbor a few regrets concerning my boxing career. In my final bout against Ali, I kept my distance in the final round. My corner told me that I was way out in front, which I was; and in hindsight, I should have poured it on against Ali. I was never fatigued in the encounter and easily could have gone another 15 rounds. To be completely frank, I don't think about it anymore. That fight is in the past, and it's impossible to move ahead if you keep looking backward.

Boxing has treated me well, and I'm happy for all of the rewards the sport has brought to me. Sometimes I wish I could have taken my career a bit more to heart. After the Holmes defeat, I could no longer get myself up mentally for competition, and it almost cost me my life against Cooney.

As proud as I am about my past achievements, I am even more thrilled with the progress of my offspring.

My eldest son, Keith, has recently relocated back to Chicago after a brief transfer to Kansas City. He is working in the computer industry and has three wonderful boys.

Ken Jr., as I already mentioned, is still knocking them down on the gridiron. Kenisha is studying communications at Saddleback Junior College and recently has applied for her real estate license. Kene Jon is a senior in high school at Dana Hills and will be attending college next year. He hopes to pursue baseball and football while in school. I am blessed to have such a great relationship with all of my offspring.

Kenisha Norton: *I admire my dad a lot, in the way that he is always down to earth and the way he treats people so kindly. I have the opportunity to witness many celebrities who have the power of making or breaking someone's heart, and my dad never refuses anybody. I remember one time in Atlanta during the Super Bowl where he was flooded by autograph seekers, and he signed for everyone. He just adores the public. I have learned so much from my dad and am honored whenever people see similarities between us.*

I pride myself on keeping in peak physical condition, but it had not always been that way. I began partying heavily immediately following the conclusion of my ring career. I was confused about what direction to take and looked to the bottle for answers. I never turned into a drunken ogre, but I managed to go out on the town almost nightly. One evening, a close acquaintance of mine advised me that I had something on my chin. I quickly brushed my hand over my mouth and then my friend said, "No, the other chin!" My weight had ballooned to more than 270 pounds and that little wisecrack made me take notice. My family members had also remarked about my expanding waistline.

I cut way down on my alcohol consumption and started intensifying my gym workouts. I always attempted to maintain a positive aura, and it didn't take me long to snap out of my rut. Outside of when I was laid up with my accident, I had always attempted to maintain a high level of fitness. My motto has always been "a healthy body makes for an invigorating spirit."

I have always taken great pride in fooling people about my age. I was born August 9, 1943, but during my career, my age was always a constant question mark. Once I turned 32, I remained that age for at least five years. Heavyweights mature later in life and reach their athletic potential around 30. Psychologically, I wanted my competitors to think I was near peak-fighting age. I remember Cobb hammering this point across at our press conference in the twilight of my career. He tried to make my blood boil by announcing to the press, "I'm glad to be fighting Norton, who was listed at 32 for the fifth year in a row. Norton is past his prime!"

I had been through many megafight press conferences where I let comments like Cobb's casually roll off my back, but it wasn't until my good friend, Bobby Moore, ribbed me about my age that I took notice.

Bobby Moore: *Ken brought me back to his high school reunion in Jacksonville. When I got to the party, I was laughing my fool head off. Ken came over and asked me what was so damned funny. I told him, "Either there are two reunions going on or you've lied about your age because there are so many older-looking people here." Ken is really in great shape!*

I think it's safe to say that I am still a tad bit vain. It does bother me when I see former champions, who at one time were the fittest human beings on earth, let themselves blow up to grotesque proportions once they've retired. These former gladiators are revered by the public and should exhibit more self-control.

Retirement has treated me well, for the most part. Outside of the automobile accident, life has been pretty sweet. I recently opened Ken Norton's Restaurant & Nightclub in Irvine, California, near John Wayne Airport. The restaurant is decorated with boxing memorabilia from my years in the ring. What could be better than to have a place of your own where the food and booze is free? And if the patrons get drunk or rowdy, who's going to complain to the owner? Yes, the Knuckle Sandwich is also on the menu.

All in all, I'm extremely proud of how my career progressed. What started with little fanfare at the old downtown San Diego Coliseum in November 1967 exceeded my wildest expectations. Six years after my debut, I broke Ali's jaw, and the rest is history. But the more you dwell in the past, the more the future does not happen. The experts said that I did not belong in the same ring with Ali. They also predicted that I would never walk again. I ended up going the distance with Ali three times, and with the accident, I am in the process of going the distance.

I believe that many of life's outcomes are determined by your attitude. By keeping a positive outlook, an upbeat spirit, and a confident belief in my abilities, I overcame obstacles few people gave me a chance of defeating.

Just remember: What the mind can conceive, the body can achieve. Whatever you do in life, always go the distance!

In the Ring

Record: 42-7-1

Date	Opponent	Site	Result/Rounds	Title
11/14/67	Grady Brazell	San Diego, CA	KO/3	-
1/16/68	Sam Wyatt	San Diego, CA	W/6	-
2/6/68	Harold Dutra	Sacramento, CA	KO/3	-
3/26/68	Jimmy Gilmore	San Diego, CA	KO/7	-
7/23/68	Wayne Kindred	San Diego, CA	TKO/6	-
12/5/68	Cornell Nolan	Los Angeles, CA	KO/6	-
2/11/69	Joe Hemphill	Woodland Hills, CA	TKO/3	-
2/20/69	Wayne Kindred	Los Angeles, CA	KO/9	-
3/31/69	Pedro Sanchez	San Diego, CA	TKO/2	-
5/29/69	Bill McMurray	Los Angeles, CA	TKO/7	-
7/25/69	Gary Bates	San Diego, CA	KO/8	-
10/21/69	Julius Garcia	San Diego, CA	KO/3	-
2/4/70	Aaron Eastling	Las Vegas, NV	KO/2	-
3/13/70	Stanford Harris	San Diego, CA	KO/3	-
4/7/70	Bob Mashburn	Cleveland, OH	KO/4	-
5/8/70	Ray Ellis	San Diego, CA	KO/2	-
7/2/70	Jose Luis Garcia	Los Angeles, CA	KO/8	-
8/29/70	Cookie Wallace	San Diego, CA	KO/4	-
9/26/70	Chuck Leslie	Woodland Hills, CA	W/10	-
10/16/70	Roby Harris	San Diego, CA	KO/2	-
4/24/71	Steve Carter	Woodland Hills, CA	KO/3	-
6/12/71	Vic Brown	Santa Monica, CA	KO/5	-
8/19/71	Chuck Haynes	Santa Monica, CA	KO/10	-
9/30/71	James Woody	San Diego, CA	W/10	-
2/17/72	Charlie Harris	San Diego, CA	KO/3	-
3/17/72	Jack O'Halloran	San Diego, CA	W/10	-
6/5/72	Herschel Jacobs	San Diego, CA	W/10	-
6/30/72	James Woody	San Diego, CA	TKO/7	-
11/21/72	Henry Clark	Stateline, NV	KO/9	-
12/13/72	Charlie Reno	San Diego, CA	W/10	-
3/21/73	Muhammad Ali	San Diego, CA	W/12	Won NABF-H
9/10/73	Muhammad Ali	Los Angeles, CA	L/12	Lost NABF-H
3/26/74	George Foreman	Caracas, Venezuela	KO'd /2	For World-H
6/25/75	Boone Kirkman	Seattle, WA	TKO/8	-
3/4/75	Reco Brooks	Oklahoma City, OK	KO/1	-
3/24/75	Jerry Quarry	New York City	TKO/5	Won NABF-H
8/14/75	Jose Luis Garcia	St. Paul, MN	TKO/5	-
1/3/76	Pedro Lovell	Las Vegas, NV	KO/5	-
4/30/76	Ron Stander	Landover, MD	KO/5	-
7/10/76	Larry Middleton	San Diego, MD	TKO/10	-
9/28/76	Muhammad Ali	New York City	L/15	For World-H
5/11/77	Duane Bobick	New York City	TKO/1	

9/14/77	Lorenzo Zanon	Las Vegas, NV	TKO/5	-
11/5/77	Jimmy Young	Las Vegas, NV	W/15	-
6/8/78	Larry Holmes	Las Vegas, NV	L/15	WBC-H
11/10/78	Randy Stephens	Las Vegas, NV	KO/4	-
3/23/79	Earnie Shavers	Las Vegas, NV	TKO'd/1	-
9/19/79	Scott LeDoux	Bloomington, MN	D/10	-
11/7/80	Randall "Tex" Cobb	San Antonio, TX	W/10	-
5/11/81	Gerry Cooney	New York City	TKO'd/1	-